Remaking America:
The Values Revolution

Remaking America:
The Values Revolution

Paul D. Knott, Ph.D.
Colorado Family Services

Library of Congress Catalog Card Number: 93-71174

ISBN Number: 1-880651-02-5

Published by Colorado Family Services
P.O. Box 101535
Denver, Colorado 80210

Printed and bound in the United States of America.

First edition, May, 1993.

Acknowledgements

I express my deepest thanks to the following people:

To Roberta, my wife (known to all her friends as Robbi), for all the hours she put into proofreading, editing and typing the manuscript.

To my three children, Adriana, Michael and Joel, for being there.

To Mark Lusky and Heather Higbee for their editing, proofreading and consultation.

To Mary Elizabeth Newman, Bernard Spilka, Bill Hodges (now deceased), Steve Tattum, Andre Radatus, Ed McManis, and Jamie Gordon for reading parts or all of the manuscript and for their many helpful criticisms and suggestions.

To Robbi, Adriana,
Michael and Joel

Table of Contents

Introduction

By the beginning of this century, conventional religion had fallen from grace in Europe and among most intellectuals worldwide. While the Judeo-Christian belief system had served the Western world for many centuries, the emerging scientific view of the world called for a new mythology. "Modern Man" needed a new concept – a new myth – to guide and inspire, in place of the old myth of religious worship of a supernatural being. Since men and women cannot live long without myth, which gives hope as well as purpose, this new myth had to have heroes and grand themes that could bestow meaning and dignity to life.

Enter the 20th Century Myth, predicated on the belief that reason and science had shown the old myth to be false. Especially false had been the belief in an Absolute guiding the universe. Modern men and women had discerned that all was relative. Since no absolute could be found, there was no reason to believe in God. God was increasingly seen as a childish concept, a throwback to primitivism.

In the new 20th Century Myth, Man was the focus. Man and his methods were the measures of all things. Man would master the universe and solve all his social problems as well. He would create heaven on earth and save himself. Man would be his own hero.

Indeed, the new 20th Century Myth was often presented as if it were scientific fact, not just a new set of assumptions. It created its own ethic (its own sense of right and wrong), as myths always do. The fostering of each person's full human potential was thus acknowledged as the supreme value of life. But here a major problem was encountered: How can people realize their potential when some are hungry and dominated by fear?

The 20th Century Myth required that all people be fed and free from fear. Their security needs must be met first so that self-actualization might then occur.

Clearly, since all people are brothers and sisters and all are of equal value, it followed that all people should have equal economic resources. Since equal access to economic resources does not lead to equal outcomes, as some people are more effective than others, the resolution was for government to step in and guarantee equal outcomes for all.

The 20th Century Myth invested great power, the supreme power, in human government – instead of religion. The State was looked to as the resource to solve human problems. Worship of the State (as the embodiment of the worship of Man) became the focus. Yet, since the 20th Century Myth assumed that all truth was relative to the observer (as there was no longer any absolute force), how could Man worship the State, when, by definition, he can only really know himself?

The answer was to insist that all people in the State think alike. In totalitarian societies, this took the form of "group think" – no ideas that deviated from the party line would be tolerated. In more democratic societies, the same process occurred through attempted enforcement of "politically correct" thinking.

Left and right wing totalitarian, collectivist societies were spawned worldwide by the 20th Century Myth. It raised social engineering to new heights of effectiveness as its chief method. It guaranteed equal outcomes while proclaiming the fulfillment of all human potential as its chief goal and value. Thoroughly grounded in the here and now – in the world of material needs and wants – it offered no hope for anything beyond this life, for by definition it could not. Since all standards and values were relative to the individual's perspective (expressed as a consensus in the State), the 20th Century Myth easily slid into self-worship. Worship of Self replaced worship of God.

> The criticism of religion disillusions man, to make him think and act...like a man who has...come to reason, so that he will revolve around himself and therefore round his true sun.
>
> Karl Marx
> 19th Century

We now have a century of experience with the effects of the 20th Century Myth, even here in the United States – which by 1990 had seen her families, her schools, her most basic social institutions corrupted by the values of the 20th Century Myth. America's social foundations are being eaten away by a thousand different maggots, all escaped from the same Pandora's Box of misbegotten concepts – the 20th Century Myth.

Yet, this corruption can be reversed. A reversal will require a return to our heritage, in particular a return to the very best of our traditional values as found in the *ancient wisdom* that fosters personal, spiritual growth based on trusting the idea that the universe is grounded in an eternal absolute – God. This is not a simplistic return to old ways. Many lessons have been learned over the past century and these must be incorporated into our applications of our higher values. The goal is our true emancipation, not our binding again in old chains.

So that we may go forward, not backwards, it is necessary to look first at the mythology that generated the dominant values of the 20th Century.

Paul D. Knott, Ph.D.

Chapter One

The 20th Century Myth
Roots and "Relatives" of the 20th Century Myth

In Gotha, Germany, in 1784 this message was placed in a church steeple for posterity to read:

> Our age occupies the happiest period of the eighteenth century. Emperors, kings, and princes humanely descend from their dreaded heights, despise pomp and splendor, become the fathers, friends, and confidants of their people. Religion rends its priestly garb and appears in its divine essence. Enlightenment makes great strides. Thousands of our brothers and sisters, who formerly lived in sanctified inactivity, are given back to the state. Sectarian hatred and persecution for conscience' sake are vanishing. Love of man and freedom of thought are gaining the supremacy. The arts and sciences are flourishing and our gaze is penetrating deeply into the workshop of nature. Handicraftsmen as well as artists are reaching perfection, useful knowledge is growing among all classes. Here you have a faithful description of our times.
>
> Do not look haughtily down upon us if you are higher and see farther than we; recognize rather from the picture which we have drawn how bravely and energetically we labored to raise you to the position which you now hold and to support you in it. Do the same for your descendants and be happy.[1]

This statement typifies the optimism about the human condition brought about by the Age of Enlightenment and Reason in the late 1700s. At this same time the United States was being founded on the Enlightenment principles of the "natural rights" of man to justice, to freedom of thought, to the pursuit of happiness and property. Liberty, equality, fraternity – these were the ideals not only of the French Revolution, but of all thoughtful persons of this period. Man, and human society, were perfectible through the application of reason and its main method, science.

Only a century later, in 1886, the 20th Century was ushered in when the German philosopher, Friedrich Nietzsche, declared, "God is dead."[2] God had been put to death by the application of reason and science, the same two forces heralded a century before as the liberators of mankind. Thoughtful persons, said Nietzsche, could no longer believe in God. He had been a product of ancient poets and mythmakers. Prescientific man had "needed" God for solace, for comfort, for ideals and values, for cosmology, for meaning and salvation from death. Modern man now knew this was all myth, a fanciful dream. Man now had to face a cold cosmos on his own. He had to re-create himself as a god, or as Nietzsche put it, as a "superman." This new man would not cringe and collapse because God had been found out to be a myth. He would rise above this hard, tragic, cruel reality to create a new world. This new man, the superman, would be a fighter, domineering and unyielding to nature. He would be without tender compassion, humility and love, for these Christian values, said Nietzsche, could never win the promised land. Nietzsche turned the ancient assumption on its head: it was not God who had created man, but man who had created God.

Not surprisingly, the Nazis later favored Nietzsche's views and bent them to their own ends. Nietzsche himself, however, was distraught over the loss of God and anxiously sought an alternative to take his place, a new ideal for man. In this he was joined by two other Germanic thinkers, Karl Marx and Sigmund Freud.

These three Germans, Marx, Freud and Nietzsche, all atheists and all products of the 19th century, laid down the major theoretical bases for social and personal change in the 20th Century. Germany thus spawned the thinkers who had the greatest impact on the 20th Century, but again, this is no surprise. At the start of this century Germany had the highest level of education of any country, great universities, a prosperous middle class and a level of industrialization comparable to the United States and England. It was, in many ways, the most advanced, the most modern of all nations.

Ironically, only 28 years after Nietzsche's declaration that "God is dead," Germany, the most modern of states, helped plunge the world into the first of the two World Wars, the greatest bloodbaths in history. The 20th Century subsequently has been marked, especially in intellectual and artistic circles, by a brooding pessimism that easily slides into cynicism. What a contrast to the ringing optimism of that statement placed in a German church steeple in 1784.

As Nietzsche foresaw, God's death meant that man must create his own heaven, his own salvation. This heaven could not be otherworldly, for there was no longer any reason to hope for life after death. Man was merely a material creature, dust to dust.

Marx's ideas were thus perfectly suited for this new ethic, the new spirit to dominate the new century. Communism offered a purely materialistic definition of the world. Religion had been an opiate, but now men and women could take their fate into their own hands, by force if necessary, and create a world in which equality would be the supreme value. Equality was mainly defined as sameness of financial rewards. Class distinctions would evaporate as all people shared equally in the products of their joint labor. So great would be the new commitment to the group, to the common good, that even the need for government would eventually disappear. In the meantime, as Lenin and Stalin saw more clearly than Marx, government would need to be all-powerful to bring about these splendid changes. This all-powerful State would be controlled by a ruling elite, a small group of philosopher kings who truly understood Marxist theory. Democracy, the people, could not be trusted to run the State during this critical period of transition because only the elite understood the inner workings and mysteries of communist theory. Communism was a new form of Gnosticism, of esoteric knowledge, since the real forces that determined human destiny were underneath the surface and could only be known by those trained in and dedicated to the Marxist view of the world. These new "priests" would interpret the secret knowledge for the people. The eerie similarity of the communist ideologues with the priests of the medieval church was palpable. Social engineering, the use of State power that treated people not as individuals, but as members of a group, was quickly determined to be the most efficient method to bring about the required changes. Since life was short the changes had to be made fast, and all changes focused on the materialistic world, since that was all there was. People, as individuals, mattered only to the extent that they fit into Marxist ideology since *it* was all-knowing and all-truthful.

Communism thus encompassed the main ideas that became the central themes of the 20th Century – the use of a powerful State to force individuals to conform in their everyday lives to the precepts of man-made ideologies designed to establish equal material conditions for all. Salvation was attainable through material progress and power in this life, the only life. These same themes took many forms and quickly spread around the world in the first half of the 20th Century. They dominated all talk of progress and change. Intellectuals of all nations took to these themes as ducks to water.

Central to the above themes was the notion of *relativity* of values, of morals, of cultures. This notion had been gathering steam for 200 years; it burst upon the 20th Century at full speed. This was the idea that there were no absolute standards underlying truth, beauty and goodness, hence no absolute, or "real" values or morals. Values were merely a product of perspective, of one's viewpoint and prejudices acquired through the particularities of one's training.

The notion of moral and social relativism was provided one of its biggest boosts by another great German scholar, Albert Einstein, when his theory of relativity was popularized in the 1920s. Einstein regretted this extrapolation of his concepts, "there are no absolutes in the universe, even time and space are curvilinear, everything is relative to the observer," for he was not an atheist and he believed in an ultimate right and wrong. But, many people inferred that there were no absolutes in the social as well as in the physical universe. The new social sciences, eager to gain respectability as real sciences, proclaimed relativism as fact. Moral and social relativism then provided the framework, in democratic societies, for the vivid, daring liberation of man from the last constraints of traditional religious belief. Man was set free to pursue his life, or "lifestyle" as it came to be known, in whatever manner he pleased. In non-democratic societies, moral relativism provided a rationale for the State to abrogate the rule of law and then impose on its citizens its new vision of man. Moral relativism, the notion that truth is merely a matter of personal perspective, readily became a foundation stone in most of the social changes of the 20th Century.

Moral relativism cannot exist within the context of the Judeo-Christian ethic of individual responsibility. The two are incompatible. Relativism asserts that our actions are products of our unique perspectives, our past training. There is no absolute standard of right and wrong. The Judeo-Christian ethic, however, asserts that we are accountable to God, who ultimately judges our actions by *His* absolute standard of right and wrong.

Moral relativism readily became a dominant theme of the 20th Century, especially among the learned. The Judeo-Christian ethic of individual responsibility, hence individual guilt, was downgraded in importance. Freud and Marx were early leaders of this denigration of the old ethic. Both were determinists who taught that individual free will was a fiction, much as God was a fiction, that in fact man was controlled by unseen forces that led him about much as flotsam on the sea.

The psychologists of the US and USSR, who opposed Freud on other counts, joined him in this deterministic view. They argued that man was controlled by his environment and could be understood through the study of the principles of conditioning. Most social scientists agreed with some version of this latter view. A person's fate was determined by his environmental conditioning that produced his unique perspective and reactions. The individual could not, then, be held truly accountable for his actions. In the ultimate sense he was the "victim" of his circumstances. No one person was guilty of misdeeds and harming others. We were all guilty because we were all responsible for the social environment that had ultimately "caused" the individual's misdeeds. Group guilt, societal guilt, thus replaced individual guilt. Society was responsible for our actions, not we as individuals.

This new view of man, of the human condition, brought about radical changes in how morals and values were viewed in the 20th Century. Moral relativism was energized by this new definition of man's nature. Together, moral relativism and social guilt (rather than individual guilt) became the guiding lights for enlightened social change in the 20th Century. But was this progress? Some argued that this was regression to earlier, more primitive mores and values masquerading as progress. Wasn't it true that collective accountability had been typical of the ancient world? Just how valid was the "new" definition of man and of the human condition?

Both Freud and Marx taught that man's destiny was controlled by unseen, subterranean forces. In a strange sort of way, they were "conspiracy" theorists. Marx replaced the unseen hand of God with the unseen hand of economic determinism. Freud replaced it with the suppressed and sublimated drive of sexual energy. All human behavior, said Freud, could ultimately be explained as manifestations of libido. His theory was also Gnostic. Only specially trained "priests" (psychiatrists) could truly understand the hidden workings of the libido on the human psyche. These priests would liberate people from their neurotic torments caused by the rigid or ritualistic suppression of sexual desire.

Whereas Freud saw sex as man's energy source, Nietzsche saw power, the need and lust for power, as man's driver. Nietzsche taught that the drive for power had been constrained in earlier times, for most people, by the Christian teachings on humility, love for others and submission to a higher power, God. Those personalities, however, who in earlier times craved power over love of God had ironically gravitated to the churches, since in religious eras the most effective way to exercise power over others was often through the venues of organized religion. Nietzsche saw the demise of religion around him and accurately predicted that in the 20th Century political zealotry would replace religious zealotry as the primary avenue for power-seeking personalities. He foresaw that in our century those same personalities who in earlier times had pursued power over others through the Church would now pursue power over others through the State. Lenin, Hitler, Mussolini, and many, many others of lesser stature soon arose to confirm his predictions.

Humanism — Centerpiece of the 20th Century Myth and Man's Substitute for Religion

The ethic driving most social change in the 20th Century has been humanism, the idea that people can attain all their goals of dignity and self-realization by their own efforts and abilities. As the century unfolded, religion declined in importance as a resource for social change. There were a few exceptions, such as the early civil rights movement led by Martin Luther King, but for most reformers religion was encrusted in dogmas that seemed out of touch with modern realities. Also, the growing power of government made it increasingly attractive to social reformers. In the 19th century, most social activists had worked through churches or set up private organizations. The Salvation Army was a prototype of 19th century activism, as were the many hospitals, orphanages and universities founded by various churches during that period. In the 20th Century, though, activists increasingly turned to government, for the State had shown itself capable of great power. It could tax people and thus raise huge amounts of money that could be redistributed to good causes. It also could pass laws, and enforce them, that made people behave the way social activists wanted them to behave. It could effect change much faster than the old ways. The State was irresistibly powerful. Social change through State power and the growth of the State fed off each other, while church and family receded into the background as resources for self-help.

The 20th Century Myth often incorporated the highest humanistic values, many of which had been derived from the Judeo-Christian ethic. In this regard, the 20th Century Myth was not as radical a break from the old traditions as it appeared to be at first glance. And humanism, in a rather amorphous way, became the ethic the majority of Europeans and North Americans referred to as the source of their everyday morals and values. This change of reference is evident in our everyday conversation. As a boy I remember the old folks, who had been born in the 19th century, referring to acts of goodness or charity as "the Christian thing to do." A man might be described as "a Christian gentleman." These expressions sound antique to us today. Nowadays, in describing the very same acts, we say they are "humanitarian." This changeover in perspective from religious to humanistic was, for most people, not so much a matter that God was "dead"; rather, he was simply excluded from everyday thinking and living. In a secular society, one may regard religion as interesting but not truly relevant to everyday life. God is a removed or merely historical figure lacking contact with the "real problems of the real world."

Humanism speaks to modern men and women with its emphasis on human dignity, the rights of each person, equality and tolerance for all, and world citizenship, even to the point of pacifism. Humanism celebrates life and encourages people to fulfill all their potentials while enjoying every delicious nuance of this life. The old canons and beliefs of religion, which were being battered on all sides by science and scholarly research, were hard put to compete for people's hearts with this new, seemingly more positive view of the human condition.

Humanism, however, is not a product of the 20th Century. It has a long, rich and colorful history going back at least to Aristotle. Its proponents in the Renaissance led the revolt against the medieval Church's concept of man as a fallen, depraved creature. They asserted the essential dignity of each person. They were often bold in their assertions. Lorenzo Valla, in his treatise *On Pleasure* (c. 1431), declared that the prostitute was better than the nun because she made men happy while the nun lived in barren, shame-ridden celibacy. Rabelais (c. 1534), through his writings on the adventures of a lusty monk, encouraged a society in which everyone slept late, where there were no clocks, where all forms of bigotry and prejudice were banned, where everyone was rich and at liberty to express his free will as he wished, where all ladies were lovely and all men were handsome, where conversation was always bright and lively, and where the only rule of life was *"do what thou wilt,"* a worthy precursor to that adage later popularized in the 1960s, *"do your own thing."* Rabelais taught that truly free men would always choose that which benefited the common good, for people were intrinsically good and lovely, a belief about the nature of man shared by a later, great humanist, Rousseau. The spirit of the Italian Renaissance, which rebelled from medieval Christianity to delight in all forms of beauty, was well stated, purportedly, by Cosimo de Medici: "You follow infinite objects; I follow the finite. You place your ladders in the heavens, I on earth, that I may not seek so high or fall so low." This is but a more eloquent expression of the popular beer commercial of our time that encouraged TV viewers to "go for the gusto, because you only go around once."

The 20th Century mind resonates to the humanism of Shakespeare, whose richly drawn characters are moved by their own inner vitality and who are often oblivious to the struggles of philosophy or theology of their own or any other era. His humanism centered on a practical interest in human nature with little concern for man's beliefs beyond this life. It is not for lack of competition that Shakespeare is still our most popular playwright; he fits well into the 20th Century.

Sometimes this keen interest in human psychology led to an obsession with magical mastery over self and others, as expressed in *Doctor Faustus* (c. 1587) when Christopher Marlowe has the good doctor say:

> Philosophy is odious and obscure
> Both law and physic are for petty wits;
> Divinity is basest of the three...
> 'Tis magic, magic, that hath ravished me.

Doctor Faustus was Marlowe's creation who sold his soul to the devil so that he could know, feel, and experience everything. These same drives for self-power and to "experience it all" are vital components of the 20th Century spirit.

Humanitarianism reached the apex of its development later on in the Age of Enlightenment, as seen in the works of Voltaire and Rousseau in France, Goethe in Germany, Hume, Bentham and Adam Smith in England and Thomas Jefferson in America. It stressed that all men have equal rights to happiness and liberty. It awoke a revulsion at human slavery and war. It preached tolerance, pacifism, cosmopolitanism. Patriotic prejudices were to be despised because all men were equal parts of the whole of humanity. And society was forever progressing toward an ideal state because man was essentially good; he was perfectible. The central theme was the pursuit of happiness in this life, perfectly captured by the esteemed Bishop Joseph Butler in this quote from his *Sermons* (c. 1750):

> "It is manifest that nothing can be of consequence to mankind... but happiness. We can therefore owe no man anything but... to promote his happiness. And therefore... to endeavor to do good to all... is a discharge of all the obligations we are under to them... And this entitles the precept, *Thou shalt love thy neighbor as thyself*, to the preeminence given to it."

The idea of a "natural order" that led to the "natural, inalienable rights of man" was best expressed by the Utilitarians (Bentham): that each man, in seeking his own best interest, worked with all other men to produce the best possible happiness for the whole of society.

Humanism in the 1700s adopted as its own the main principles of Christian morality, as earlier recommended by the most brilliant of the Renaissance humanists, Erasmus. Erasmus (c. 1505) had proclaimed "the philosophy of Christ" with its emphasis on the brotherhood of all men. He saw in Jesus an enlightened teacher of morality wherein reason was warmed by love for all men. In his incisive satires he poked fun at the excesses of the Church, which removed it, he said, from the essential teachings of Jesus. Erasmus "lost out" in his battle with the reformer, Martin Luther, for men were not yet ready to disavow the Church in order to take up the philosophy of Jesus. They did as they had always done – they exchanged one superstition for another. But Erasmus seemed vindicated two centuries later when his ideas took hold and became a basis for the exciting principles of the Enlightenment. This excitement can be felt in the quote that opens this chapter, and this excitement was felt over all of Europe and the Americas. The leaders of the Enlightenment adopted the morality of Jesus into their overall concept without much question or debate. It was assumed that everyone realized that Jesus's teachings were the most advanced ever pronounced to man.

But there was a glitch in all this. For even in the Age of Enlightenment the relationship between Jesusonian morality and humanism was tentative. The humanists of the 1700s started their philosophies of human society from reason, not faith. And reason has never produced an ironclad argument for the existence of God, much less the necessity for faith. By contrast, it was the teaching of faith in God that underscored all the morality teachings of Jesus. Inevitably, reason, especially when science later matured in the 19th century, could not continue to support the philosophy of Jesus as the rationale for humanitarianism. The one did not lead, rationally, to the other. Humanists increasingly had to stretch their logic to incorporate the Jesusonian teachings as the basis for their morality. Further, the Jesusonian teachings were often encased within a rigid church dogma that taught that all non-believers were damned forever. Such teachings were exclusive in their effect, whereas the spirit of humanism was inclusive of all peoples. And 18th century humanism had always stressed equal rights to the "pursuit of happiness" as the supreme virtue. But Jesus had taught that true, longterm happiness was achievable only by putting one's faith, one's trust in God's hands. Then how could one do such a thing when neither reason nor science could prove the existence of God in the first place? Happiness seemed better achieved by focusing on the pleasures of this life, that is, by fulfilling all of our human potentials in the here and now.

As society was increasingly secularized in the 20th Century, humanism distanced itself from its roots in the Judeo-Christian ethic. Humanism became increasingly *human* and *now-oriented* with little or no reference to the Jesusonian teachings that had provided its values, its "enlightenment," in the 1700s. Humanism before had taken its morality, its values, primarily from the teachings of Jesus, especially his teachings on the *brotherhood of all people*. The brotherhood concept was the foundation of humanitarian idealism: its emphasis on peace, not war; on the essential equality of all people; on justice and tolerance for all. And it is here that we come to the basic problem of 20th Century humanism. For Jesus, the most eloquent teacher of the concept of the brotherhood of all people, taught that all people were brothers *because they were all sons and daughters of God*. The commonality, and essential dignity, of each man and each woman was due, Jesus said, to the truth that each was a son or daughter of God, and that God loved each of his children equally and with a fullness beyond our comprehension. Since all had the same parent, all were brothers and sisters and were to love one another as they wished to be loved. All were members of the same family.

This potent, profound teaching slowly but surely loses its power for good when the brotherhood of man concept is cut off from its root concept of the fatherhood of God. This is what happened in humanistic thought in the 20th Century. The root concept – of God as a loving, caring Creator Parent to all beings – was deemed no longer relevant or necessary to humanism's goals and values.

Without this foundation, the idea of the brotherhood of man must sustain itself on the basis of the supposed "natural goodness" of man, or on the basis of some global concept such as "we're all in this together because we share a common destiny – we're all going to die," or "we're all in this together because we all must live on the same planet."

These general appeals to a common ground for humanitarianism rarely have the ability to sustain idealism for very long. They suffer from the same defect – that in their definition of the brotherhood of man, man himself is the measure of all things. There is no standard outside of man for appeal. When man is the only measure, most people extend themselves for others only as long as little personal cost to themselves is involved. But as the personal cost adds up, which it inevitably does, man draws back into himself. For it is *his* happiness, *his* pleasure, *his* rights that must come first, that must be protected at all costs. Ultimately, there is nothing to call him outside of himself. He joins with others of similar prejudices and together they fight for "our" rights or on behalf of another group that's been identified as needing "our" help. But then it quickly becomes a matter of "us" vs. "them" (all those who disagree with our version of our rights). The adversarial posture becomes the automatic position to take. The pie is limited and must be fought over. Whoever ends up with the biggest piece wins. Being of service to others is distorted into power politics.

Promoting the brotherhood of man without the root concept of the parenthood of God is much like a family where the mother and father have left the children alone for an extended period. Stripped of the support and discipline provided by loved and respected parents, the children take to incessant fighting among themselves over their limited resources, even though they are all "brothers."

Twentieth Century humanism, with few exceptions, is a regressed form of 18th Century humanism. It is humanism without a foundation. It typically is based on the precepts of moral relativism. It is permeated with materialistic desire and the demand to have it all, *now*. It readily deteriorates into power politics. It does not hesitate to use the concepts of moral relativism and collective guilt to place one group of people over another group of people. It is often characterized by good intentions, but as a force it has lost its fountainhead, its very rationale for being.

Modern humanism, however, is a wonderful ethic for those who see the pursuit of pleasure as the chief goal of life. It has become so suffused with moral relativism that it can be used to justify anything. "Do your own thing as long as you don't hurt anyone else," the clarion call of the 1960s, was a child's version of moral relativism. It blithely ignored the fact that the initiator of the "thing" had set himself up as the sole judge and jury of its effects on others. It was and is narcissism without constraint. It leaves the final judgement of what is good or bad exclusively to the individual (much as did the sophists of ancient Greece and the existentialists of our times). Old fashioned self-centeredness then can be justified under the guise of self-development or self-expression. The noble humanism of the 18th century, now stripped of its base, readily degenerates into a childish morality play.

Modern humanism is shallow, for it does not address the central question of life, which is death. How a person deals with his own death and the issue of his personality survival has always been the central question from which all others follow. Twentieth Century humanism, which ducks and hides from the eternal questions, is a puny specimen compared to the major philosophies and religions of earlier ages. It caters to children, while being a disservice to them, and leaves the mature adult, who can no longer delude himself on the imminence of his own death, with a hollowness upon awakening in the middle of the night.

God Doesn't Die After All

As historian Paul Johnson points out, the "outstanding non-event" of the 20th Century "was the failure of religious belief to disappear."[3] If religion is defined broadly, we can even say that interest in things spiritual is as great today as in most other eras. Indeed, psychological research over the past few decades indicates that religious persons are both mentally healthier and more courageous in the face of adversity than the non-religious, but more of this in the third chapter. Suffice to say at this point that religion has not resolved the problems that caused it to lose importance over the past 100 years. The problems remain, and yet so does religion.

Carl Jung, another early 20th Century Germanic scholar, disagreed with the prevailing view that religion would disappear in the 20th Century. Jung argued that religion occurs in all societies in all ages because it is an instinctive attitude that expresses universal truths. Religion can be suppressed, but it will simply reappear in a new form: *"Naturam expellas furca tamen usque recurret* (You can throw out Nature with a pitchfork, but she'll always turn up again)."[4] In his brilliant essay on modern man, *The Undiscovered Self* (1957), Jung pointed out that worship of the State and its masters, so common to the 20th Century, was in reality the religious instinct expressing itself in another form. Jung also argued that religion could not be destroyed by reason and science because it is the product of man's inner, "irrational" life, thus not subject to validation by man's rationalized, external criteria. Jung asserted that religion's problems were due to most religionists' accepting their traditional creeds without authenticating the underlying truths through their own inner experiences with God. Thus their religion was strictly conventional, based on *unreflected belief*, and easily decimated when subjected to rational, scientific scrutiny. This was more true than ever in the 20th Century, since the old mythologies that enshrouded the traditional creeds looked more and more ludicrous in light of man's advancements in knowledge. The underlying eternal truths were thus harder to discern unless one was willing to attempt authentication through one's inner experiences, i.e., through making a "leap of faith" and then experiencing the effects on one's life. Since this is something few are willing to do, Jung concluded that religion would be viewed as increasingly irrelevant by most people, although it would of course emerge in their lives in strange ways, since it was an instinctual drive that could not be denied.

Clearly, religion has many problems of credibility in a scientific age such as ours. Nevertheless, religion flows right through the 20th Century like a great river moving down the middle of a continent. It will not be denied. It will not go away. Deprive people of it and they will find their way back to it. Whatever it is, it is a powerful force in human behavior. This, too, is one of the great lessons of the 20th Century: religion does not disappear merely because men and women adopt a materialistic, humanistic view of themselves and the cosmos.

Religion is often slow to adapt to new knowledge, but it has shown itself capable of eventual change. In this respect religion has many great traditions on which to call. One example is Jesus, who was a revolutionary of the first rank. He shattered tradition, threw out established dogma, and criticized the clergy and organized religion of his time. He called people *not* to mass action, but individually to take a stand on the meaning of one's life based on his expanded teaching of the fatherhood of God and resultant brotherhood of all people. George Bernard Shaw may have been right after all: "The only trouble with Christianity is that it has never yet been tried."

The Vacuum Remains

If 1886 were the true beginning of the 20th Century, then 1989 may have marked the start of the 21st Century. The year 1989 saw the incredibly rapid fall of one collective state after another as each of these entities struggled to regain a sense of the individual's rights to liberty, justice and freedom of thought. Religion appeared to be on the rise in all these states. The spirit of the 20th Century, the long, dark winter of regressive collectivism, appeared to be coming to an end. No one could be sure what the spring thaw would bring – more regression in another form, or true progress.

In 1850 thoughtful persons earnestly debated what would happen to world society with the fall of the great monarchies. Now those debates seem unreal to us. Who needs kings and queens to rule? In 2050 people will no doubt look back on our collectivist experiments, our worries over the communist scourge, and chuckle knowingly at our naivete. Why, anyone could see that collectivism was bound to fail. Such are the joys of hindsight.

At the end of the 20th Century it is clear that the 20th Century Myth has not captured the hearts and minds of the majority of people. The new mythology was supposed to fill the vacuum created by the loss of God. But the vacuum remains. And this is the central problem of the 20th Century – the vacuum remains. In the first decades of this century the vacuum was mainly a problem for intellectuals who gravitated either to humanism or collectivism, usually to some combination of the two (as expressed in the great 20th Century Myth) to fill the void. But with each succeeding generation, the proportion of people who fell out of time with the old faiths and who thus felt the impact of the void increased. In America, a quantum leap in this proportion of the population occurred when the baby boomers came of age in the 1960s. Now the majority of people, not just intellectuals and artists, feel the vacuum keenly. The result has been increased feelings of anxiety, restlessness, fearfulness. Nothing seems settled anymore. People are not sure if they can commit to anything anymore. We are left with a restless materialism and a vaguely felt self-obsession. Our institutions, especially the family, have been wracked by this uncertainty in values and direction. Modern men and women know they need a great faith to restore meaning, direction and security in their lives, but they see few if any viable options. Our everyday humanism thoughtlessly slips into self-centered, materialistic obsessions. Let's go shopping. What else is there?

The 20th Century has been a scientific and technological bonanza for man, but in human and communal relationships there has been as much regression as progression. The common glue that's needed to hold us together, to inspire us to implement higher values, either is missing or considered untrustworthy. How to fill this vacuum is the single greatest issue facing us in the 21st Century. Until we deal effectively with this challenge, all else we accomplish will ring with a certain hollowness in our inner ear.

Summary

The spirit of the 20th Century, as expressed in its great myth, was a product mainly of the disillusion felt by many European intellectuals at the end of the 19th Century. The New Myth fostered collectivism, State worship, and looked to moral relativism for its ethical basis. On a finer level, humanistic self-worship was elevated to a central focus.

The humanism sanctified by the 20th Century Myth expressed many of the highest values found in the Judeo-Christian traditions. But since God was now "dead" there was no absolute or ultimate reality to sustain these higher values. In essence, it was every man for himself. Without the fatherhood of God the brotherhood of Man too readily deteriorates into power politics and unforgiving selfishness. It is doubtful that the 20th Century Myth, seemingly so modern in its time, can in fact provide a real and enduring basis for the healthy development either of individuals or states. Something else is needed.

Chapter Two

The 1960s: The 20th Century Myth Comes to America
Personal Expression Replaces Traditional Values

The 20th Century has often been called "the American century." By the 1940s it was evident that the U.S. economy was the strongest in the world. At the end of World War II the U.S. was the strongest country militarily (a whole new experience for America) and "owned" the atomic bomb. In the 20 years after 1945 the U.S. economy experienced an unprecedented boom that allowed America to dominate the world stage as no nation ever had done before.

Ironically, of all the leading nations, America most staunchly had resisted the 20th Century Myth: collectivism, State worship, abrogation of individuals' rights, moral relativism, etc. At mid-century, when this era was first being acknowledged as the American century, the U.S. actually functioned as a throwback to an earlier era. The U.S. stood for the traditional values and beliefs derived from the 18th and 19th Centuries – the values of the Enlightenment, the Judeo-Christian ethic, and Adam Smith's essays on capitalism. The materialism of America was often softened by traditional religious beliefs and a strong social service ethic based on individual voluntarism. In values and ideals the U.S. stood in sharp contrast to the world's other leading societies of Germany, the U.S.S.R., Japan, China, and most of what would later be called the "Third World." World War II heightened the differences between America and the majority of the rest of the world. Only England and some of her former colonies seemed compatible in values with the U.S., although even they were more prone to experimentation with the 20th Century Myth than America. The U.S. was a mighty repository of the earlier Enlightenment ethic, and yet, intriguingly, the leading nation in the 20th Century.

In the 1930s, however, the U.S. became more receptive to the kind of social experimentation by then commonplace in the rest of the world. In response to the economic depression of the times, U.S. government intervention into people's lives and some social institutions occurred on a fairly large scale. Most of these programs, especially the work programs, were terminated as soon as the economy recovered. However, Social Security for the aged and Aid for Dependent Children (originally set up for children of widows) were two programs originated in the 1930s that continued on. Continued government intervention into the economy, however, was highly questionable since it had not brought an end to the economic depression. There was no compelling evidence to support the notion that the Hoover-Roosevelt interventionism of the 30s brought recovery to the economy. Indeed, it could be argued that government interventionism prolonged the economic depression.[5]

The U.S. economy,however, was stimulated by the outbreak of war in Europe in the fall of 1939. It was not until 1941 that the dollar value of U.S. production caught up with and passed 1929 levels. With the onset of World War II, the U.S. quickly returned both to prosperity and to its traditional values. For the remainder of the 1940s, 50s and early 60s the U.S. proudly retained its role as "the last Arcadia."[6] The U.S. was committed to the continued implementation of the values and ideals of the Enlightenment.

There was one group of Americans, however, whose underlying ethic had been permanently changed in the 1930s – her intellectuals. Many American intellectuals were aghast at the economic events of the 30s, especially the greater impact for the worse on the working classes and small farmers. John Steinbeck's novel, *The Grapes of Wrath*, later captured in a brilliant 1940 movie by John Ford, perfectly expressed the concerns of Americans on these matters. Intellectuals naturally wondered if there was something fundamentally wrong with the American system. They looked toward the U.S.S.R., which had been widely advertised by many European intellectuals as the new society, the wave of the future that was already working, and which guaranteed economic equality and full employment for all. Some American intellectuals began to dabble with communism and other aspects of the 20th Century Myth. As a group, American intellectuals, artists and media personnel were well informed on the changes going on in the rest of the world. They were tuned in to the 20th Century Myth as it was being expressed in the cultural arts and thought of the older European societies, for which they had great respect. The upshot of all this was that as America recovered from the 1930s, many of its intellectuals were left with lingering doubts about American institutions and values, and with the disquieting feeling that America was a philistine out of touch with the rest of the world. As noted by Mortimer Adler, by 1940 students in the rarefied atmosphere of the University of Chicago were addicted to "...subjectivism and relativism about all questions of value, about the principles of morality...".[7] The American intelligentsia moved decidedly to the Left in the 1930s and stayed there, long after the majority of Americans returned to their traditional values. This development later proved critical in bringing about the dramatic changes of the 1960s.

The "American century" reached an apex in the 1950s, or more accurately in the 20 years from 1945 to about 1965. There was far more to this than worldwide economic dominance. America had come into its own in the theater, in literature and in all phases of popular culture. The generation of American writers, playwrights and moviemakers that had come into maturity in the 1920s and 30s was now in full bloom and respected worldwide. New York City, the ultimate American city (which later disgraced itself in the 60s and 70s) was in the 1950s the center of the world in nearly all fields. U.S. schools and universities were strong, especially the latter, due in part to an influx of German scholars who had fled from the Nazis and relocated in America. Politically and morally the U.S. stood on high ground. It led the free world, seemingly the only force that could stand up to the rising tide of collectivism. It protected the old, tired nations of Western Europe. And the U.S. had demonstrated wise, ethical leadership in assisting Japan and West Germany to restart their economies after World War II and rebuild their political institutions along democratic lines. The U.S. was a conquering nation truly rare in history: it resisted the temptation to plunder the defeated. The U.S. was strong and seemingly invincible. Then came the 1960s.

In the 1960s a *Zeitgeist* swelled into a tidal wave of change that engulfed the whole of American society. No one in 1959 could have predicted accurately the nature of the U.S. in 1969. The changes were too sudden and too dramatic. This *Zeitgeist* was created by six contiguous and somewhat interrelated factors.

First, the Vietnam War became the most unpopular war in U.S. history. The country was divided angrily over the validity and viability of the war effort. It eventually became the only major war in U.S. history not won.

Second, the modern civil rights movement, begun in the 1950s, exploded into the 60s. Black Americans were angry and determined. White Americans were on a roller coaster of conflicting emotions. Many were resentful that blacks were placing such demands on U.S. society. Many later felt guilty as the justness of many of those demands became more and more difficult to deny. Then some elements of the movement changed from the non-violent, Christian inspired moralism of Martin Luther King to the strident, at times violent, nature of the Black Power advocates. Some whites responded to this change in tactics with more feelings of guilt, while others became more resentful and angry. The nation was split not only black versus white, but also white versus white. By 1969 there were riots in the streets and parts of cities were burned out, a new and foreign experience for most Americans.

Third, a trio of assassinations shook most Americans badly. Regardless of what one thought of the two Kennedys and Martin Luther King, people were shocked by their cold blooded murders. America seemed to have deteriorated to the ethics of a third-rate dictator republic. The rule of law, with its intrinsic promise of tolerance for differing views, was crumbling before American eyes.

Fourth, the poor were rediscovered. The book, *The Other America*, presented a dismal picture of America's poor. The U.S. had been in an economic boom for so long that it was easy to forget that some people had been left behind. John Kennedy was moved by this book to initiate legislation that would later be the nucleus of Lyndon Johnson's "War on Poverty." The nation was split both on how much should be done for the poor and how it should be done.

Fifth, student activism in the nation's universities erupted as never before in the U.S. These college students, the "baby boom" kids, were the most numerous and the most widely educated of any American generation. All of America's good fortune and affluence had been showered on them, and now they were saying terrible things about U.S. society. If these kids no longer believed in America, then who could? They were angry about the poor, the assassinations, the treatment of blacks and most of all about Vietnam, for that affected them most personally. They wore long hair, spoke openly in obscenities, used drugs and had sex seemingly when they felt like it. Their elders recoiled in horror. Something was very, very wrong in America. Part of this strong reaction was due to naivete since, in fact, the student activists were carrying on, even dressing, in much the same manner as student activists of other countries in prior centuries.[8] Another part of this reaction was due to the eerie similarity of this activism to the mass actions seen heretofore only in totalitarian societies. When the students sacked deans' offices, threatened violence if they didn't get their way, made professors recant unacceptable views and didn't hesitate to intimidate others who disagreed with them, their actions seemed to fly in the face of the most basic American values. The student activists began to look more and more like the student activists of Germany in the 20s and 30s, who had brought down the great German universities and inadvertently helped to set up German society for Hitler's takeover.

These five factors led to the sixth and decisive factor. The American intelligentsia looked upon all this and declared America sick. The country was, they said, sick to its very roots. America had failed; failed its young, its women, its poor, its blacks, its other minorities, nearly everyone.

Nietzsche's 1886 pronouncement that God was dead was rediscovered while the New Morality, based on "all is relative," was said to be the enlightened way out of our sickness. Now, to be sure, this was the same America that only a few years before had been seen as ethical, mighty, rich, the leader of the free world. The objective reality of all this was still true. Nevertheless, America was proclaimed rotten to its core and in need of a total overhaul.

It is important to remember that the American intelligentsia had been radicalized in the 1930s. These tendencies had been reinforced by the "red hunts" of the early 50s. Through all this, American intellectuals had become comfortable in their role as the chief critics of American society. Their job had a noble purpose – to keep Americans from becoming smug about their institutions, history and values. Now, in the 60s, all forms of activism were exploding in the very front yard of intellectuals – the university. Unbelievably, student activists were accusing their professors of being part of the "establishment." They were claiming that the cream of the intelligentsia was just as corrupt as the rest of American society. The only way to avoid this scathing criticism was to agree with the activists' critique of American society. The professors had to make a choice: either join the activists or oppose them. There were no gray zones since the activists, in the tradition of zealotry, would not allow any. For many in the intelligentsia the decision was easy. They joined with the students and together they declared America a sick society that needed restructuring from top to bottom. Ironically, these statements were being made when the U.S. was at the very acme of her wealth and powers – the mid and late 60s.

These statements, however, packed a lot of punch. Pronouncements by intellectuals usually do, especially in societies like the U.S. that place a high stake on education. The ongoing Vietnam War, the civil rights protests, the assassinations, and the rebellion of the nation's brightest young people left many Americans vulnerable to charges of corruption. Massive changes quickly occurred throughout American society. The door suddenly had been thrust open, allowing the 20th Century Myth to rush inside. If America were rotten to its core, then the only sensible thing to do was to turn to those ideas and concepts dominant in the rest of the world, especially the "New Myth" that promised instant equality for all.

These sweeping changes always were justified on the basis that they were the fulfillment of the American dream of equal rights for all. And there was much truth in this assertion. But the changes initiated in the 1960s and 70s also had a dark underside to them, a direct reflection of the 20th Century Myth that had suddenly bored its way into American thought:

- When student activists demanded and received courses on black and female history they were acting well within the scope of traditional American ideals. But, when they demanded to dictate content of courses and to define acceptable versus unacceptable ideas, they expressed the collectivism, the "group think" ethic of the 20th Century Myth.
- When the courts demanded integration of all public schools, they were acting out the finest of traditional American ideals. But, when they required forced busing as a quick fix, they employed the favored method of the 20th Century Myth – social engineering.
- When activists demanded and received affirmative action for minorities and women in the job marketplace, they were acting within the scope of traditional American attitudes of fair play and help to the underdog. But, when they twisted affirmative action to mean preferential treatment and quotas set aside for preferred groups, they were acting out the meanest side of the 20th Century Myth – the denial of individual rights by the redefinition of people into preferred versus non-preferred group categories.
- When feminists demanded no-fault divorce they thought they had made divorce quick, relatively painless and equitable. But, in eliminating the concept of individual blame, hence individual responsibility, they created a monster that has impoverished millions of women and children.
- When activists taught young blacks that blacks were all victims of society, they acted with good intentions. But, in removing from blacks the "burden" of individual responsibility and replacing it with the collective guilt of all whites, they unwittingly afflicted blacks with a double stan-

dard that diminished the incentive to acquire the skills blacks needed to compete with whites in the marketplace.

The examples go on and on. A bumper crop of Karl Popper's "Law of Unintended Consequences" was created. In nearly every major social change that came out of the turmoil of the 1960s, the positive basis of the change was in part negated by inclusion of components of the imported 20th Century Myth. Traditional American values, the ones that had made America a source of light and strength through the first half of the 20th Century, were diluted by the incorporation of the 20th Century Myth into almost every aspect of social change.

One of the more destructive effects of the New Myth can be seen in the change in emphasis from the individual to the group. Social engineering inevitably focuses on group category, not the individual, as the identified unit to undergo social change (especially ironic when we consider the 20th Century Myth's insistence that the only knowable reality is the Self). Social engineering has been the favored method for bringing about the social changes required by the 20th Century Myth. State power is used to move people about, as members of groups, to effect radical change. Stalin in 1929 thus ordered the forced movement of peasants onto collective farms resulting in 5 million people murdered by State authorities while 10 million others were placed in forced labor camps. Mao in 1958 ordered over 100 million Chinese onto communes in his "Great Leap Forward" to establish communism overnight, with the result that millions died from starvation. On a more benign level, the U.S. government, today, defines millions of school children strictly by race category and then orders them bussed to schools other than their neighborhood schools to achieve prespecified ratios of racial quotas. Most social engineering in this century has been rationalized by good intention; it has been designed to accomplish equal conditions for all.

When moral relativism combines with the notion of collective responsibility, then any view can be readily rationalized. When group identity becomes the focus of change, the social atmosphere is poisoned as group is set against group to fight over limited resources. In the 1960s, the traditional American emphasis on empowering the individual was shifted to empowering individuals via group identity (race, sex, etc.). We thereby regressed from the more advanced ethics of individual responsibility to the more primitive ethics of collective responsibility and collective guilt. Patricia Raybon notes:

> Race has become a red flag. Wave it around and see what you get — maybe guilt, maybe an arrest, maybe even an invitation to speak at a college graduation.

> Last week in New York a mob of black men chased down and almost beat to death a Vietnamese man they thought was Korean. This was no simple

case of mistaken identity. It was a shameful, barbaric act of terrorism.

And that, indeed, is the horror of "mistaken identity" based on race. It rips from people their selfhood. They cease to be themselves. They become their race – whatever that may mean to other people – and usually it means something profoundly different from who that person really is.

And it cuts both ways. As a black American, I can't afford to look at white skin and think "problem" – any more than a white American can look at black skin and imagine something just as demeaning.

The issue, really, is respecting individuality.[9]

With hindsight, it is tempting to look back on the 1960s and conclude that the intelligentsia and students hysterically over-reacted to problems that were in reality the normal growing pains of a still young republic unaccustomed to being a world power. They thereby stampeded the country into poorly conceived, instant "solutions" to social problems. Paul Johnson refers to this as America's attempt to commit suicide.

But you had to be there. The 1960s were a time when hysteria was the order of the day. Student activists had a ball. (I know; I was one of them.) Many activists now look back on those days in the same manner as some veterans look back to World War II – as the best years of their lives. It can be great fun to parade one's self-righteousness and demand instant, radical solutions without being responsible for the long-term consequences.

What activists didn't realize, with their anti-historical bias, was that our approach to social problems was a replica of previous student activism in Europe going back over several centuries. One of our predecessors had been the *Neue Schar*, the German student activists who sprang up in 1919 in reaction to World War I.[10] They were the original "hippies." They wore sandals, long hair, disdained baths, practiced free love and handed out flowers at their mass meetings. They danced to the guitar, studied Zen Buddhism, Siddhartha, and read Herman Hesse as well as Lenin. They were anti-capitalist, anti-bourgeois, and believed that German society was corrupt to its bones, that democracy and liberalism were part and parcel of the whole rotten system, that tolerance was out of date. And, as always, there were admiring adults who supported them in their attitudes. This movement demoralized Germany's universities, thereby helping to set the stage for Hitler's later takeover of Germany. There has always been a dark as well as a bright side to student activism.

It has been argued that youth revolt harms society more than it helps. Lewis Feuer, among other historians, asserts that the Russian student activists of the 1880s irretrievably set back that country's then growing trend toward liberal, constitutional government and thereby set the stage for the later Communist takeover of Russia in 1917.[11] The German student movement of 1815-1819, the *Burschenschaften*, similarly set back the cause of German liberalism for at least 30 years.[12] Bosnian student activists kicked off World War I when one of their members threw the bomb that assassinated Archduke Ferdinand in 1914. And on and on the examples go. The idea that generational conflict is the mainspring of history goes back at least to Plato, but few scholars have ever argued that youth activism brings social change free from major defects.

The American student activists of the 1960s and 70s were unique in at least one respect. As historian Walter Laqueur noted in 1969, "Youth movements have come and gone, but … never in the past has an older generation been so disconcerted by the onslaught of the young."[13] Not only did American elders over-react to the youth revolt of the 60s, in many important ways they caved in to it. The youth activists actually succeeded in changing America. Remember, these were the "baby boom" kids – the biggest and most highly touted and analyzed generation in America's history. And they had their way. By the early 70s customs that would have seemed unthinkable only 10 years before were rapidly becoming commonplace in American life. Couples now lived together openly before marriage, and their parents had to accept it whether they liked it or not. Drug usage at parties became as commonplace as alcohol use. Relationships, even marriage, had to conform to the new ethic: if one partner no longer pleased the other, then the grounds were adequate to terminate the relationship. The old goal of assimilation into American culture was debunked as ethnic groups asserted their own sub-cultures and "rights" to preferential treatment. Standards in schools were lowered and grade inflation became the order of the day. Core curricula were declared irrelevant and dropped. In the mad scramble to assert newly discovered "rights" the legal system became everyone's favorite dumping ground for all kinds of social and relationship problems. Mothers started leaving their infants at the newly developed day care centers so they could resume their careers quickly. The fabric of American society unraveled at an astonishing pace as the old values were discarded and "me-firstism" became the dominant theme. None of this would have seemed possible even a few years before. Everything seemed affected, suddenly and profoundly, by the ramifications of America's youth revolt of the 60s and 70s: families, relationships between the sexes, race relations, uses of law, schools and philosophies of education, work habits, America's whole way of looking at its society and its traditional liberal values born of the Enlightenment 200 years before. The founding fathers were now described as racists and chauvinist patriarchs; no longer were they beacons of enlightened values and farseeing wisdom. A pessimism set in that was far more than a reaction to Vietnam or Watergate. The student activist bias that America was corrupt became standardized as conventional truth. More and more people turned into themselves as the "me generation" was born. The only thing that didn't change was America's traditionally rampant materialism. Indeed, by the 1980s materialism seemed to be America's sole ethic.

To balance this perspective, it is well to remind ourselves of the good that's been accomplished since the 1960s – more opportunities for fraternal race relations; more and better job opportunities for people of color and women; more educational opportunities for people of color and women.

But we must also look at the negative spinoffs from the changes in values that took place in the 1960s, namely: the deterioration in the care of our children; the deterioration of our public schools; the increased hostility between men and women; the increase in dysfunctional families; the greed and lack of ability to delay gratification resulting in mindless materialism; and, in many urban areas, the loss of a sense of community.

When we blame "society" or "government" for this deterioration, we are like children pointing fingers. When our politicians run up out-of-control deficits they are representing us – the *us* we have become. We can change this only by changing ourselves first and to do this requires a re-examination of our values. In particular, the values spun out of the 20th Century Myth must be questioned, for they have had a negative effect on ourselves and our society.

Worship of Self: Chief Legacy of the 20th Century Myth

The 20th Century Myth fosters a person who vacillates between State worship and Self worship. It is the State that must equalize all resources and save man from the trials, hardships and inequalities of life. When this approach fails, as it always does, the New Man easily falls prey to self-centeredness. His self is the only thing he can know is real since he operates on the assumption that all other things are relative to him, to his self, to his perspective. He knows the dangers of self-centeredness, but what else is there? The 20th Century Myth offers no hope for anything beyond this life. The universe is cold and impersonal. Camus and Sartre, two leading existentialists of the century, took relativism to its conclusion and looked honestly at its end result – "a meaningless, absurd cosmos."

Moral relativism is the foundation of the 20th Century Myth: God is dead, the Absolute is no more, all is relative. This eventually leads to the notion that one view is as good as any other, for there is no real basis for discriminations and decisions based on values since all values are relative to the individual. Thus, tolerance must ultimately mean equal acceptance of all views. But at this point the real world always intrudes. For in the real world decisions must be made and resources allocated and, since no one view is better than any other, then it all comes down to who has control, who has power. The 20th Century Myth leads us back to the most primitive of all ethics: *might makes right*. This effect is seen easily in totalitarian societies. It takes subtler forms in more open societies. Many of today's universities offer examples of how the infusion of the 20th Century Myth leads to a rigid exclusivity where only currently acceptable notions are allowed; all others are shouted down. This is a dramatic change from the university as a "marketplace of ideas," where all ideas were to be heard with respect and subjected to the same standards for truthfulness; a concept derived from traditional liberalism. The new rigidity seen in intellectual circles, masquerading as the new tolerance, is one of many prices we pay as long as our social glue is weakened by the principles of thc 20th Century Myth.

The best of our traditional values, by contrast, demand individual, not group, accountability. The very finest of our traditional values require that the individual learn self-discipline, learn how to delay his own need for gratification, so that he may better serve others – his family, his friends, his community. Free choice and voluntarism are paramount, not coercion based on ideological assumptions. All of society is beholden to the rule by law, which is based on Natural Law. And Natural Law, that wonderful concept which runs along many lines from Plato through the Enlightenment, presumes the existence of moral absolutes in the universe. It therefore presumes that the universe is somehow grounded in an Eternal Being, the ultimate source of all truth, beauty and goodness. It assumes that each individual has the inherent right to pursue this Ultimate Reality in his own way. It therefore insists that each person's search for God be protected, while it bestows dignity on this search by asserting that each person is equally valued in the eyes of this same God. It insists that we are all brothers and sisters, and thus obliged to nurture each other, precisely because we are the sons and daughters of this great God. These are the most basic assumptions underlying our brilliant heritage. And this ennobling heritage is precisely what our present education no longer teaches (along with how to read and write).

A Dutch writer, commenting on Rosenstock-Huessy's *Out of Revolution*,[14] notes that "We all know we are in common need for a universal future. But how many people know that the creation of a universal future depends on the creation of a mutual past?"

Natural Law provides us with a mutual past as well as a universal future, for it leads us to the great principle that each of us, in his own way and in his own time, is on a pathway to the same Ultimate Truth. Natural Law thus teaches us tolerance and respect for each individual conditioned on the presumption of a moral absolute. In this view, each person stands as the embodiment of the supreme value of life. This traditional ethic teaches us tolerance of and respect for differing views since they are the inevitable result of the brotherhood of all people, for each of us, in his own way, is on a quest to be reunited with the Source of us all.

The highest expressions of the traditional view all converge on this point – that the universe is grounded in an Absolute, that subsequently there is an absolute right and an absolute wrong. But we are highly limited beings. Our limitations are so great that no single one of us can know the absolute right or the absolute wrong. It is here, but only here, that the traditional view and the 20th Century Myth agree. The two different believers can empathize with each other at this juncture. Then the two views quickly diverge again. The believer in the 20th Century Myth is likely now to retreat into himself, for he must rely on himself since his self is the only reality of which he can be sure. By contrast, the believer in the traditional myth, if he is true to his ethic, must now go outside himself, for *his* ultimate reality resides outside of his own self.

The believer in the traditional ethic must now make a leap of faith. If he chooses not to make this leap, then his faith is likely to calcify into an increasingly rigid belief system. He thereby chooses "the easy way out" by fixating on established belief. But if he chooses instead to take the leap, then he presumes the reality of an Absolute Power in the universe while accepting the notion that he and other believers are highly limited in their understanding of the Absolute. He thus accepts Plato's dictum that man in his current state is capable of perceiving only the "shadows" of the Divine Reality. As for the rest of it, he must rely on his faith in his idea. He is now ready to begin in earnest the quest for the meanings of truth, beauty and goodness, for he now believes that the source of all truth, beauty and goodness really exists and underlies the universe. *There is something to search for.* This is the beginning of the "hero's quest," which requires a rebirth of the individual, for the quest cannot begin until the new hero consciously chooses to make the leap of faith that somewhere, someplace, sometime there resides Ultimate Reality.

The hero's quest is nearly always carried on in the realm of everyday life. Our hero is rarely a monk in isolation from the world. His relationships with other people are often his paramount concern, his supreme value. And this concern to be of service to others comes about because our hero finds himself slowly, inevitably falling in love with the Divine Essence that he pursues. The more constant his courtship, the more he falls in love. And the more he falls in love, the more he aches to serve that Divine Essence which he now recognizes in nearly every person he encounters. So it happens that the realization of the Fatherhood of God breathes warm life into the Brotherhood of Man. Each day becomes a new adventure into this realm of limitless possibilities. Once the adventure is embarked upon in full and tested faith, it becomes increasingly evident that the adventure is infinite; that the drive to reunite with the Loved One never ends, it simply leads to one adventure after another. Our destiny is great, which we could easily see except that we insist in putting on our self-made blinders.

How many persons in the next generation, and in the next century, will choose to go on the hero's quest? There is certainly a growing restlessness, a growing disenchantment with things as they are. Paganism has about run its usual course. Materialism, sensationalism, hedonism always end up running, then exhausting, those who are thereby obsessed. There is a growing number of people who grow increasingly curious about the hero's quest. It has been said that our world "...is now quivering on the very brink of one of its most amazing and enthralling epochs of social readjustment, moral quickening and spiritual enlightenment."[15]

> Goethe was right when he said that the deepest distinction between...historical periods is that between belief and disbelief, and when he added that all epochs in which belief dominates are brilliant, uplifting, and fruitful, while those in which disbelief dominates vanish because nobody cares to devote himself to the unfruitful.

> Erich Fromm

Interestingly, the largest pool of potential seekers may reside within the very generation that so forcefully imposed the 20th Century Myth onto America – the baby boomers. The "boomers," by the sheer force of their numbers, injected and then overwhelmed American life with their version of the 20th Century Myth. But that was in their youth. Now the boomers are in their 30s and 40s. They are entering that period of life in which one must start facing one's own death. A re-evaluation of one's life may then occur at some level of consciousness. Carl Jung and others have noted that for many people this becomes the first time in their lives that they truly question their own first assumptions, the very meaning of their lives. The first wave of boomers is now coming into this time of their lives and a few of them will open the door into their own souls. Those boomers who have been most committed to the 20th Century Myth are likely to feel an eventual, aching hollowness. It is this same dry hollowness, especially when it comes in the middle of the night, that can compel a person to seek earnestly a higher wisdom than that which previously satisfied him. At the turn of the coming century, baby boomers may well be in the forefront in the search for spiritual meaning.

They will find a great many resources to fall back on, for throughout the 20th Century there have been many who sought after spiritual meaning, even in the midst of the cynicism fed by our era's leading intellectuals and artists. They can read, for example, the works of Emmet Fox[16] or Eric Butterworth[17]; or the works of C.S. Lewis and many of his "inklings" contemporaries, that rare group of intellectuals and mythologists who convened at Oxford University in the 1930s and 1940s (and which contained such luminaries as Tolkien and T.S. Eliot). Or they may read the works of Lewis's 19th Century predecessor, George MacDonald.[18] Though MacDonald is sometimes difficult to read, his searing insights on the relationship of God and man often surpass those of Lewis. Then there are the charming *Joshua* books for children by Joseph F. Girzone.[19] Or they can read what has been called the "masterpiece of all anthologies," Aldous Huxley's *Perennial Philosophy*,[20] a book that in the 21st Century will be recognized as one of the great achievements of the 20th Century. They may choose to read the works of the transpersonal psychologists. Early precursors to this school of thought were Carl Jung and Victor Frankl. Some representatives of the current generation are Ken Wilber, Scott Peck, Gerald Jampolsky, and Stephen Covey. These psychologists reject the notion that man is only a material creature. They posit that man's most common psychological affliction is spirit sickness – the fear, loneliness and ego-domination caused by man's separation from God. *A Course in Miracles*[21] is in this same school of thought. Or they may read the literature generated by Alcoholics Anonymous, which provides a fascinating study of personal redemption in an arena of great difficulty for 20th Century persons – drug and chemical dependency. Or they may wish to tackle the most comprehensive resource, *The Urantia Book*.[22] And there are many, many other resources as well, stretching back into previous ages, including the enlightened studies of the world's great religious books. The adventure is endless. Each author dips his cup into the great river of spiritual truth, derives his own unique contribution from it, then places the cup back into the great river.

In nearly all religions there are great sources of truth that lie ready to be tapped, though admittedly these truth sources are often covered over with manmade rules, creeds, rituals, dogmas, ancient cosmologies and all the accumulated products of the ecclesiastical bureaucracies. Nevertheless, the great truths are there; they have been partly unearthed by at least a few people in almost every place of worship in every land.

This quest for spiritual meaning is called "the quiet revolution." It does not yearn for television cameras to mug for. It eschews violence. It is unique for each individual. It is the most revolutionary of all changes, for it transforms forever one's view of the world. It is "the road less traveled." Many are called, few choose to go. This, however, will not always remain so. In the new era of spiritual awakening, more and more people will respond to the urge to embark on the great adventure. And these same people will slowly, surely, change the world for the better.

How can so few change the world? The history of the 20th Century (and all other centuries) is replete with examples of a few individuals, working singly or in small groups, who brought about true change in the world. We are all familiar with the great evil, the horrible harm to others, that can be brought about by one person bent on evil doing. But it is easy not to see the great good that flows, ripple like, from the person who lives out spiritual truth in his everyday life. Such people (and we are all that person from time to time) are the "salt of the earth" who enable life to continue on. It is our everyday kindnesses which hold us together. A few people, living out spiritual truth, can transform the world, for nearly all people instinctively respond to the "fruits of the spirits" when they see these in others. Such is the nature of the Quiet Revolution.

Households, cities, countries and nations have enjoyed great happiness, when a single individual has taken heed of the Good and Beautiful...such men not only liberate themselves; they fill those they meet with a free mind.

Philo, 1st Century

Summary

In the U.S., the 20th Century Myth exploded into full view with the tumultuous rebellion of the 1960s, where it infected and subtly corrupted that decade's well-intentioned social and personal changes.

This view reached its apex with the "me first" decade of the 1980s, wherein individuals rationalized that what was in their best self-interest benefited all, since a strong "me" then has the ability to help others. Manifestations of this philosophy were rampant materialism to satisfy "me" needs; abandonment of relationship and family values to get "my act together"; and disintegration of America's organizations and institutions as factions fought for "their" best interests, higher purposes be damned.

Now, in the last decade before the millennium, people across the nation are re-evaluating their circumstances. Materialism has propelled us into an abysmal consumer debt, and the same selfish mechanism is apparent at the government level, where special interest "me first" spending has created a huge federal deficit. Our families, cities, organizations have all been infected by the same virus – runaway self-centeredness.

This has led to a new search for what we value, and what we want to create as individuals, as organizations, as a country. It can lead to the Quiet Revolution, a quest for a higher, spiritual meaning to our existence. In the process, it examines what needs to be done to rebuild the fabric of this society – with individuals charting a course for self-growth that leads to rebuilding the health of our families and institutions.

The Quiet Revolution is based on the value of helping others, established by thousands of years of empirical evidence as the most self-fulfilling program of all. At the same time, much is to be learned and integrated from the lessons of the 20th Century Myth – so that a return to traditional values can incorporate the finer features of the social changes of this century.

Chapter Three

The Quiet Revolution

Ancient Wisdom: The Modern Basis for Personal Growth

The quintessential revolution is that of the spirit, born of an intellectual conviction of the need for change. A revolution which aims merely at changing official policies and institutions with a view to an improvement in material conditions has little chance of genuine success.[23]

> Aung San Suu Kyi, Burmese revolutionary and winner of the 1991 Nobel Peace Prize – written while she was under house arrest in her homeland.

All our wisdom is ancient wisdom. The essential truths are with us always. But the 20th Century has been the noisiest of centuries. It has produced one loud, violent revolution and war after another. All our chest-beating and mouthing of political and social platitudes have served to obscure one of the more elementary facts of human experience – that man primarily changes society by first changing himself. True revolution, that which creates lasting change for the better, always begins and ends with the individual. This is the quiet revolution, the one that occurs from within. For this revolution to succeed, the individual must be willing to challenge his own first assumptions, which naturally contain the prejudices and biases he holds as precious parts of his selfness.

> The Grand Augur, in his ceremonial robes, approached the shambles and thus addressed the pigs. "How can you object to die? I shall fatten you for three months. I shall discipline myself for ten days and fast for three. I shall strew fine grass and place you bodily upon a carved sacrificial dish. Does this not satisfy you?"
>
> Then, speaking from the pigs' point of view, he continued: "It is better perhaps after all, to live on bran and escape from the shambles."
>
> "But then," he added, speaking from his own point of view, "to enjoy honor when alive, one would readily die... in the headsman's basket."
>
> So he rejected the pigs' point of view and adopted his own point of view. In what sense, then, was he different from the pigs?
>
> Chuang Tzu
> Taoism, 4th Century, B.C.

We all have much in common with the Grand Augur, for it is a normal part of the human condition to be entrapped by our own self-serving beliefs and biases. How do we break out of these molds? One way is to turn to the study of the ancient wisdom and the essential truths contained therein. Aldous Huxley did just this in his study of the *Perennial Philosophy*, which he defined as the recognition of "…a divine Reality substantial to the world of things and lives and minds."[24] It is the study of the Highest Common Factor to be found in the "traditional lore of primitive peoples" as well as in the highest expressions of values found in nearly all the world's religions over the past 2,600 years. These more highly evolved expressions of spiritual truths must be differentiated from the lower expressions, which also can be found in all the religions of the world. The latter are the debased forms of the higher truths and are often expressed through the dogma, rules, and rituals of religion. Sometimes these rules and rituals contain elements of truth, but all too often they express past and present superstitions and local prejudices.

Those who have taught the perennial philosophy have sometimes been mystics and many were at odds with orthodox religion. The most curious aspect of these far flung rebels from many different lands is the commonality of themes found in their teachings. One puts more emphasis on this point rather than that point, but they all end up saying much the same thing.

This study of the ancient wisdom is inexhaustible. Its examples occur time and again in the world's literature. Its themes are found in all lands and in all centuries. Its truths are available to all persons at all times. Yet, these truths comprise no stultifying dogma, but instead lead to a dynamic psychology that embraces life in all its positive potential while minimizing fear and prejudice. They celebrate the dignity and uniqueness of each person. They always have been with us and always will be with us.

Only a few, however, in each generation have been willing to undertake the adventure that leads to the great truths. The reason for this is elementary – the first step is very difficult to take. Buddhism, Christianity, Hinduism, indeed most of the major religions of the world are in agreement on the nature of this difficult first step. There must first be a "dying to self," a conscious decision to move away from the normal life of self-interest, of self-aggrandizement, of "egocentric thinking, feeling, wishing and acting." This letting go of the old self, the "old man" in each of us, is the first step that then frees us to begin the journey toward the eternal ground of truth, beauty and goodness.

The Buddha, for example, taught that "all life is sorrowful," but that we can escape from sorrow into health through Nirvana. In his original teachings, the Buddha taught that Nirvana was release from egoism (not release from life). He then taught the Way to be released from egoism, the Eightfold Path, so that one is eventually moved from within, not by the external authorities of the material world. The Buddha's teachings were later modified and somewhat corrupted by others – a fate that has befallen all the great teachers – but his original ideas are in the great traditions of the ancient wisdom found worldwide.

Know that when you learn to lose yourself, you will reach the Beloved.
There is no other secret to be learnt, and more than this is not known to me.

Ansari of Herat
Islam, 11th Century

God expects but one thing of you, and that is that you should come out of
yourself in so far as you are a created being and let God be God in you.

Meister Eckhart
14th Century

This "dying to self," though it is the key to personal growth, is the most challenging of jobs. It arouses great "dread," as the Danish philosopher Kierkegaard noted in the 19th Century. The most difficult thing to ask of any human being is to ask him to give up his normal preoccupation with self, with his own ego. C.S. Lewis, in *The Great Divorce*, pictures our ego as a great weight that we carry around on our backs or on a heavy chain; and this thing, this ego, is the very obstacle that continually isolates us from others.[25] Fear drives us away from the task of "dying to self" – fear of losing control over our own lives, our own selves, our own destiny. That ultimate control is to be turned over to the Unseen Force is an idea that occasions "fear and trembling." This is especially true for those who believe in the 20th Century Myth. This Myth presumes that each person can, and should, create himself by himself; and besides, the "unseen force" is not an absolute, but is relative to the individual's perspective and training. It is not so much real as it is personal projection. In the 20th Century Myth, personal growth becomes a matter of finding the right technique. And this approach, as Stephen Covey points out, quickly regresses into a "personality ethic" where positive mental attitude and good public relations take precedence over development of integrity and fidelity or what Covey calls the "character ethic."[26] But the ancient wisdom refutes the modern approach to self-development based on the 20th Century Myth. It asserts instead that personal growth, self growth, becomes a reality only when we pierce our dread and give up our focus on our own inner potentials; we choose to forget ourselves.

This idea, that the sure and lasting route to personal growth is in forgetting about ourselves, has always boggled the mind, but even more so in modern times, for in the 20th Century we have been taught to put ourselves first, which brings to mind this story, as told by James G. Johnston:

The self putting itself first is much like the story of the servant living in Persia. The story portrays a servant who, while walking through the courtyard of the home of his master, encounters "Death." The servant turns and runs in abject terror. He finds his master and begs him to loan him his best horse so that he may ride to Tehran to escape "Death." His master gladly grants his request, inviting him to take whatever he needs for the journey. Later, the master also walks through the courtyard and sees "Death." The master confronts him, "Why did you frighten my servant?" And "Death" responds, "I did not mean to frighten your servant. I was only surprised to see him here. I expected to see him tomorrow in Tehran."

As Johnston notes, the self is always looking for the fastest horse to Tehran. The addiction to "me first," to selfishness (in its many guises – self-righteousness, prejudice, greed, vanity, envy, intolerance, slothfulness) destroys relationships and families. The ancient wisdom has always taught instead that selfishness is the acme of ungodliness. But the 20th Century Myth fosters the notion that we must always put our selves (or our group) first. It ignores one of the great lessons taught in the ancient wisdom – that we become who we are, not by what we get in life, but by what we give away.

Growing Toward a Higher Plane

In the 20th Century, one of the more straightforward and practical expressions of the ancient wisdom is found in the Alcoholics Anonymous literature. Though A.A. grew up to meet the needs of those who had become alcohol and drug dependent, the A.A. model of "treatment" (or personal redemption, if you prefer) speaks to all who seek to break free from the old, selfish self to a higher self (which includes nearly all of us, sooner or later). Let's look at the words of Bill Wilson, co-founder of A.A.:

> I had met my match. I had been overwhelmed. Alcohol was my master.
> Fear sobered me for a bit. Then came the insidious insanity of that first drink, and on Armistice Day, 1934, I was off again. Everyone became resigned to the certainty that I would have to be shut up somewhere...
> My musing was interrupted by the telephone. The cheery voice of an old school friend asked if he might come over. He was sober.
> I pushed a drink across the table. He refused it.
> He looked straight at me. Simply, but smilingly, he said, "I've got religion."
> I was aghast. So that was it – last summer an alcoholic crackpot; but now, I suspected, a little cracked about religion. But bless his heart, let him rant: besides, my gin would last longer than his preaching.
> But he did no ranting.[27]

The example of his friend caused Bill Wilson to ruminate on his own spiritual development:

> With ministers, and the world's religions, I parted right there. When they talked of a God personal to me, who was love, superhuman strength and direction, I became irritated and my mind snapped shut against such a theory.
>
> The wars which had been fought, the burnings and chicanery that religious dispute had facilitated, made me sick. I honestly doubted whether, on balance, the religions of mankind had done any good.[28]

In these statements Bill Wilson is the quintessential 20th Century man. He was not an atheist; it was just that religion, for many reasons, had little positive meaning or value for him. Like many another modern person, he had seen the follies of conventional religion and had thereby developed an extreme prejudice toward all spiritual concepts.

Bill Wilson had been a successful man on Wall Street, but his financial gains had been wiped out by the erratic behaviors caused by his increasing dependence on alcohol to make it through the day. By the time of this conversation with his old friend he was "down and out." But he was still not ready to turn away from his old self, the "old man" inside him, in large part because God to him was a negative idea, certainly not a loving, caring, merciful father-mother. Then his friend suggested something that turned out to be a bit of genius. He said, "Why don't you choose your own conception of God?" As Bill Wilson then states,

> That statement hit me hard. It melted the icy intellectual mountain in whose shadow I had lived.
>
> It was only a matter of willing to believe in a Power greater than myself. Nothing more was required of me to make my beginnings.[29]

And this is still one of the cornerstones of A.A. No one is required to believe in anyone else's concept of God. Each person is free to define or "see" God in whatever way he chooses. The individual may thus define God as Father, Mother, Parent, First Cause, Source of Energy, Higher Power, Ultimate Reality or whatever.

> We are operating a spiritual kindergarten in which people are enabled to get over drinking and find the grace to go on living to better effect. Each man's theology has to be his own quest, his own affair.[30]
>
> Bill Wilson

Yet, A.A. is clear on this point: that to experience the benefits of the approach one must willingly give up his selfishness (his need to run his own life and solve all his problems himself), and instead turn control of his life over to the Higher Power (however he may define the Higher Power). As Bill Wilson explains:

> I was to test my thinking by the new God-consciousness within. Common sense would thus become uncommon sense. I was to sit quietly when in doubt, asking only for direction and strength to meet my problems as he would have me. Never was I to pray for myself, except as my requests bore on my usefulness to others.
>
> Simple, but not easy: a price had to be paid. It meant destruction of self-centeredness. I must turn in all things to the Father of Light.
>
> The first requirement is that we be convinced that any life run on self-will can hardly be a success. On that basis we are almost always in collision with something or somebody, even though our motives are good. Most people try to live by self-propulsion. Each person is like an actor who wants to run the whole show; is forever trying to arrange the lights, the ballet, the scenery and the rest of the players in his own way. If his arrangements would only stay put, if only people would do as he wished, the show would be great.
>
> Selfishness — self-centeredness! That, we think, is the root of our troubles. Driven by a hundred forms of fear, self-delusion, self-seeking, and self-pity, we step on the toes of our fellows and they retaliate. Sometimes they hurt us, seemingly without provocation, but we invariably find that at some time in the past we have made decisions *based on self* which later placed us in a position to be hurt.
>
> Neither could we reduce our self-centeredness much by wishing or trying on our own power.
>
> This is the how and why of it. First of all, we had to quit playing God. It didn't work. Next, we decided hereafter in this drama of life, God was going to be our Director. He is the Father, and we are his children. Most good ideas are simple, and this concept was the keystone of the new and triumphant arch through which we passed to freedom.
>
> We cannot subscribe to the belief that this life is a vale of tears, though it once was just that for many of us. But it is clear that we make our own misery. God didn't do it. Avoid, then, the deliberate manufacture of misery...[31]

These principles and ideas are the foundations of the A.A. movement and all its associated movements based on the 12-step approach to personal spiritual growth. Alcoholics Anonymous is one of the more remarkable phenomena of the 20th Century. Its impact has been enormous worldwide (but quiet; A.A. stresses anonymity in all its works). It is not a church; it has no ecclesiastical structure or functions. Yet, it is one of the most spiritually endowed and enriched movements to have originated in the 20th Century.

> A drunken man who falls out of a cart, though he may suffer, does not die. His bones are the same as other people's; but he meets his accident in a different way. His spirit is in a condition of serenity. He is not conscious of riding in a cart; neither is he conscious of falling out of it. Ideas of life, death, fear and the like cannot penetrate his breast; and so he does not suffer from contact with objective existence. If such a security is to be got from wine, how much more is to be got from God?
>
> Chuang Tzu
> 4th Century, B.C.

Lest we think that the above model is useful only to those with drinking problems, let's look at the words of Gerald Jampolsky, a transpersonal psychiatrist who was moved to leave behind his "old man" by the study of *A Course in Miracles*:

> For most of my life, without fully recognizing it, I've had expectations that I wanted other people to fulfill. I wanted them to fit into a mold of my making. In a sense, I was saying that the world would be a wonderful place if everyone would just do things my way. If they did things my way, they became my friends, and if they did not measure up to my expectations, I no longer wished to have them around.
>
> The way I looked at things, it was always the other person who had to change if our relationship was to be healed – never me.
>
> In my late fifties, as I look back, I realize that my life has been one of intense seeking without knowing what it was I was looking for. At times I sought after such things as health, self-esteem, money, material possessions, prestige, social status, professional recognition, security for the future, and friends I could trust and love. Despite my success in pursuing most of these, I never experienced the happiness they were supposed to bring.
>
> It never occurred to me that I had the wrong goal, and that by searching for happiness outside myself, I was looking in the wrong place. I had absolutely no conscious awareness that I was suffering from a self-imposed state of spiritual deprivation, that I was starving myself and suffering from spiritual hunger and thirst. (I recognize now that the condition of spiritual deprivation is not unique to me, and that everyone seeks for something constant and everlasting that can be found within.) Little did I realize that the love, joy, and peace of mind that I was looking for outside myself were already bountiful within me. They were simply blocked from my awareness by the fear that I alone had manufactured.[32]

The experiences reported by Bill Wilson and Gerald Jampolsky, while similar, are in no way unique to them. Similar statements are found throughout the world's literature written by people who had exhausted the means of their ego and its accomplice, the material world; then they suddenly found themselves confronting the other world, the spirit-led world, which existence they had earlier denied or ignored. This confrontation can occur at any age, but as Schopenhauer suggests, it is most likely to occur during the second half of life: "The first forty years of life furnish the text, while the remaining thirty supply the commentary; without the commentary we are unable to understand aright the true sense and coherence of the text, together with the moral it contains."[33] Jung agreed with Schopenhauer and became one of the few psychologists to place emphasis on the second half of life. Jung asserted that it was mainly then that most people had the greatest opportunity to grow and expand their persons (or otherwise calcify), and thereby give meaning to their lives.

It is in the second half of life that most people begin to realize that the rational, materialistic, scientific way of approaching life is somehow lacking. It doesn't produce the hoped-for happiness and soul comfort, despite the successes enjoyed by the person in his pursuits. But for many of these same people, conventional religion offers no solace either, so they are left confused, anxious, wondering. These were the people especially addressed by Jung in his work, for he felt they represented most accurately the dilemma of 20th Century men and women. Jung asserted that modern man, enshrouded in scientific materialism and an often misguided religious system, had lost contact with his own roots as a spiritual being with a spiritual destiny. Modern man had lost contact with the perennial philosophy – the idea that the essential truths have always been with us. It is each person's adventure to rediscover the great truths in her or his own way. Jung thus was fascinated with the ancient mythologies of all cultures since he saw in their similar content and spirituality the earliest expressions of the *archetypes*, the sources of the ancient wisdom. Jung helped to inspire Joseph Campbell, who studied the common themes of mythologies from all over the world. Campbell proposed that each person can choose his own hero's quest based on the spiritual archetypes that have been with us since the beginning of time.

Jung in Europe was also a direct inspiration to Bill Wilson in America in the beginning years of Alcoholics Anonymous.[34] The A.A. concepts of self-redemption are in close accord with Jung's ideas that the personal growth of the individual depends on his choosing to implement spiritual meanings and values in his life. Otherwise, man is constricted in his personal growth by the fear of death and aging.

> Among all my patients in the second half of life...there has not been one
> whose problem in the last resort was not that of finding a religious outlook
> on life. It is safe to say that every one of them fell ill because he had lost

what the living religions of every age have given to their followers, and none of them has been really healed who did not regain his religious outlook. This of course has nothing whatever to do with a particular creed or membership in a church.[35]

Carl Jung

You are asking yourself, as all of us must: "Who am I?... "Where am I?... "Whence do I go?" The process of enlightenment is usually slow. But in the end, our seeking always brings a finding. These great mysteries are, after all, enshrined in complete simplicity. The willingness to grow is the essence of all spiritual development.[36]

Bill Wilson

Everything Alcoholics Anonymous represents stands in contrast to the man-made "religion" of the 20th Century – the 20th Century Myth. The focus of A.A. is on the innate dignity and uniqueness of each person; not on membership by race or class or gender. It rejects moral relativism while explicitly founding itself on a faith in an Absolute Ground of the universe. It is non-bureaucratic, non-ecclesiastical, almost totally decentralized in its functions. It eschews all use of government power. It is strictly voluntary, there is no coercion at any point in the process. It is open to all of all beliefs. It is a voluntary, person-to-person approach built on a foundation of eternal spiritual truths. It is a simple expression of the ancient wisdom.[1]

And A.A. is far more likely to endure and prosper into the 21st Century than all the social change programs generated by the 20th Century Myth.

The model for social change offered by A.A. and similar self-support groups is based on the old idea that enduring social change comes about only through individual change and growth, and that the individual cannot remake himself by himself; he can do this only by turning to the eternal Ground of all Reality. The main purpose of the group is to support each person's quest of the Higher Power. This "turning away from self" at first requires a heady price – the move away from our normal self-centeredness. This same model for personal growth has been taught by the great spiritual teachers throughout the ages. And as these same teachers often have noted, this process of "turning to God" is fraught with dangers and pitfalls:

> Some people want to see God with their eyes as they see a cow, and to love Him as they love their cow – for the milk and cheese and profit it brings them. This is how it is with people who love God for the sake of outward wealth or inward comfort. They do not rightly love God, when they love Him for their own advantage. Indeed, I tell you the truth, any object you have in your mind, however good, will be a barrier between you

and the inmost Truth.

Meister Eckhart
14th Century

Would you know whence it is that so many false spirits have appeared in the world, who have deceived themselves and others with false fire and false light, laying claim to information, illumination and openings of the divine Life, particularly to do wonders under extraordinary calls from God? It is this: they have turned to God without turning from themselves... Now religion in the hands of self... serves only to discover vices of a worse kind than in nature left to itself. Hence are all the disorderly passions of religious men, which burn in a worse flame than passions only employed about worldly matters; pride, self-exaltation, hatred and persecution, under a cloak of religious zeal, will sanctify actions which nature, left to itself, would be ashamed to own.

William Law
18th Century

"Turning to God without turning from self" – the formula is absurdly simple; and yet, simple as it is, it explains all the follies and iniquities committed in the name of religion... They are tempted... to practice magical rites, by means of which they hope to compel God... to serve their private or collective ends. All the ugly business of sacrifice, incantation and what Jesus called "vain repetition" is a product of this wish to treat God as a means to indefinite self-aggrandizement... Next, they are tempted to use the name of God to justify what they do in the pursuits of place, power and wealth.[37]

Aldous Huxley
20th Century

The history of man on the eternal quest has been a strange odyssey. In his search for the "holy grail" man has looked everywhere and in vain, but he has failed to look within himself. Occasionally, a prophet came, talking of the world within. But instead of following him into the deeper experience, men invariably made a god of the prophet—worshiped him and built monuments to him. They then trapped themselves in a religious practice that had no within. How many times has this happened? How many religions are there in the world?[38]

Eric Butterworth
20th Century

The minute I figure I have got a perfectly clear pipeline to God, I have become egotistical enough to get into real trouble. Nobody can cause more needless grief than a power-driver who thinks he has got it straight from God.[39]

Bill Wilson
20th Century

There is also the temptation to dwell on mystical experiences. They can be sought after and worshiped for their own sake. When this happens, the mystical experience is the same as an idol, for it has become an "object in the mind" that stands in place of God. In its extreme form, the worship of the mystic experience can result in personality isolation and withdrawal from everyday life, which is the very antithesis of spirit-led living.

And then there are the dangers of codifying the spiritual experience, of reducing and restricting it to a set of rules and "correct beliefs," i.e., of shrinking it into a dogma, a religious ideology that must be adhered to or else damnation follows. The dogmatic, ideological approach to spiritual development inevitably reinforces our focus on *time*, on the here and now, for religion becomes a matter of who has the "correct belief" and who has not. Religion then becomes a contest to see who is right and who is wrong, which is why the ideological approach to spirituality always leads to war-making in some form or another. When Jesus said, "Woe unto you lawyers," he was expressing his consternation with those who would codify religion and thereby reduce it to a set of prescribed rules and righteous beliefs.

Jesus taught instead that the spiritual life consisted of opening oneself up to the eternal God within, that is, to the "kingdom of God" that waits patiently within each human being. He never taught that the spirit-led life consisted in the pursuit of "correct beliefs." The great teachers have all taught that "belief fixates" while "faith liberates," for faith is dynamic: "...it is God-knowing and man-serving."[40]

But then, reliance on rules and ideology instead of faith is the easy way out; one thereby circumvents the dying to self essential to spiritual growth. And this tendency to fixate on dogma as a way to maintain the me-first approach to life has been a curse to all the world's religions.

Those who lack discrimination may quote the letter of the scripture; but they are really denying its inner truth. They are full of worldly desires and hunger for the rewards of heaven. They use beautiful figures of speech; they teach elaborate rituals, which are supposed to obtain pleasure and power for those who practice them. But, actually, they understand nothing...

Bhagavad Gita
Hinduism, 2nd Century, B.C.

Religionists have often confused dogma, doctrine and creed with religion – a mistake that often leads them to worship the dogma rather than God. True reli-

38

gion, according, for example, to the precepts of Judaism, Christianity and Islam, is found in the individual's relationship with God. But religionists early on begin to associate this precept with the doctrines that grow up around the precept. It is then an easy step to substitute the doctrine for the precept. In Christianity, for example, its teacher, Jesus, never spoke to the issues of abortion, divorce, birth control and sexual conduct. Later adherents of Christianity formulated their own ideas on these issues or took ideas from ancient sources. These other ideas were accepted by some churches as doctrine. And in many minds the doctrine became the religion. So much so that many people define themselves as Christians because of their specific doctrinal beliefs on abortion, divorce, birth control, sexual conduct, etc. This definition of religion too easily deteriorates to the concept of God as stern schoolmaster whose main job is to administer exams. If you pass his exam, if you have the "correct" doctrinal beliefs, you pass *go* and get to go to heaven. If you have the wrong beliefs, you fail and go somewhere else. This view of God is not only wholly inconsistent with the teachings of Jesus on the nature of God, but also leads to self-righteousness. And the pose of self-righteousness, of "we're right in our beliefs and all others are heathens," has led to more harm and violence committed in the name of religion than any other factor. It also establishes the conditions wherein worship of church and/or worship of scripture take the place of developing a loving relationship with God.

And what of those who stay aloof from the messy problems caused by the desire to have a spirit-led life? They readily fall into progress-worship, or technology and gadgets-worship, or social/political ideology worship, or state worship, or revolutionary-future worship, or glorified-past worship, or money worship, or pleasure worship, or fashion worship, or food worship, or humanistic self-worship. There is as much worship of false idols today as there was in Moses's time; it is only that idolatry is somewhat more sophisticated now than then.

Growth of the Real Self

Personal growth is ultimately dependent on spiritual growth, and our spiritual growth is stunted to the degree we hang on to the "old man" inside us. Only when we let go of the old self can the Real Self come alive, but more of this later. For now, we need to look closer at what is involved in letting go of the old self.

This is a daily exercise, for "dying to self" is rarely accomplished by some magical, once in a lifetime experience as noted by the first of the great American psychologists, William James, in his classic work, *Varieties of Religious Experience*.[41] It is, instead, an ideal, a value, to which one must recommit every day. The key to this daily recommitment is simplicity of motive:

In the world, when people call anyone simple, they generally mean a foolish, ignorant, credulous person. But real simplicity, so far from being foolish, is almost sublime. All good men like and admire it... I should say that simplicity ...prevents self-consciousness. It is not the same as sincerity, which is a much humbler virtue. Many people are sincere who are not simple. They say nothing but what they believe to be true, and do not aim at appearing anything but what they are. But they are for ever thinking about themselves, weighing their every word and thought, and dwelling upon themselves in apprehension of having done too much or too little. These people are sincere, but they are not simple. They are not at ease with others, nor others with them. There is nothing easy, frank, unrestrained or natural about them. One feels that one would like less admirable people better, who were not so stiff.

To be absorbed in the world around and never turn a thought within, as is the blind condition of some who are carried away by what is pleasant and tangible, is one extreme as opposed to simplicity. And to be self-absorbed in all matters, whether it be duty to God or man, is the other extreme, which makes a person wise in his own conceit – reserved, self-conscious, uneasy at the least thing which disturbs his inward self-complacency. Such false wisdom, in spite of its solemnity, is hardly less vain and foolish than the folly of those who plunge headlong into worldly pleasures. The one is intoxicated by his outward surroundings, the other by what he believes himself to be doing inwardly; but both are in a state of intoxication, and the last is a worse state than the first, because it seems to be wise, though it is not really, and so people do not *try* to be cured. Real simplicity lies in a *juste milieu* equally free from thoughtlessness and affectation, in which the soul is not overwhelmed by externals, so as to be unable to reflect, nor yet given up to the endless refinements which self-consciousness induces. That soul which looks where it is going without losing time arguing over every step, or looking back perpetually, possesses true simplicity. Such simplicity is indeed a great treasure. How shall we attain it? I would give all I possess for it.[42]

Fenelon
17th Century

Huxley's comment on this passage says it all, "Nothing is more difficult than to be simple." Yet, this goal, this forgetting of self so that God may be God within us, is the most enriching of all human activities. It generates dynamic self-development. It is the essence, the meaning and the end-all of personal growth. It is what Jesus meant when he said that to enter the kingdom of God we must enter as little children. To commit to this goal, no matter how difficult and long of attainment, is the greatest of adventures.

Yen Huei said, "I'm improving!"

Confucius said, "How so?"

"I've forgotten...righteousness!"

"That's good. But you still haven't got it."

Another day, the two met again, and Yen Huei said, "I'm improving!"

"How so?"

"I've forgotten rites and music!"

"That's good, but you still haven't got it."

Another day, the two met again, and Yen Huei said, "I'm improving!"

"How so?"

"I can forget myself while sitting," replied Yen Huei.

Confucius looked startled and said, "What do you mean by that?"

"I have freed myself from my body," answered Yen Huei, "and by thus getting rid of my body and my mind, I have become One with the Infinite. That is what I mean by forgetting myself while sitting."

"If you have become One," said Confucius, 'there can be no room for bias. If you have lost yourself, there can be no more hindrance. So you really are a wise man! I trust to be allowed to follow in your steps."

Chuang Tzu

Is Confucius gently chiding the ardent Yen Huei, who in his pursuit of self-lessness is perhaps still too concerned with his own selfness? The attainment of simplicity, of self-forgetfulness, is difficult for us to comprehend. It is a mysterious process and somewhat different for each person.

The great teachers of the ancient wisdom have always taught a dynamic psychology of seeking forgiveness from God that prevents our normal conflicts with others from growing into grudges and prejudices toward others. This daily *forgiving*, of oneself as well as others, also prevents the person from falling into the trap of blaming others for his problems, which is one of the more common traits of those whose personal growth is retarded. An important part of this daily inventory of "crimes against others" is prayer and meditation in which the person humbly asks the Higher Power for an understanding of His will, the power to carry it out, and a petition to remove one's defects of character. This method for character development, in general outline, has been used since the beginning of recorded time by persons attempting to lead a spirit-led rather than a self-led life.

Man has the capacity to escape the self-binding caused by being a tied-up ball of fear, anxiety, selfishness, pride and resentments. But can he do this alone, by himself? Hardly.

No one knows why one person deals with his fears and resentments by excessive drinking or drugs, while another deals with them by withdrawing from life, while another deals with them by trying to control everyone and everything in his life, while yet another deals with them through a myriad of obsessive-compulsive behavior patterns. Theories and research abound, but the differentiating factors among individuals are not known. These questions pose great challenges for 21st Century psychologists. But this we know: people can and do grow out of their problems. Personal growth, though too often a self-delusion, can be real and lasting.

All the great teachers of the ancient wisdom have asserted that personal growth cannot be attained if we try to serve two masters, though this teaching has never stopped any of us from trying to do just that. Our old self is our first master, and we cling to this old man by every means, conscious and subconscious, we can dredge up. The eternal Ground is the other master. We choose between the two masters. Though God is a patient and persistent suitor, he will not force himself on us. His respect for our free will, our dignity, seems to be infinite. But this is clear – we are all in service to some master, and it is up to us which master we serve. And this appears to be true: those who take up God's yoke, *in simplicity*, seem to breathe easier and freer than those who cling to their own self-yokes. This leads to a form of personal growth that not only endures, but grows wiser, stronger, happier with each passing season.

> Jampolsky describes this transition from the ego-led life to the spirit-led life by noting that when he was self-led the world was based on fear and guilt. It is a depressing world where we believe that sooner or later bad things are bound to happen to us, and our unhappy experiences from the past will repeat themselves in the future. It is a world in which relationships are often troubled and short-lived, and the way we handle disharmony in our relationships is to get out of them. It is a world that believes in judgement, unforgivingness, and punishment; a world in which others are seen as guilty and responsible for our problems.
>
> What I used to believe seemed very real to me, and there didn't seem to be any other way of looking at the world. It was not until I began to be on a spiritual pathway that I began to consider the idea, as many have before me, that there are two ways of looking at the world, and each of these requires a totally different belief system…different ways of looking at cause and effect, truth and illusion, life and death.
>
> The commonly shared thought system of the world is the thought system of the ego. It is based on perceiving a world of separation, guilt, fear, attack and unhealed relationships. It is a world of misperception.
>
> The opposite of this belief system is the thought system of love…a world where relationships are healed. It is a world based on God's love – a world in which (mis)perception has been corrected through forgiveness.[43]

A peculiar aspect of personal/spiritual growth is that the person himself is not aware of growing spiritually. Just as a young person cannot feel his body growing, the person growing up spiritually cannot feel his own growth. This lack of self-consciousness generally characterizes personal/spiritual growth. These people come to emanate personal strength while not exhibiting egoistic exaltation. They report that they work steadily at unselfish prayer, but then go about their daily jobs in the trust that they will continue to grow in the ability to do God's will. They don't fret about it or make a big commotion about it; they just do it. They themselves are not entirely clear on what's happening, but it appears that they are letting go of their selfness enough to allow "God to be God" within them. This process is another one of those "mysterious ways" in which God works. But this is evident – the eternal Ground will not force itself upon us; we must consciously choose to let this happen.

Another aspect of personal growth based on spiritual growth is that the person becomes more *real* as he grows. The old self shows itself to the world as a *persona*, or mask. Phoniness is the hallmark of the persona. The person still dominated by his old self, his persona, is thinking: how can I manipulate that person, or impress this person, or flatter that person, or prod yet this other person, so that I may feather my own nest. And this is hard work to maintain the needs of the mask; nothing seems truly natural, certainly not simple. The mask precludes our having healthy relationships with others. As long as we are ruled by our persona we never feel altogether real, except perhaps for those fleeting times when we're "high" on something. The mask is essentially defensive in nature, for the old self is predicated on separation from others; it must be on guard at all times to protect its own interests, biases and territories. Whether the persona is being aggressively friendly, or shy and withdrawn, its driving impulse is to protect its own welfare, happiness and interests. The persona is the outward expression of the old man within us, which was initially born of our childish fears, abuses and anxieties over what's due us versus what's due the others.

As we begin to grow up spiritually this old self is allowed to die away. It is slowly, often haltingly, replaced with the Real Self. As the Real Self begins to emerge from its cocoon, we become less phony both to ourselves and to others. The Real Self is based on spiritual reality; that is, it is grounded in ultimate reality, God. The Real Self is a gift from God. Each person has been granted his own unique combination of personality potentials. But as long as the old self dominates, we only see the shadows of the Real Self potentials. As the person begins to "die to self," the clouds casting these shadows slowly dissipate, thus allowing the real personality potentials to emerge. When we allow "God to be God" within us, we're providing the condition required for our Real Self to begin this process of emerging. It is then that we begin to feel more at home in the world, no longer so separated or isolated. We begin to feel more real because we have finally aligned ourselves with Ultimate Reality. Now it becomes easier to see the realness in others. Interestingly, the unrealness of others becomes less offensive, less threatening, less likely to provoke anger. For the more we align ourselves with Ultimate Reality, the more we realize that It is forgiving and merciful, and thus it becomes more natural for us to forgive both ourselves and others.

This great gift of our own, unique personality comes about in partnership with the spark of God within us. Man has always acknowledged the presence of a divine something within him, something that was growing or trying to grow, something that endured beyond bodily death. The Hindus defined this spirit as the *atman*. The ancient Chinese differentiated this into the spirit and the soul, which they called the *Yin* and the *Yang*. The Egyptians and many African tribes believed in the *ka* and the *ba*. The ka was a spirit-genius that tried to guide the person into the better life on earth and then waited for him to be reunited again after death. In all lands and in all times and in all tongues one finds a word designating the concept of the *soul*. This concept is an integral, universal part of the ancient wisdom.

The Real Self is the Real Me, our true and lasting personality potentials, a gift of the Light within. To the degree that the person allows his Real Self to emerge is the degree to which he becomes sure that he will survive beyond bodily death, for the eternal value and growth potential of the Real Self are undeniable. Those persons who are the most real, the most simple, are also likely to have the least anxiety about the survival of their persons. They *know*, in an unprepossessing way, that they will survive death, thus death holds little or no fear for them. Their faith in this matter is quite unlike that of those religionists who are obsessed with salvation, especially their own. These latter individuals are often those who have "turned to God without first turning from self." They are still self-obsessed, and thus exhibit the "strained overeagerness of the zealot for salvation."[44] Such people, in their great anxiety, can do much harm to others. They are most likely to be found in those theologies that see God as a demented, monarchial scorekeeper scrupulously toting up pluses and minuses for each of our actions and taking delight in catching us in wrongdoing. By contrast, those who have "died to self" and thus allowed their Real Self to emerge are invariably less anxious on this matter, for the more the Real Self emerges the more self-evident it becomes that one's personality naturally survives beyond death. I have had the good fortune to know some remarkably mature people for whom this issue is simply not an issue any more. Such people go about their daily affairs doing good, looking for opportunities to do God's will with no thought to their own salvation, for eternal life is already a reality to them.

As the Real Self emerges the person also begins to realize that his body is *not* truly correlated with the Real Self. The body will pass away, but the Real Self will not. He becomes more forgiving of his body as well as those of others. The body loses its power to obsess us. And this brings us to another idea always found among the teachings of the ancient wisdom, or perennial philosophy, as Huxley called it. Namely, the idea that by aligning ourselves with the Divine Mind we enter into eternity, now. Our perception of time thus changes.

When we are self-led, time is our enemy. As Butterworth comments, "We feel that we are chained to a relentlessly moving treadmill: 'Time marches on. It is later than you think. With every passing moment the supply is depleted, and what will we do tomorrow?'"[45] We worry about what we shall eat or how we shall be clothed or housed. Life is viewed as a short, hurried, stress-laden journey between two points. We have to get all we can of it *now*, before we dry up and are gone. People thereby "...make themselves unhappy now, in trying to keep from being unhappy in the future."

This sad, constricted view of time changes as people become more spirit-led. The person begins to realize that he has already entered into eternal life and that his adventure will never end. He can relax more and enjoy the moment more, especially relationships with others. Every day is a new adventure in growth; one's potentials are unlimited.

All this is not to say that the spirit-led life is free of problems, anxiety or even guilt. For one thing, the person who has discovered the God within is still an imperfect being fully capable of many mistakes and of falling off the spirit-led wagon. He is merely beginning his journey and has a long, long way to go. For another thing, he lives in a world of self-led persons who daily exercise their God-given free will. Sometimes these exercises in free will lead to harmful results for others either because they are in the wrong place at the wrong time or because they are seen as standing in the way of the desires of the other person. The spirit-led person thus continues to suffer both for his own mistakes and at the hands of others. But there is a world of difference in how he now views these problems. Whereas before they would have made him angry and resentful or jealous and depressed, he now responds with an inner assurance that "all things are possible" and that the adversities of this life are rarely very important; certainly they are rarely what they seem to be. The great adversities are even seen as great opportunities for personal growth. This new attitude does not come easily. The person pays a price by recommitting himself at every juncture with unselfish prayer and a continual "dying to self" so that his fears can be given over to the Divine Mind. As the individual continues to do this, it becomes easier and easier to do as he again and again experiences the positive results of giving control of his life over to God and trusting in His direction. I have yet to talk with anyone well along in the transition from the self-led to the spirit-led life who would even consider going back to his old fear-driven ways. Once a person has tasted the "fruits of the spirit" it is inconceivable that he should go back to letting the "old man" control him.

Another common source of guilt is that spiritual ideals often grow at a much faster rate than the ability to live up to them. The guilt subsides only when the person realizes that the Divine Light understands our dilemma infinitely better than we do, and that God is merciful and forgiving beyond our comprehension. This is where the brilliance of Jesus's teachings is especially noticeable, for "the most original of his teachings was the emphasis of love and mercy in the place of fear and sacrifice."[46]

> ...it is not so much what mind is like as what mind is striving to be like that constitutes spirit identification...What you are today is not so important as what you are becoming day by day..

> God the Father deals with man his child on the basis, not of actual virtue or worthiness, but in recognition of the child's motivation...

> Urantia Book
> 20th Century

Nurturing the Real Self

We are now going to do a presumptuous thing. We are going to reduce the psychology of love and self-worth to a formula. We begin with the repeated experiences of "dying to self" and realization of our spiritual impoverishment, which open the door to experiencing God's forgiveness and mercy. We start allowing "God to be God" within us. In some unknown, not conscious way we then grow in the capacity to understand and forgive others, and this is love in action. We begin to lose our fears and resentments of others. As we repeatedly experience this reality, our self-worth is augmented and our perception of time changed as we come to know that this adventure in personal growth will go on forever. We are energized as we glimpse the great destiny God has planned for us and for our fellows. We are liberated and more courageous, for this truth sets us free. And all this is based on growing experience with the Divine Light. Spiritual, personal growth is based on spiritual experience, not on theology. And since each person's experience with God is uniquely his own, in accordance with his own God-given personality potentials, then each person's "religion" is uniquely his own in the sense of how he interprets this experience. Spirit-led persons can thus experience unity of goals and supreme values, but not philosophic uniformity. The spirit-led person sees and feels unity with others while slowly losing his fear of their diversity. He comes to adore unity rather than uniformity. But there is no spiritual growth without psychic conflict and agitation. And this growth does not lead to a static, blissful state of mind. It is based on "decisions, decisions, and more decisions" and results in a dynamic life in which service to others is predicated in an increasing way on simplicity of motive and self-forgetfulness. Loving others is no longer seen or felt as an assumed attitude; it comes about when the time is put in to understand the motivations, sentiments, and circumstances of the other person's actions, especially his noxious actions. Love is more than mere feelings; it is seen for what it is – action for the sake of others. Adversity may be his lot, but the spirit-led person finds that at the worst of times great courage is bestowed on him. Slowly he comes to see that the world is not dark with occasional rays of light, but that it is bathed in a brilliant and warm light only occasionally marred by darkness.

Jung referred to this process of personal, spiritual growth as *individuation*. He noted that as a person grows the shadows caused by his old self, which had always blemished his personality before, are transcended by the emergence of the Real Self, which is created from the "God-image" within. Other teachers in the tradition of the perennial philosophy have used different terms to denote this rare but remarkable metamorphosis of personality. Why so rare? Most people feel they are too busy making their way in life to devote time or energy to such a quest. Little do they realize they have missed the main point of life, much less the lasting satisfactions. And too, there are few people around who naturally model this process in its true simplicity. But all this is about to change. For if we have read the portents of change correctly, a small but significant increase in the number of persons who opt for the Great Adventure will occur in the next few decades.

The Scientific Objection

Of course one can look upon all this and remark on how subjective it is, how unscientific it is, how very old fashioned it is. Is it not, after all, a process of sophisticated self-delusion, that is, a subconscious fulfilling of one's own projected prophecy? Where's the proof of it? The proof, as always, is in the pudding, but as yet no scientific studies have been done comparing the "mental health" of those who are simplistically spirit-led with those who are not. We are left with this response to the skeptic who doubts the idea of a Loving Divinity, "how do you know that I do not know?" Within the acceptable bounds of scientific logic there is no good answer to the above question. And there is another, major problem for the proof-oriented person as well.

Early in the 20th Century the more thoughtful of scientists realized that they had reached a sort of invisible barrier in their attempts to penetrate the secrets of the universe. Then they acknowledged that they too were dealing in inference and "leaps of faith" in their desire to understand ultimate reality. In short, the proof-demanding person is demanding the impossible, for there is no man-made method that can yield indisputable proof as to the true nature of ultimate reality. All such questions inevitably come down to statements based on inference and belief.

The revolution in science wrought by such notables as Einstein and Max Planck in the first decades of the 20th Century caused great excitement but also a new sense of unknowing and awe of the true nature of the universe. All science operates on the assumption that only that which can be measured and objectively verified can be *known* by science. But in sub-atomic physics the components of the *atom* (supposedly the reality of realities; the irreducible element of nature) are observed to be such particles as, for example, electrons. And electrons cannot be measured accurately because they weigh so little that they are always changed in the act of trying to measure them. This observation brought forth the Great Ghost that hovers over all of modern science, the Heisenberg Uncertainty Principle, which in everyday language comes down to this statement by the physicist Eddington:

> *Something unknown is doing we don't know what* – that is what our theory amounts to. It does not sound a particularly illuminating theory. I have read something like it elsewhere -
> … the slithy toves
> did gyre and gimble in the wabe.[47]

Another physicist puts it this way,

> …the solid substance of things is another illusion… We have chased the solid substance from the continuous liquid to the atom, from the atom to the electron, and there we have lost it.[48]

The truth is that science cannot "know" the ultimate reality hidden within and basic to even a simple wood table. It can only draw inferences and theorize. No matter how we approach the definition of and knowing of Ultimate Reality, we come up against the necessity of making a leap of faith sooner or later. The materialist, though he may not like it, is in the same boat as the spiritualist on this particular river. Bertrand Russell viewed this predicament and noted, "The world may be called physical or mental or both or neither as we please; in fact the words serve no purpose."[49]

Science eventually ends up postulating an unknowable First Cause. The First Cause of science, and the Divine Mind who fosters personal growth and survival, are one and the same in the teachings of the ancient wisdom. The division between the material and spiritual worlds is seen as more fiction than reality since both worlds are derived from the same Source. The "war" between science and religion is a man-made squabble and irrelevant in the bigger scheme of things.

But all such argumentation as the above is so much folderol. For those who have not yet experienced the Light within can never be convinced by mere logic, while those who have experienced God require no arguments. It has been forever true that, "Human things must be known in order to be loved, but divine things must be loved in order to be known."[50]

Almost 2,000 years ago a young man from India traveled around the Mediterranean countries with his father, who was a successful importer of goods, on his way to Rome to conduct business. During the course of this trip, the boy was exposed to the then new teachings of Jesus. This perceptive lad grasped the meanings of these radical teachings – that in forgetting about ourselves through dedication to God we become more serviceable to others and find our own destiny. In the following excerpts from the young man's writings he states in his simple, childlike way the essential truths of the ancient wisdom:

> By this new faith I know that man may become the son of God, but it sometimes terrifies me when I stop to think that all men are my brothers, but it must be true. I do not see how I can rejoice in the fatherhood of God while I refuse to accept the brotherhood of man. Whosoever calls upon the name of the Lord shall be saved. If that is true, then all men must be my brothers.
>
> Henceforth I will do my good deeds in secret; I will also pray most when by myself. I will judge not that I may not be unfair to my fellows. I am going to learn to love my enemies; I have not truly mastered this practice of being Godlike.
>
> But first of all I am going to practice worshiping God by learning how to do the will of God on earth; that is, I am going to do my best to treat each of my fellow mortals just as I think God would like to have him treated.
>
> God is not only all-powerful but also all-wise. If our earth parents, being of evil tendency, know how to love their children and bestow good gifts on them, how much more must the good Father in heaven know how wisely to love his children on earth and to bestow suitable blessings on them.
>
> When men begin to feel after God, that is evidence that God has found them, and that they are in quest of knowledge about him. We live in God and God dwells in us.
>
> With our heavenly Father all things are possible. Since he is the Creator, having made all things and all beings, it could not be otherwise. Though we cannot see God, we can know him. And by daily living the will of the Father in heaven, we can reveal him to our fellow men.
>
> This new religion of ours is very full of joy, and it generates an enduring happiness. I am confident that I shall be faithful even to death, and that I will surely receive...eternal life.[51]

This has been a cursory look at a few expressions of the perennial philosophy, or as I prefer to call it, the ancient wisdom. This ancient wisdom calls us back to our roots, for it is easy to forget that in the 20th Century we have done a radical thing – we have thrown out the old God-centered mythology and replaced it with a man-centered mythology. This has never been done before, at least not on such a grand and bold scale. Before, man always built his myths about the nature of Ultimate Reality on belief in the gods. The question is – how valid is our new myth? How real is it? The contention here has been that the

20th Century Myth is replete with erroneous assumptions, which result in false values and great difficulties in our lives. Yet, the old myths are still so encrusted with dogma and local prejudice that they fail to inspire, truly inspire, many modern men and women. The suggestion has been to reexamine the ancient wisdom so that we may recapture the very best, the very finest features of our traditions. We may then use this wisdom as the foundation for a new mythology for the 21st Century – one that provides the ennobling ideals and inspiring vision we long for.

This process is required for the re-making of America. As long as we persist in implementing the 20th Century Myth we will continue to erode the very roots of our culture. Only by re-examining the finest of our traditional values, those derived from the ancient wisdom and well expressed in the time of our founding – the time of Enlightenment – can we hope to re-establish the very basis on which America attained its current position in the world.

While perusing the ancient wisdom one gets the impression that the germ of the idea is quietly passed on from one generation to the next, and that this germ will continue to gestate until humankind matures enough to cultivate it and implement it on a widescale basis. Then, and only then, will we see the full strength and beauty of the human race.

On Happiness

The ancient wisdom disputes the central message of both modern humanism and popular psychology. These latter two schools of thought, each expressing aspects of the 20th Century Myth, contend that man must first make his own self happy before he can be happy with others or make others happy. Each person is thus encouraged to develop his or her potentials to the utmost, to focus on his own self-development, to "go for it." Man, truly, is the measure of all things in this scenario. Whole generations have now been brought up on this philosophy of life.

Interestingly, the available data do not support this modern view on happiness. Indeed, the data lend considerable support to the views found in the ancient wisdom. Bernard Rimland, for example, tested Mother Teresa's idea that happiness comes not from seeking material goods and self-aggrandizement, but from forgetting about self in service to others. He asked over 200 people to rank another 2,000 people (who were known personally to the 200 evaluators) on both their happiness vs. unhappiness and their degrees of selfishness vs. unselfishness. He found that 70% of those judged unselfish were happy people. Of those judged to be selfish, 95% were unhappy. Obsession with self does not bring lasting happiness.[52]

There is a growing body of evidence further indicating that those people who commit their lives to the Divine Light are both happier and more successful in life. Psychological research comparing the happiness of those who are religious versus those who are not religious consistently finds that the religiously involved are happier and more content with their lives than the non-religious.[53] Religious persons also report greater satisfaction in their marriages and home life and a much lower divorce rate.[54] Interestingly, they even report greater happiness with their marital sex lives.[55]

Clearly, the greater happiness reported by the religiously involved is not due to any immunity from life's hardships and disappointments. Religious folk experience as much adversity as non-religious folk. But the available data indicate that the religiously involved seem to bear up much better to adversity than the non-religious.[56] They are, psychologically, both happier and stronger than the non-religious.

Of course, the above conclusion does not apply to all religious people. Some people who define themselves as religious are unhealthy people by any definition. The above differences are *averages*. Yet, these average differences between the religious and the non-religious are reliably reported in study after study.

Research over the next few decades will no doubt help to delineate the distinguishing characteristics of those persons in the religious population who account for the differences in health and happiness between the religious and the non-religious. We anticipate that much of this difference will be found to be attributable to those who are more simplistically spirit-led. Or, to use a phrase often used in this field of research, the beneficial results accrue mainly from those who are *intrinsically spiritual*, in contrast to those who are *extrinsically spiritual*.[57] The intrinsically spiritual experience an ongoing, lively, highly personal relationship with God, in whatever way they define him. They may or may not be churchgoers, but this they share in common: they have authenticated their beliefs by making the leap of faith and then experiencing the fruits thereof. The extrinsically spiritual, by contrast, base their religion on a set of beliefs and practices taught to them that they have accepted as valid. But their religion has very little inner life of its own, except perhaps on special occasions. The proposition here is that most of the observed difference in psychological health between the religious and the non-religious will be found to be accounted for by the intrinsically spiritual. For the extrinsically spiritual are more likely to have had difficulty in "turning to God without turning from self." The simplistically spirit-led, by contrast, are more likely to have forgotten self in their pursuit of the eternal Ground. Healthy service to others is then inevitable. And so are strength and happiness as we become as concerned for the happiness and welfare of others as for ourselves. The sense of a caring community is derived from this process of rebirthing individuals who then model caring for others in their daily lives. It hardly comes from government mandates imposed from the top down.

The ancient wisdom, when truly searched for, is always found and always validated. But it is found only when we search beyond our selves. One may penetrate his inner self in pursuit of the Divine Light, but this act is in the service of discovering something far wiser, far stronger and far finer than mere self.

> To begin with oneself,
> but not to end with oneself;
> to start with oneself,
> but not to aim at oneself;
> to comprehend oneself,
> but not to be preoccupied with oneself.
> Hillel
> 1st Century

Summary

In the quiet revolution, personal growth is thwarted to the degree we focus on our self-development. Instead, it is determined by how we forget our own ego needs, by how we "die to self". This concept flies in the face of most modern humanistic thinking on self-growth. It is, though, very much in the tradition of the ancient wisdom (perennial philosophy).

Personal growth, according to the ancient wisdom, is a matter of "dying to self" while also granting ultimate control of our lives to a loving, caring Higher Power. This is a difficult, rather mysterious process that requires daily re-comittment to its goals and values. This process may occur inside or outside of conventional religion, but in either case it leads to more tolerance of others and a heightened motivation to be of service to others in a self-forgetting, simple way. The quiet revolutionary is increasingly drawn to sharing these experiences with others, but in doing so he is less interested in uniformity of thought, more interested in celebrating unity of supreme values.

Though such persons are hardly immune from life's difficulties, their personal strength and sense of happiness are often impressive. It is proposed here that societal improvement that is lasting, that is real, has always been primarily the work of quiet revolutionaries, and that even more opportunities for real improvement lie in the 21st Century, provided that even more people choose the Great Adventure.

---

[1] I wish to state here that I am not, nor have I ever been, an A.A. member. In making the above statements about A.A., I am not therefore violating their pledge of anonymity. I am, however, an admirer of the A.A. approach to personal and spiritual growth as a means by which to treat certain psychological difficulties.

Chapter Four

The Family
Egocentrism & the Family – A Plague of Dysfunction

They were an attractive, animated, intelligent, charming couple. They were one of my first cases requesting marital counseling. They were both 30 at the time and had been "hippies" only a few years back (it was now 1974). They had been married for nearly four years and had two children, ages 1 and 2. They had come for therapy because she was sometimes depressed and her depressions were becoming more intense and frequent. They wanted to return to their previously happy state.

It didn't take long to get to the root of her depression. He was seeing other women, sometimes two, three evenings per week. She knew about them. He wasn't good at hiding the facts of his liaisons, nor did he really try. They both believed in total honesty in marriage.

It wasn't that he now found her unattractive. She was plump from two pregnancies, but she confirmed that they had sex, good sex, almost as often now as when they were first married. He stated that no one woman, no matter how loved or lovely, could satisfy all his sexual and emotional needs. It was clear they still loved each other and both were very caring toward their two children.

I asked to see the husband alone in the next session. Before this session I mapped a variety of behavioral techniques the husband could employ to bring his impulses under control so he could stop hurting his wife and family. Eagerly, and with great confidence, I outlined the first technique. He rejected it. He then rejected the second method, then the third. It began to sink in that this outwardly charming fellow had no interest in changing any of his own behaviors.

At this point I sat back and let him do the talking. He told me he had not come to therapy to change anything about himself. He was very happy with his life. But he was concerned for his wife. Her depression affected the children. He had agreed to come to counseling in the secret hope his wife could learn to deal with their situation more effectively. He wanted her to accept him as he was. He talked about how happy they had been in the 60s and how they had both subscribed to the views of Fritz Perls on relationships. He could still quote this passage, which had served as a "psalm" for the kids of the 60s:

> I do my thing,
> And you do your thing,
> I am not in this world
> To live up to your expectations.
> You are not in this world to live up to mine.
> I am I, and you are you.

And if by chance we find each other,
It's beautiful.
If not, it can't be helped.

I did not tell him what I really thought of this humanistic "prayer": that it was childish and egocentric, much less nihilistic. It claims all rights for the individual while granting no responsibility for the concerns or needs of the other person. This "psalm," in poster form, had been on the wall of every other college dorm room in the 60s. It was, in its own way, as pathetically tragic as this popular bumper sticker of the same period – "I don't get mad; I get even." Imagine, for a moment, how cold and unstable a society built on the above, self-centered prayer would be; yet this poem expresses the aloneness and self-centeredness fostered by the 20th Century Myth.

He stated his belief that each person in a marriage should be free to develop his own unique self. He was sure he could continue to live with his wife even if she chose to have an affair, or simply a one-night stand. It was up to each person, he said, to define and develop his own means to happiness. I was shrugged off when I suggested that his view of happiness was one-sided and self-serving, and his actions were bound to hurt his wife and children if he continued having affairs. By the end of the session it was evident I had nothing to offer this fellow. All he wanted from me was to help his wife feel better about his activities.

Selfishness is at the root of most marital breakdowns. In this case, the selfishness of the husband was simple, easy to see, raw. There was little attempt to hide it or confuse the real issue. This turned out to be a rare case, but only in its bare-boned rawness.

"Immaturity" is a nicer, more clinical sounding term than selfishness, but when we say someone is immature we are usually describing aspects of self-centeredness. "Selfishness" more directly goes to the point. If one (much less both) of the marriage partners is unduly selfish, then that family is in trouble. This means that most families of today are in trouble. Some will grow up and out of trouble; many will not.

Usually the underlying issue of one partner's selfishness is obfuscated by rationalizations, or by elaborate intellectualizations, or by projections of one partner's problems onto the other. Most people take more care to cover up their selfishness than the husband of the above example.

Selfishness as the cause of marital discord is nothing new. What is new is the respectability lent to selfishness after World War II, especially in and after the 1960s by the infusion of the 20th Century Myth into our family lives. Prior to the Second World War, abject selfishness in marital relationships had been respectable only among some circles of the rich and famous, but in the 60s it became not only respectable but almost canonized for everyone; selfishness was democratized.

The 20th Century Myth reinforces the "me first" approach to human relationships. It assumes that the only reality is the here and now, that therefore only the things of the material world matter, that all knowable things are relative to the perceiver, that indeed all values and standards are relative; therefore the only reality of value is me, the perceiver. My needs, my growth, my development must be my first priority, for I am the only thing that can be truly known, at least by me. The 20th Century Myth fosters the greatest of rationalizations – *that only by meeting my own needs first can I then become capable of loving others*. First, I must be happy; then I can make others happy. Now, we human beings hardly need encouragement to be self-centered; nevertheless, that is the effect on us when we build our lives around the 20th Century Myth. And, of course, the more respectable our selfishness, the more difficult it becomes to make commitments to others last, once made.

When both partners have areas of selfishness interfering with the happiness of the marriage, then the problems are more than doubled; they are exponentially increased. The fate of such a marriage can resemble a horror movie. Danny DeVito's 1989 film "The War of the Roses" was not that far off the mark. When two people, both accustomed to being indulged on every important point, come together in marriage a recipe for disaster is written.

When one of the marriage partners becomes obsessed with career and then neglects the marriage relationship; when one insists that the children must be treated and reared a particular way or else; when one holds a grudge and cannot let go of past grievances; when one must always win the argument and the other must always give in; when one consistently mishandles the family's money and refuses to change; when one uses alcohol or other drugs to medicate feelings of resentment toward the other; when one or more of these occurs, the marriage is in trouble. Everyone has his or her areas of selfishness or "pride." Inevitably, these areas of selfishness interfere with our development of healthy relationships with others. The question is, can the person let go of his selfishness to the degree required to allow the couple to work through the adversity together? This requires self-sacrifice and humility, old-fashioned values not currently in favor.

In other eras the prevailing ethics often called people away from their natural selfishness to something greater than themselves. These ethics did not always work. Sometimes they were so heavy-handed they made matters worse. But they existed, and they were typically reinforced by all the significant institutions of the society.

Now, however, there are no agreed-upon ethics reinforced by all of society's major institutions. Everything is relative. Now, it is every person for himself. It is not so much that there are more inherently selfish people today. It is, instead, that selfishness has become a social norm, an expected standard of behavior.

This change in social norms has resulted in more people acting more selfishly. Hedonism, instant self-gratification and obsession with materialistic goods, has always been with us, but now it too often reigns paramount in our galaxy of values. Its competitors have been weakened, shoved aside, or dismissed altogether. In recent Gallup polls, 89% of young adults stated that they were more selfish than the young people of twenty years ago, and 82% said they were more materialistic. In 1970 only 39% of entering freshmen, in over 500 colleges surveyed, rated being *well-off financially* as a "very important" life goal. By the mid-1980s this figure had risen to nearly 80% of entering freshmen. Our social norms, our normative values, have slipped in many critical areas. This happened so easily, so readily, so thoughtlessly, that we barely noticed. Suddenly, as we moved from the 1960s to the 1970s, our social norms were turned inside out.

Sacrifice for others, duty to a higher ideal, patience, delay of one's own gratification to serve the more immediate needs of others – all these values, always hard to achieve, were dismissed as ancient, irrelevant, even laughable. Self-centeredness, dolled up as self-development or self-expression, quickly became the reigning virtue of the day. This cynicism was caused by the exhaustion and collapse of the old ethic. This old ethic – humanism based on Judeo-Christian principles – lost its power as the dominant spiritual and ethical force in society. The ethic of the 20th Century Myth was thrust into this suddenly-created vacuum, but this ethic does not reliably call man to something higher, bigger, better than himself. Its inherent nihilism ends up reinforcing every self-centered, materialistic tendency of man. Once this "new" social norm took over, it became every man for himself, which of course is the oldest, most primitive of social norms. That which was touted as progress, as emancipation of the individual, turned out to be regression to a more primitive state of affairs. The family was in serious trouble. Very quickly, divorce rates soared and dysfunctional families established new norms.

Now here's the rub: Most people do not want to go back to the old ethic. Too much of the old ethic depended on fear and intimidation to control people and motivate them to act as they "ought to." Most of us really can't go back to that home again. Our spiritually-based and values-producing institutions seem for the present exhausted, incapable of generating a new ethic that would motivate modern men and women by the positive ideals they long for.

In the meantime we face all the implications of the ancient truism: *as the family goes, so goes the society.* The strength of any society is directly dependent on the strength and nature of its families. Japan and Germany bounced back quickly from the devastation of World War II in no small part as a result of their strong family units. Their families produce a high percentage of persons capable of sustained, intelligent work and the ability to fulfill obligations to others. In contrast, the American family has deteriorated since the 1960s, and this deterioration is nowhere more evident than in the growing numbers of children from dysfunctional families. These children are handicapped from parental neglect, or the effects of alcohol and other substance abuse by their parents, or physical and mental abuse by parents resulting in emotional scars that preclude healthy relationships with others. The results are alcohol and substance abuse of their own, heightened tendencies toward crime and other anti-social behaviors, increased teenage pregnancy outside of marriage, poor health, and lack of basic skills and work habits requisite to hold down a job. These children are often said to be "at risk." At risk to do harm to themselves and others. At risk to perpetuate these same problems into the next generation when they have children of their own.

A report prepared for the Florida legislature suggested that by the year 2000 over 50% of that state's children will be definable as at risk.[58] Data provided by the Education Commission of the States, in Denver, show that since 1960 drug and alcohol problems among teens have increased 60 times over, a blood curdling statistic. At the current rate of deterioration only two or three more generations will be required to remake the U.S. into a second-rate nation. Children of dysfunctional families have a heightened tendency to produce dysfunctional families of their own. An exponential effect is thus generated that eventually affects the majority of society.

At-risk children pose many problems for society at large, in part because they do not have the skills and work ethic required to perform adequately in the marketplace. As their numbers grow their cumulative effect is to bring down both the quality of all lives and the productivity of the nation as a whole. A Japanese company (Honda), for example, started a manufacturing plant in Ohio. It planned on using the same management and procedures utilized in Japan. It soon found, however, that it had to change back to less productive work methods because many of the American workers did not have the math skills to implement the Japanese methods. Production was thus lowered. Less was produced for the same amount of labor. The American workers then lost out on the higher wages that would have been generated by higher productivity.

From 1947 to 1973 American productivity and real compensation per hour increased at a 3% per annum rate. The standard of living thus doubled, per worker, every 24 years, or about once every generation. Since 1973 our annual growth in productivity per worker has been 1% per annum while real compensation has grown at a 0.4% annual rate. Six generations, 180 years, are now required for the American worker to double his standard of living.

The top half of American workers are still competitive with those of such societies as Japan and Germany. But the bottom half of American workers have fallen far behind their comparable numbers in these other societies, thus producing a dramatic, overall decline in American productivity. *Dysfunctional families in combination with poor schools* are mainly responsible for this ineptness of many American workers. Too many of today's adult workers cannot compare with the adult American workers of the 1940s, 50s and 60s, a high percentage of which were products of strong family units, reasonably competent schools, and the old ethic.

This decline in our ability to compete in the international marketplace is minimal, however, when compared to the human misery caused by dysfunctional families – the heartache, loneliness, and fear caused in children when they are neglected, abused, used as tools of manipulation by two warring parents, exposed to substance abuse at an early age, and provided little or no training in morality, job and person skills, let alone other "ideals" except those of self-gratification and materialistic aggrandizement. If our goal were to destroy children's lives, then we have found the formula.

Since family dysfunction is at the root of so many of our current social problems, one might say all of them in the ultimate sense, it behooves us to look more carefully at what's happened to the American family, at one time a source of great pride of the nation. We look first at the effect of family dysfunction on children and then at the issue of child care. Then in a subsequent chapter we'll look at those principles that by contrast provide healthy bases for both marriage-building and child-rearing.

Modern Family Life: Debilitating Effects of Divorce

Divorce is the most visible feature of modern family life, especially in the U.S. where far more children are affected by divorce than in any of the other 12 highly industrialized nations of the world.[59] Divorce, single-parent homes and children born out of wedlock have combined to create a world in which at least half of all children born in the U.S. after 1980 will spend part or all of their childhood in a single-parent (usually fatherless) home. If Americans in 1960 could have been informed of this 1990 statistic, they simply would not have believed it. Few Americans in 1960 could have comprehended that such a massive deterioration in traditional American family life was about to occur. There was nothing to predict it. No one knew that the 20th Century Myth was about to replace traditional values. Then, throughout the 1960s the divorce rate, proportion of single-parent homes and children born outside of marriage slowly but steadily increased. These increases exploded onto the American scene in the early 1970s as the first wave of baby boomers came into their child-bearing years, bringing with them all the ramifications of the 20th Century Myth. We can now look back on at least 20 years of research on these unexpected changes.

The research on the effects of divorce on child development must be approached with some caution. A strange but true "law" exists in psychology: the more important the research topic, the more poorly done the research. We psychologists are without equal in the study of rats coping with mazes. Our research on such weighty matters exemplifies the highest scientific standards. But when we turn to the study of divorce and childcare our research is often poorly designed and inadequately implemented. Sometimes, however, we make up in quantity what we lack in quality. Hundreds of studies have now been done on the effects of divorce on children. By carefully sifting though the mountains of data, while looking at the better designed studies for consistencies, we can arrive at some reliable reports.

In looking at the *short-term* effects of divorce on children (the first two years after divorce), the most consistent finding is that *boys are more adversely affected than girls*. This report shows up time and again and takes on many different expressions:[60]

- The deterioration in schoolwork subsequent to divorce is more prevalent among boys and lasts longer with boys than girls.
- Boys are even less happy and more likely to be depressed than girls.
- Boys are more aggressive and distractible at school after divorce.
- Boys are more often than girls described by their mothers as "out of control" at home after the divorce. Teen-age boys are much more likely than teen-age girls to hit their mothers and to be abusive both physically and verbally.
- Boys show these overt effects of divorce for a longer period of time than girls do.
- Even ten years after divorce boys are much more likely than girls to express anger and resentment toward their mothers and even express the belief that the mother "drove the father away."

It would be a tragic injustice to infer from the above findings that girls are impervious to the negative fallout of divorce. Girls are deeply affected by divorce. Over the short run boys are more overtly affected than girls. Over the long haul, however, there is good reason to believe that girls are as dramatically affected as boys. The effects are somewhat different for the two sexes. This will become clearer when we look at the long-range effects of divorce on adolescent and adult development. For now we need to look at why boys appear to suffer more than girls in the first one to two years after divorce.

In the overwhelming majority of divorces the father leaves, not the mother. The boy thus loses his father; the girl does not lose her mother. This basic fact, with all its ramifications, explains much about the greater overt effect of divorce on boys. The boy loses his father, the primary male figure in his life. In some cases the boy may have secretly wished for the father to go away. Still, he hurts in a hundred different ways when the father disappears. Since the woman usually keeps the house, it is easy for the boy to surmise that the father "lost out" to the mother, and was thus pushed out of the mother's territory. Boys (and girls) may believe this and be resentful toward the mother even when they know the objective facts are to the contrary. I have known teenagers who knew their fathers had been abusive toward their mothers while married, but who nevertheless persisted in their belief that the mother had somehow driven the father out of their lives.

Most boys see their fathers even less after the divorce than before. If the relationship had not been good before, it rarely gets better after the divorce. This is especially true when the mother maintains custody of the boy. Sadly, in most cases, the father does not want custody. To make matters worse, mothers are hard hit financially by divorce. The financial condition of both the mother and the children who stay with her is usually greatly worsened after divorce, a fact that's been exacerbated by the implementation of "no-fault" divorce in the last two decades.[61]

On other dimensions, however, it is the father who is hit harder by the consequences of divorce. The research shows that the death rates of divorced men, rates of disease, accident rates and homicide rates are much higher than those of married men. Their suicide rate is three times higher than that of married men.[62] Both boys and men are in many ways more adversely affected by divorce than women and girls. There is some truth to the feminists' claim that females are better off outside of marriage than in.

Women experience more stress than men prior to divorce, whereas men seem to experience more stress after divorce. Women are twice as likely to initiate divorce.[63] Divorce is usually a matter of one partner's becoming unhappy with the marriage, trying to do something about it, and feeling frustrated in his or her (usually her) efforts. Women are more likely to be unhappy in the time leading up to the divorce, finally reaching a point where they initiate the divorce.

In 1980 I saw again the woman of the couple discussed at the start of this chapter. She came to one of my workshops on parenting skills and stayed afterwards to chat for a while. She told me she had divorced her "ex" two years before. She was still not happy, but she was relieved to be out of the "living hell" her ex-husband had put her through while they were married. She was not through with him, however. She told me they were constantly fighting over child support and money and when he could see their two children. This is common to divorces where children are involved. The two former partners are never truly divorced; they continue to feud with each other over children and finances.

Boys, even more than girls, show the impact of father-loss by being less happy and more resentful at home, more aggressive and distractible at school. The boy is left wondering, what's wrong with me that the main man in my life does not want to be with me? He is not there at the game, or the school play, or at home when the boy needs to be disciplined. The love and discipline that a father provides are gone.

As William Hodges points out in his superb review, the effect on boys' school performance is significant even after taking into account the many flaws in the research.[64] In the most carefully done study, boys from two-parent homes "...were absent less often, had higher peer popularity...had higher internal locus of control, and had higher full scale IQ's and ... reading and spelling scores" in contrast to boys from divorced homes.[65] Another study reported that children from single-parent homes were twice as likely to drop out of school and three times more likely to be expelled as children from two-parent homes.[66]

These reports are even more compelling when they focus on father absence in the home. A large number of studies over the past 40 years have indicated that masculinity in boys is often affected by father absence. These studies report that father-absent boys are relatively less masculine, more dependent on peers, less trusting, less industrious, feel less confident, perform more poorly in school and score lower on indices of moral development than boys from intact homes. And the greater the post-divorce conflict the more feminine both boys and girls tend to be.[67]

All this should not be used to infer anything about the effects of mother-absence, since there have been only a handful of studies that have looked at mother-absence. Until recently mother absence was such a rare occurrence that it didn't seem to call for research. We can only guess at its effects, perhaps by looking at cases of abandonment by mothers. Over the past two decades I have seen hundreds of cases of total or near total father abandonment, but only a few cases of total mother abandonment. These few children, abandoned by their mothers sometime after the age of two years, were among the most pathetic children I've ever seen. They seemed to be crippled for life. Abandoned children have confided to me that they still grieve over the missing parent years later and they search the faces of strangers in crowds hoping to "see" the missing parent, even after they have forgotten the face of the lost parent. It is remarkable how often parents underestimate their impact on their children's lives.

One of the most common concerns of college students today seeking counseling is this: does my father truly love me? A good friend of mine, who died early at the age of 43, was often depressed even though on the surface he seemed to "have it made." He was good-looking, highly intelligent, had a loving wife (no children by choice), was financially successful and howlingly funny when he chose to be so. When we would talk about his depressions he would always return to the topic of his family, especially his father. Once I asked him if he could recall any good times with his father (who had been a financially prominent man). Yes, he said, he often thought of one summer the family had spent together in a cabin in Northern Michigan when he was 10 or 11. It would have been 1947 or 1948. The father was on the phone all day doing business. But early in the morning he would get his son out of bed and they would run together in the woods before breakfast. The son couldn't remember if this had happened once, twice, or several times. It was all a blur now, but he still remembered how warm and secure he felt at the time. I asked him why. He said it was the only time he could recall when he had felt that his father *truly wanted to be with him.* Now we are raising a generation of children where many, many of them wonder if their fathers ever want to be with them.

In one of the largest studies ever done, which involved several thousand teenagers and their families, these three factors emerged as the main causes of juvenile delinquency:[68]

(1) A low degree of communication between fathers and their children;

(2) A low degree of affection between both parents and their children;

(3) A low degree of mothers' supervision of their teenagers.

The long-term effects of divorce, it turns out, are not all that different from the short-term effects. These effects have been brilliantly and compassionately documented by Judith Wallerstein and Sandra Blakeslee. In their book *Second Chances*,[69] Dr. Wallerstein reports on her 10- to 15-year follow-up of children of divorced families. This book is advised reading for all married couples as well as couples contemplating marriage. Wallerstein's research suggests that the negative effects of divorce on children can be mitigated by a successful remarriage, by frequent visitations by the missing parent, by grandparents helping out, and many other factors as well. But the research also shows that divorce has a lifelong impact on children. It may be more or less, good or bad, but divorce is for the child's lifetime. Anyone who has worked for a long time with the children (and later adults) of divorce knows this to be true.

An overwhelming result of Wallerstein's research is that the long-term effects of divorce may be good for the adults, but rarely for the children. Divorce "…is almost always more devastating for children than for parents" and as a result "…we are allowing our children to bear the psychological, economic, and moral brunt of divorce."[70]

Divorce stays in the mind of the growing child. Sometimes the experience is buried and the child leads a normal life for a while, but it stays close to the surface of the child's thoughts. Children and adolescents talk about how they miss the structure, the discipline, the feeling of being protected from the outside world they sometimes felt in their previously intact home. A nagging sense of vulnerability pervades their lives. Sometimes this feeling seems to go away, but it never really goes away.

Children of divorce are haunted by the modeling effect they have lived through, which causes much fear about their own abilities to maintain relationships with others. Even though they may eventually accept the idea that their parents are better off not married to each other, they are left with this modeling – that when things get tough in a relationship, you leave it. They wonder – will I do the same or will the same happen to me? They worry about other people. Can "they" be trusted to keep their commitments or will "they" take a hike if the relationship becomes inconvenient or emotionally difficult?

Wallerstein talks about a "sleeper" effect she has observed in girls. In the short run, as previously noted, many girls seem to snap back from divorce rather quickly, certainly faster than most boys. These girls often identify strongly with their mothers and even become their confidants and friends at an early age. Their schoolwork and achievements are usually not affected by divorce.

As they reach adolescence, however, and especially upon later separation from Mom, these girls often show a resurgence of the anxiety they experienced right after the divorce. This sleeper effect often occurs even if the mother has successfully remarried. The girl, now a young lady, worries if she can have and hold a good relationship with a man. Her fears are not unfounded. Many studies have reported that girls from divorced families are more sexually active and overtly flirtatious than girls from intact families.[71] These girls often appear to be trying to prove something about their sexual attractiveness and their ability to hold on to a male. These girls worry about the statistic that the children of divorce are more likely to experience divorce themselves. Some studies have reported that the divorce rate for adult women who have experienced divorce in childhood is almost two-thirds higher than for women from intact homes.[72] Other studies have reported that women from divorced parents are four to five times more likely to undergo divorce themselves than women from intact families. And, women of divorce are more likely to cohabit with men outside of marriage and often report a larger number of sexual partners.[73] These young women thus enter into relationships with men and marriage with a different set of expectations and fears than most other women. Wallerstein is convinced from her work over the past 20 years that over the long run girls are as negatively affected by divorce as boys.

Many boys from divorced families exhibit what I call the "rudderless ship effect." Boys, unlike girls, do not catch up with boys from intact families in school performance. Many such boys drift along, not developing the "stick-to-itness," the self-discipline required to achieve their goals successfully. Wallerstein reports that when she later observed them as young adults, about 40% of the boys in her study were still drifting with little sense of direction in their lives. Wallerstein, however, was viewing the long-range effects of divorce on a predominantly white, middle class population. Over the past 25 years, I have observed in my work thousands of families breaking up, a significant proportion of which were minority and/or lower income. In my experience the proportion of boys of divorce who are "rudderless" is closer to 50% of the total group. Many of these boys I have been able to observe well into their twenties and thirties. They find it very difficult to come out of their pattern of drifting along. It is hard for them to stay with jobs, with school, or with relationships with women for very long. They are often bright and inherently capable young men. But they lack the ability to stick things out, to persevere, to do what's necessary to achieve their goals. These boys often have lofty ambitions but lack the motivation, discipline and follow-through required to achieve their goals. Subsequently, they experience repeated frustrations which reinforce their low self-esteem. Growing numbers of these young men are among us today. They are more often seen among black males, since fatherless homes are more common among blacks, but can be seen in increasing numbers among all ethnic groups. The "rudderless effect" is not an automatic product of fatherless homes, but it is a high-probability effect.

With the above experiences in mind let's look at a case study of a somewhat "typical" divorce. The woman was nearing 40 and had been unhappy in the marriage for several years. She and her husband had three boys – ages 12, 10 and 7. Her husband had few interests outside of his work and paid scant attention to her, though he showed some interest in the boys' activities. Her work life was much more satisfying than her home life. At home, she felt the emotional distance between herself and her husband growing larger all the time. She feared her "looks" were diminishing and life was passing her by. She longed for some romance in her life, some passion. She felt she had sent her husband many signals of her unhappiness with him, but he never responded to her signals in the way she hoped he would. Finally, after many talks with her friends, she decided to divorce him, especially after she became friends with a recently divorced man at work who was definitely interested in her. Some of her friends warned her that her sons would be devastated, but she felt that after the boys got over the initial shock they would be better off because she would be happier, hence they would be happier.

Her husband was shocked when informed of her decision; he asked for marital counseling. She said no, her mind was made up. Four years after the divorce she and all three boys were in therapy. She said she was "a little happier" than before, but admitted that her new husband had not turned out as well as she had hoped. He showed many of the same tendencies as her former husband. Her older son was "out of control" and she was attending *tough love* groups to try to learn how to cope with him. Her middle son had developed severe migraine headaches, and her youngest insisted on sleeping with her every night. All three boys' school grades had fallen significantly. The boys became excited, however, when planning a weekend with their biological father who had not remarried. She often thought the boys would be better off staying full-time with their father, but she was wracked with guilt if she thought too much about it.

The woman in this case was better off than most. She remarried almost immediately and never suffered financially. Nevertheless, this example has many characteristics common to other family break-ups of today. A minority of divorces are due to philandering or physical abuse – the more sensational causes of divorce. Most divorces are due to one partner's expectations not being met by the other person. One partner feels that his or her needs are not being fulfilled by the other person, and then seeks a way out of the marriage, which raises this question: Was the small increment in the mother's personal happiness worth the negative impact on her children? And this question: had the wife in this case truly exhausted all possible means to rejuvenate her marriage? It was clear that as a result of the divorce her sons were worse off; it was not clear that she was better off. These questions bring us to the first of five modern "myths" that need addressing:

Modern Myth #1 – Children Are Improved by Divorce in Contrast to Maintaining Them in an Unhappy Home.

We do not know if this statement is true or false. Nevertheless, this bromide is often stated as if it were a universal truth. It is critical to the excuse-making that's necessary in justifying divorce involving children. Psychologists and other counselors are especially fond of this statement since they are very concerned not to raise undue guilt on the part of the divorcing partners. This notion was another product of the 20th Century Myth. Prior to this new myth, the old-fashioned bromide stated that children were better off if the two parents "stuck it out together" (despite a less than happy relationship), at least until the children were grown. By contrast, the 20th Century Myth fosters the belief that our own personal happiness must always precede the happiness of others. The old bromide was thrown out in the 60s and quickly replaced with the new bromide. Which view is closer to the truth? We do not know. It is a matter of belief.

There are a few studies that seem to support the new notion. One widely quoted study, for example, reported no significant differences in self-concept in young children from intact, single-parent and remarried families. The critical variable observed in this study was the degree of family conflict.[74] Low self-esteem correlated with high family conflict regardless of the makeup of the family. This and a few other studies have formed the "scientific basis" on which Modern Myth #1 has been justified.

These few studies, however, have not directly addressed the question raised by the statement. A well-designed, longitudinal study is called for that could be replicated by other investigators (to see if the results hold up beyond the one sample – remember that in social science no one study proves a point). Such studies have not been done. Longitudinal means that the same sample of children would be followed over a long period of time so that effects over time could be studied. This is quite different from the usual "snapshot" approach used in psychological research wherein, for example, a questionnaire is handed to the teachers or parents of children one time only, one year after the divorce.

This hypothetical, longitudinal study would require at least three groups of children. One group would be comprised of children of divorce. Another group would be comprised of children from intact families which stay intact for the 10 or 20 year duration of the study. This second group would be split into two groups: intact families with high degrees of conflict vs. intact families with low degrees of conflict. Yet other variables would have to be "controlled" (equalized) across the three groups to make this a sound study. If we were to follow these children over 10, 15 or 20 years into adulthood, then we should be able to construct some defensible statements about the effects of divorce on children in contrast to maintaining them in high-conflict but intact homes. But such studies have not been done.

Wallerstein's research certainly indicates that the long-term effects of divorce on children are often pernicious. Unfortunately, her study did not include comparison groups from intact families. Thus, again, we are uninformed as to the reality of Myth #1.

Despite our great ignorance on this important matter, we perpetuate Myth #1 and act as if it were the gospel truth. We need this myth. Otherwise, we would have to face the guilt caused by the opposite statement – that often we put our personal quest for happiness above and beyond the happiness of our own children. The guilt of facing this would be unbearable. Baby boomers always have been taught to avoid guilt at all costs. Guilt is "unhealthy" (a proposition originated by Freud at the beginning of this century). Sometimes guilt is unhealthy. Sometimes, however, guilt is based on reality and is a necessary experience that provides the opportunity to learn from our mistakes. A degree of wisdom and self-knowledge (based on self-honesty) are required to know the difference between the two kinds of guilt. Is there truth to Myth #1? Again, we do not know. I suspect we'll discover that in a minority of divorces the children are truly better off, but that this is not the case in the majority of divorces. Hopefully, guidelines would emerge from well-done research that might allow families to differentiate between the minority conditions versus the majority conditions. We have a long way to go, however, before reaching this desirable point. In the meantime, caution is advised for those who continue to promote the notion that children are better off in a broken home than in an intact but unhappy home.

Modern Myth #2 – Although the Children May Be Harmed, at Least the Adults Are Better Off After Divorce.

This notion would seem to be on stronger grounds than Myth #1. Several studies have reported that adults state they are more satisfied with their lives after divorce. But this "finding" also requires several qualifiers. For one thing, what else can we expect adults to say, especially those who initiated the divorce in the first place? Of course they report being more satisfied, especially when children are involved. We can only imagine the guilt if one were to say, years later and after seeing the children suffer in the meantime, "Well, I blew it; I would have been better off staying married to old so-and-so." Human beings aren't built that way. There is a psychological process called *dissonance reduction* whereby we convince ourselves of the rightness of our decisions once it seems that other options are no longer available to us. Aesop's tale of "sour grapes" was an illustration of dissonance reduction at work. At first the fox tried everything to get the delicious, fresh grapes so he could eat them. But once it became clear there was no way to get the grapes, he convinced himself they were actually sour and that he had never really wanted them in the first place.

The 20th Century Myth asserts that the only knowable reality is ourselves, and this has led to the great emphasis on self-development. This attitude places a premium on attaining one's own, personal happiness first; a philosophy that results in marriages falling apart that were in fact reparable. Many people today give up on marriage very quickly, too quickly. Lacking is the patience and resolve of both partners to make the relationship work through bad times as well as good times. The children of these divorces, as we've seen, pay a terrible price for the overweaned self-centeredness of their parents. But the parents also pay a price. They do not really escape from their relationship problems by changing partners. The disgruntled partner later discovers that his old problems reappear in new form with his new partner. He finds that in the new marriage he must pick up where he left off in his prior marriage. These recurring problems and frustrations must be dealt with or the second (or third) marriage dissolves. Typically, these problems can be resolved only by changing one's own behavior and attitudes, not by changing partners. In far too many second marriages the partners are trying to work through relationship problems that, with more patience and self-awareness, could have been worked through in the first marriage.

Myth #2 also suffers from the same deficit as Myth #1, namely the lack of well-done research addressing the basic question. More definitive studies would be longitudinal. (It is hard for psychologists to do other than "snapshot" research because the pressure of "publish or perish" in universities virtually forces them to do short-term, quick-to-publish studies.) This longitudinal research would require at least two groups for comparison. One group would be comprised of adults who divorce while the other group would be comprised of adults who decide to "stick it out" despite high conflict between them. The two groups would then be compared 5, 10, 20 years later on measures of happiness, self-concept, etc. An interesting third group would be adults who decide to "stick it out" but at the same time commit to long-term counseling to try to resolve their problems. Though this research hasn't been done, Myth #2 is perpetrated, no doubt in response to the need to justify what we have been doing to each other, our families and our children. The truth is we do not know the conditions under which Myth #2 is valid or not.

Wallerstein's research on the long-term effects of divorce probably comes closest to the truth when she points out that some adults are "winners" after the divorce while others are "losers." She notes that even 10 or 15 years after a divorce some people are still suffering from its aftermath while others have flourished. She also notes a point often observed by others – that many parents, especially mothers, suffer severe financial hardship for a long, long time after the divorce.

So among the parents, who are the winners and who are the losers? The research findings are not yet clear on this point, but they are clear enough to assert that Myth #2 is, at best, simple-minded. It is also clear that children are not often "helped" by divorce.

These critiques of myths #1 and #2 also illustrate the danger of allowing social science research to provide the rationale for social change and/or social policy. Social science research is simply not sophisticated enough at this stage in history to provide a solid rationale for much of anything, much less complicated social issues. Research can serve as one source of information on the issue in question, but it should never serve as the final arbiter. For one thing, psychological research suffers the same drawback as all other scientific research – it does not, cannot, tell us the *values* to use when making decisions that affect people other than ourselves

Review of the Effects of Divorce

No one would propose that *all* children of divorce are harmed forever by divorce. Some children benefit from the remarriage, although the research indicates that stepfathers often do not have a salubrious effect on the children of divorce.[75] Other children, though few in number, show an amazing wisdom acquired through the experience of living through a divorce. They may appear at times overly serious for their age, but they demonstrate a knowledge about people and relationships admirable at any age. These, however, are the exceptions. In Wallerstein's research, after 10 or 15 years of follow-up, half the children had gone through a second divorce – the divorce of the remarriage – and half had lived through situations where the two parents continued to fight with each other for the duration of the child's childhood and adolescence. As the data accumulate, the evidence piles up that divorce has a lifelong negative impact on most of the children who must live through it. These children not only lose financially (in most cases), but they lose also on the protectiveness, the security, the discipline and the positive modeling that families try to provide their young.

Does all this mean we should tighten up the laws and make it harder for parents to divorce each other? Probably not. To go back to a more coercive, restrictive approach to marriage is likely to make matters worse, not better. Prohibition failed because most people will not stand for being told by others they can or cannot drink. The only sure answer for excessive drinking occurs when the drinker himself decides to "let go" of his problem and chooses instead to be guided by a positive ideal that eventually replaces fear-based approaches. Similarly, marriage and family life will be energized by positive ideals and models that draw people to them. Negative approaches, based on a return to fear and restriction, offer little of real value to modern men and women.

A first step, however, in moving on to a more positive ideal is to recognize honestly what we are doing to our children. Indulging ourselves in our rationalizations and myths about the effects of divorce serves no useful purpose. Our children are being battered by the lack of wisdom of their parents. They are the least able to defend or protect themselves. They are the least capable of defending their rights to protection, security and stability. We bring them into the world. They are in our *care*. That is our starting point.

> The truth shall make you free, but first it will make you miserable.
> Author Unknown

Child Care

Child care is one of the hottest topics on the public agenda as we near the end of the 20th Century. In and of itself, this fact speaks volumes about our times, especially the changes in our basic values. In previous generations the "problem" of child care would not have shown up on anyone's list of top ten problems. Now, it's on everyone's list. In prior generations it was simply assumed that each family, no matter how poor, would care for its own children. In the last 20 years, however, two new assumptions have arisen that have replaced this old value. The first new assumption is that mothering is not very important work, at least not as important as furthering one's career or simply working outside the home to make money. The second assumption is that families today must have two paychecks to make ends meet. These two new assumptions lead us directly to Modern Myth #3.

Modern Myth #3 – Both Parents Must Work Fulltime in Order for the Family to Survive Financially.

It is a curiosity that no one questions, much less challenges, this modern myth. *For the majority of families it is easily shown to be nonsense.* Yet, so awash are we in materialism that no one dares question the sacred yearning for more material goods – the newer car, more cars than one, perhaps a boat, a bigger house, an owned house and not a rental, bigger and better stereo equipment, and on, and on, and on. Many families have sacrificed care for their children so they can put their time and energy into materialistic, careeristic, self-serving pursuits.

Prior generations were also tantalized by all the things of the "good life," but in most cases they were willing to make the sacrifices required to put time and energy into providing quality care for their own children. This ideal was suddenly discarded in the early 1970s and replaced with a previously unheard-of focus on self-centeredness by the new generation of baby boomer parents. In many families today the parents' needs come first; the children's needs are to be met later – if there is enough time.

To be sure, there are families where both parents must work fulltime just to pay the rent and put food on the table. There have always been families in that predicament. And the increase in single-parent (usually father-absent) homes has been astronomical. For many of these families there is no choice. The single parent or both parents must seek outside care for their children since they must work for money merely to survive.

However, before we are carried away by these facts of modern life, let's make sure we place them into a realistic framework. For the fact is that a clear majority of children today are still being reared, at any one time, in two-parent homes. And most of these two-parent homes are functioning above, in most cases well above, the poverty line. In fact, it is almost impossible to be poor in America if a couple attains high school degrees and stays married. The Census Bureau's poverty rate for married couples where both have high school diplomas is only 5%. Even after all the family disruption of the past two decades, most children, at any one time, are in two-parent homes with average income. These families still have choice – freedom of choice – as to where they place their time and energy. When we have freedom of choice, we show by our decisions what we truly value, what we love, by when and where we put our time and energy. This is something all human beings know; certainly, children know. We know when we are first in the heart of another. We also know, acutely and painfully, when we rank second or third in the eyes of another; we know by how, when and where they expend their energy, their time, their thought and concern for us. Most families today still can make these choices. Many families no longer believe this. They have convinced themselves that they no longer have any degrees of freedom left.

In examining Myth #3, let's look at a family I counseled a few years ago that had many typical characteristics. This couple, then in their early 30s, had many of the usual complaints. They had had some arguments over in-laws and over disciplining their children. Money was tight and sometimes they fought over money. They both felt they were losing their hold on their old love relationship. They had two children, ages 2 and 4. They weren't having as much fun together as they did in their first years of marriage. They had been married nearly eight years. They were both exhausted by evening. It seemed to both of them that all they did was work, work, and then work some more. They dearly loved their two little ones. They both cared deeply for each other and wanted to make the marriage work. There was no pathology to be found anywhere, no hidden addictions or fixated sources of selfishness. They were mainly tired. They felt they were on a fast track to nowhere.

As the first sessions went by, it became increasingly clear that the two of them were experiencing guilt over leaving their two children at a daycare center every weekday. Both parents were usually too tired at night to enjoy their "quality time" with their kids. They had all the usual rationalizations about their lifestyle but, in truth, felt guilty about shortchanging their children and themselves. They had noticed that when he was between construction jobs and could stay home with the kids, they were all much happier. She longed to spend more time with her kids; she felt that every day she was missing out on important aspects of their development. They had talked about her quitting her job, but felt it was financially impossible.

The turning point in their family counseling came about when we did a common sense overhaul of their family's economics. The husband was making about $28,000 annually as an electrician; she was making about $12,000 a year as a secretary. Their total family income was slightly above average for that time. Her $1,000 per month gross income became $780 per month after all taxes were taken out. She was paying $430 each month for child care in a local day care center, leaving her with $350 monthly in true take-home pay. We determined that her job cost the family budget at least an extra $200 in additional (1) transportation costs, (2) prepackaged food costs for home meals, (3) work clothes, (4) work lunches and (5) extra family meals eaten out. She actually netted at the most $150 a month of her $1,000 gross. This was almost exactly the difference in monthly payments between their $90,000 home bought in 1983 versus a $78,000 home they had passed on. They had to admit, with hindsight, that they would have been as happy in the $78,000 home as with their $90,000 home.

After coolly looking over these facts, they decided to take the plunge. She quit her job and started taking in typing jobs she could do at home by advertising at a local college. In about six months she was making up the $150 a month with her home typing. A year later, and then two years later in follow-up conferences, this couple reported they were far happier than before these changes. They were especially happy about the positive impact of these changes on their children and home life.

Is this couple merely an isolated example? Hardly. I have seen hundreds of couples in similar situations. I have seen many families, ranging from below average income couples to $100,000 a year couples with two Volvos in the garage, who have found ways to cut here and to cut there so that one of them could be with the kids most of the time. Mainly, it all depends upon what we value. If child care is an important priority, then families will do as they always have done – they will find the way to provide it themselves.

Young couples today, though, are so often deluded by the new myths that they have an air of unreality about them. In counseling with couples about their impending, first newborn I sometimes have the strange feeling we're talking about adding a cute little puppy or kitten to their family, rather than bringing a new human being into the world. They want the best of everything for their newborn, certainly they want the best possible daycare (kennel?). They will not tolerate, however, the notion that the child should interfere with their personal ambitions or money-making pursuits. In these very modern families it is clear that the child must accommodate himself to the personal endeavors of the parents, never the other way around.

Is the stress caused by both parents of young children working fulltime always as readily resolved as in the above example? Unfortunately, no. Some young families have plunged themselves so deeply into debt by the time the first child arrives that only a miracle could salvage them. These folks will spend much of their adult lives sacrificing their family life on the altar of their home mortgage payments. We used to lament that our "souls belonged to the company store;" now they belong to the mortgage company.

Actually, it's not fair to put all the blame on the size of today's home mortgage payments. It is amazing to see the spending binges so many young people go on as soon as they marry. Within a year they have bought a new car or two, their first house, a room full of stereo equipment, and all the furniture matches! They have charge accounts in six different stores. Of course, on their combined incomes they can do it, barely. But a few years later the first baby comes and they are trapped. They are so deeply in debt they cannot imagine existing without two full incomes. The notion eludes them that with some *common sense planning* they could have avoided being trapped.

A fair analysis of the present mess in child care requires us to go back at least one generation. For about 20 years following World War II the U.S. experienced an unprecedented boom. Real income grew much faster than inflation and cheap housing was made available to young couples via the G.I. and F.H.A. programs. Newlyweds knew they had to wait a few years to buy their first new rather than used car. They knew they had to wait a few years before they could trade up from that first, cheap home to that more expensive dream home. But, for a few golden years, it seemed that an ever-rising standard of living had been providentially decreed for Americans. As couples are wont to do, they had children. Lots of them. Times were good. So many that their children were called the baby boomers.

Now those baby boomers are today's parents, who learned at their parents' knees the idea of an ever-rising standard of living. Many expanded on the idea. No need to wait a few years, as their parents did, for that new car, or dream home, or whatever. Buy now, live it up, and let the devil take the hindmost. Maybe he'll even take care of your debts.

Today's baby boomer parents, however, are living in a vastly changed world from that of their parents. For most of the past 20 years, the U.S. economy has struggled to grow even at the pace of inflation. Real income has grown little or not at all. Cheap housing is no longer available. Our families are in debt up to their ears and few families save anymore. Today's baby boomer parents are trying to live as if they were still in the glory years (1948-1968) enjoyed by *their* parents. They are paying a terrific price for their delusion. They are making their children pay the highest price of all for that delusion: absentee parents, overworked and tired parents, poor supervision of kids, too many homes broken by all the related stresses that runaway materialism brings on.

In prior generations young families with children simply did not expect to "have it all." They expected to make material sacrifices for their children. They expected life to be often difficult financially, but most believed in the ethic that the children's needs – in particular, the child's needs for protection, stability, discipline, nurturance, moral training and love – always came before the needs of the parents. The parents were responsible for bringing the child into the world; it followed that they were responsible for properly caring for the child. Many, many young couples today, however, dig themselves into a financial hole long before the first child comes. They violate the most basic principles of family finances.

- They buy far too many goods (and "goodies") and, usually lacking capital, they buy these toys with credit cards and then pay outrageous interest rates.
- They buy new or newer cars when cheaper, older cars would do as well.
- They buy houses too soon or buy houses beyond their means. Young parents in previous generations thought nothing of renting for years. Interestingly, in most of the other advanced, industrialized nations of the world few families own their own homes. Most of these families rent, and, amazingly, they live their lives out without thinking of themselves as abused by the gods.

Modern Myth #3 asserts that a man can no longer support his family without the additional income provided by a fulltime working wife. Could it be, however, that our purchasing power hasn't changed that much, but rather our expectations, our desire for more and more materialistic goods has accelerated, thereby creating Myth #3? Let's look, for example, at 1967 as our baseline year of family purchasing power and compare it to 1987-88. We'll use as our source the most reliable data on U.S. family income, that provided by the Department of Commerce, Bureau of the Census. We use 1967 as our baseline since '67 was the last year that the old-fashioned ethic still, without doubt, held sway among young married couples starting into their childbearing years. After 1967 the ethic of the 20th Century Myth, the "me first" ethic, quickly asserted itself in child care. But in '67 most young couples still worked on the assumption that when a wife gave birth she would quit work to be the primary carer of the family's children, while it was up to both parents to make the necessary financial cuts and sacrifices so the wife could do this. In 1967 a male in his mid-20's, head of household, with wife not working, earned a median annual income of $7,611, which in 1988 dollars was the equivalent of $26,958 per year. Thus, a male head of the family in 1967 earned the same in purchasing power as someone in 1988 earning $26,958 per year. In March of 1988, using this same comparison, a male in his 20's, head of household with wife not working, earned an average (median) income of $26,800/year, virtually identical to 1967 in purchasing power. The truth is there's been no significant change in actual purchasing power of young male heads of households since 1967. If we stretch this same comparison back into the 1950s and 40s, it tells us even more about the materialistic expectations of baby boomers. Male heads in those years earned even less in purchasing power than they do today. Yet, prior to 1968 most families managed to make do on one income while providing full home care for their children. Today's families claim they can no longer do this even though their actual purchasing power, in consumer dollars, is as great or greater than that of prior generations. And this is true even when we only compare male heads (1967) versus male heads (1987). In 1960 the per person average annual income, in today's dollars, was about $8,000. Today, in the same dollars, the average per person income is $16,000, and as a result the average family today has far more material goods than in 1960. Let us speak the truth here – that today's two-parent boomer families are spoiled financially, that they want more, more now, that they are too often unwilling to make the minor material sacrifices required to provide home care for their own children.

The current crisis in child care is less a crisis of family finances, as it is claimed to be, and much more often a crisis of family values.

By 1987 this change in values had become crystallized into the new standard, the new myth. Delay of gratification was no longer viable. The new norm was set and fast. Everyone "knew" that in this day and age two full-time incomes were necessary to make ends meet. No longer was there a choice in the matter. Individuals were no longer responsible for the consequences of their decisions since they no longer had any degrees of freedom left; materialistic wants ruled the day.

Today there are increasing numbers of families where the wife makes more money than her husband. If the family decides that one parent should be the primary carer of the children, shouldn't it be the husband? This decision will, and should, vary from family to family, depending on circumstances, future prospects, and most important, a determination of which parent is better suited, by temperament, for the primary carer role. This aspect becomes more relevant every day as the numbers increase of "rudderless males" from father-absent homes. Many of these young men are not well equipped to take on the primary provider role. They do not have the self-confidence, educational tools and stick-to-itness to handle well the particular pressures of being primary provider for their families. Some, perhaps many, will marry women who will earn more than they. It is possible that some of these men could regain their self-confidence by becoming primary carers for their children. Some will, and they will heal themselves in the same context – the family – that initially failed them. Unfortunately, only a few will do this. These young men are limited by their lack of a reliable father model and by the many wounds they carry. It is problematical as to how many of them could show the stick-to-itness demanded by the complex jobs of primary parenting.

The point is this: if children are to be cared for well and properly, *they must be planned for*. It used to be that one of the chief distinctions between low-income versus middle-class families was that low-income couples simply "had" children whereas middle-class, upwardly mobile families *planned* for the proper care of their own children. Now, middle-class couples go on spending binges as soon as they're married, never plan for their children, act as if they will always have two incomes, and then are shocked when the child comes and they must turn the bulk of their child's care over to someone or something else.

This idea of abandoning children so mom and dad can pursue their "dreams" used to be the sole province of the very rich who could afford nannies. Now, thanks to the baby boomers, it has become socially acceptable for all.

Instinctively, we know this isn't right, that kids are being shortchanged. But when we've been awash in materialism and self-centeredness all our lives it's hard to change, to give it up, even when the sacrifices required to do the right thing are relatively minor in scope.

It would be a mistake to infer from all this that it's been mainly the women baby boomers who have brought about these sordid changes in child care. Personally, I have seen more families where it is the man who insists the woman go back to a paying job while the child is still an infant. The extra paycheck, in his mind, is all important, and the kid, he reassures his wife, will be "just fine." All too many men use guilt and rebuke to coerce their wives into going back to work as soon as possible. Men used to take pride in their ability to support their families so their wives could provide for the children's daily protection, supervision and welfare. No doubt this old ethic, especially when taken to an extreme, was abusive and unduly restrictive for some women. But male baby boomers have turned this traditional ethic on its head and taken it to the opposite extreme. They now demand that their women do everything – bring home the bacon, keep house, supervise the kids, and on, and on, and on.

Women and men have struggled with these same issues in every generation. There is really nothing new here. What's new is the widespread capitulation to materialistic values by the baby boomer generation. Note these words written by a woman author in 1903:

> But then it is clear that many of our modern maidens do not care to inspire poetical sentiments, for they boast of being more practical than sentimental, since they have to take into consideration the probability of having to provide for themselves—marriage having become so uncertain. ...the expenses of married life have increased at such a rate during our days that men are wisely afraid of it.[76]

Nevertheless, we now know that most couples of that generation found the way to do the right thing.

I know that much of what I'm saying about modern family life hits people hard. It arouses great guilt and, often, anger. No one with any sense of compassion enjoys making other people feel guilty. I have seen many, many articles by psychologists and other professionals bemoaning the fact that our children are being neglected and, in a peculiar way, abused by today's parental attitudes. They all point to the same factors discussed here – divorce, single-parent homes, workaholic parents, self-obsessed parents, etc. But when they get to the obvious conclusion that the only way to stop the neglect and abuse is for parents to change their actions and their values, the experts back off. They dance up to the point, then shy up and pull away. No one wants to make anyone else feel uncomfortable – better to indulge ourselves in our precious myths. It is as if there is a society-wide agreement not to face facts – too much pain is involved and, besides, we might have to give up some of our goodies, or, God forbid, some aspect of our standard of living. I don't enjoy making people feel guilty either. It's much more fun to make people feel good. But what we're doing to our children, and to ourselves, is inexcusable. It's time to grow up. We can't have it all. And this leads us directly to Modern Myth #4.

Modern Myth #4 – It's Fine to Turn the Care of Your Child Over to Others as Long as You Get in "Quality Time."

The "quality time" myth stands on an even shakier basis than the first three modern myths. Its scientific basis is nonexistent. Nevertheless, this bromide is bandied about as if it contained proven truth. The fact is we have no idea as to when, where and how quality time applies to child development. For all that's known, quality time may be nothing more than the full-fledged rationalization it appears to be – a star in the pantheon of new excuses concocted to cover up what we're doing to our children. Once the change in social norms for child care occurred, the notion of quality time had to be invented. But the truth is that there is not one iota of reliable scientific evidence to support the idea that a small amount of "quality time" is equivalent to the child with "quantity time" spent in providing his care. There are no pertinent longitudinal studies. There are only dozens of snapshot studies, most shoddily done, showing mixed results.

However, as Joan Beck has suggested,[77] quality time is such a handy-dandy excuse we should consider extending its application on a society-wide basis:

- Teachers, for example, should be allowed to put in one hour per day of quality time with students and then go home. Isn't one hour of quality time equivalent to six hours of quantity time with students?
- Employees everywhere could tell their bosses that henceforth one day per week of quality time on the job is equivalent to the old-fashioned concept of five days per week of quantity time.
- Patients in hospitals should be grateful for one or two hours per day of quality care from their doctors and nurses. Certainly they shouldn't nit-pick over the lack of care the rest of the day. They should know that a small amount of quality care is equivalent to around-the-clock care.
- If we find ourselves receiving a quality ride in a taxi, we should not be dismayed if the cabby decides to take us only one-fourth of the way to our destination while charging us full fare. Surely, a one-fourth quality

ride is equivalent to a four-fourths quantity ride.

- And especially in high stress jobs such as air traffic control, we should be delighted when controllers exercise their quality time rights. Perhaps they should only bring the planes halfway down and then leave the rest to the pilot. The controller's quality time could be applied on the first half of the descent, while the pilot could exercise his quality time rights on the second half of the descent.

Despite the blatant absurdity of the quality time myth, today's parents expect their child to understand that the hour or so they give him in the evening should be deeply appreciated because it's quality time. He should be happy that his quality time makes up for all the time they were away from him the rest of the day. The two are, of course, equivalent in the child's mind and heart. It is odd that we do to our children what we would never do to our customers, patients, clients and other business associates: we ignore them, put them on hold, and get to them when we can. By the time we get to them, we are tired and cranky from a hard day's work and hard put to enjoy them, much less be at our best.

Floating around the quality time myth are several satellite issues. For example, what does it do to a child to have a succession of caretakers, most of whom aren't related to him? We don't know for sure, but the available data aren't pretty. The research suggests that when a developing child experiences a succession of broken dependencies with a series of caretakers he may find it increasingly difficult to develop loving, trusting relationships with others.

Then, there is the notion that no one should be expected to stay home with children – that such an activity is too dull for intelligent, ambitious adults. The flip side of this argument leads us to conclude that all outside jobs provide the exciting, stimulating work environments adults crave and need. This flip side is, of course, patent nonsense. Few jobs offer adventure and high degrees of stimulation. Parenting offers at least as many opportunities for adventure as other human activities. If a couple finds the idea of rearing children too dull to consider, don't have them. Children need and deserve far better.

Equally sad with the effects on children are the effects on the parents themselves. So many parents I have seen are depriving themselves of the pleasures of parenthood. More important, in neglecting their children they are also depriving themselves of invaluable learning experiences. Parenthood can be an invaluable learning experience. It has the capacity to turn fools into wise men. This cannot happen, however, unless we value parenthood. And it doesn't happen on the quick. When parenting is approached with the time and respect it deserves, we learn much about ourselves, our strengths, our weaknesses, how our personalities interact with other, growing personalities and our capacities for love.

We can even learn a great deal about the nature of the universe. The surest way to discover the meaning of the concept of God as a loving Father-Mother is to become a loving parent yourself. All this, however, must be experienced to be real. Words are not adequate to express these meanings except to say that when we truly love our child we discover the depth and meaning of unselfish love. A truly loving parent comes to know that if necessary he would give up his own life for his child. When this knowledge is applied to the notion that God loves us as *his children*, then the meaning of many of life's mysteries becomes clearer to us. Parenting is a means by which to outgrow our youthful self-centeredness. Parents who choose to deny themselves these experiences because they are too busy with other things are denying themselves the essential value of parenthood.

And, as people have always known, children grow up incredibly fast. The years fly by and once missed, cannot be recalled. By the time each generation relearns this ancient lesson it is too late to recoup that which has been lost unless one has had the good wisdom, or good luck, to know the great value of being there during the child's development.

Review

Our values about children, child care and parenting versus career started changing in the 60s and then accelerated into the 70s and 80s. As the 20th Century Myth replaced the traditional ethic it became easier and easier to rationalize all forms of self-centeredness. We are now dealing with the wreckage caused by these changes in values. We delude ourselves when we say these changes are due to current financial conditions. Most families in most generations have struggled with limited financial means in trying to provide for their children. Never before, however, has virtually a whole generation of parents chosen materialism over the care of their own children. The degree of abandonment and neglect of children going on in today's homes is unprecedented in modern civilization (the human societies of the last 300 years). This wholesale neglect of children has engendered a society-wide delusion to protect its adherents from guilt. This delusion is based on the four myths discussed above and their satellite concepts. It is true that the proportion of parents who no longer have any choice except to work outside the home has risen significantly. But it is also true that this proportion is nowhere near as large as the adherents of the delusion claim. The truth is that the majority of parents today still have degrees of freedom in which to make choices as to where their time and energies will be placed. Many, many are choosing to neglect their children, even to demand that government subsidize their neglect, while preferring to pursue their own interests and materialistic goals. But best not to dwell on this point. When the rationalizations are stripped away and the truth of the matter stated plainly, great, almost unbearable guilt is generated. Heat replaces light.

Is there hope for the modern family? Yes, there are many sources of strength to call upon to bring about a resurgence in family life. One such source is the simple fact that the demise of the traditional family has been greatly exaggerated, which brings us to Modern Myth #5.

Modern Myth #5 – The Notion that Only 7% of Today's Families Fit the Old-Fashioned Model of Breadwinner Father and Homemaker Mother

This, again, is utter nonsense and easily disproven. Yet, the adherents of the delusion that "everyone" is handing child care over to other people or institutions thrive on this misleading statistic. The facts are these: of families with preschool children, 33% (not 7%) fit the traditional model of father works, mother is at home. In another 16% of families the mother works part-time. In another 10% of families either a single mother or househusband is at home full-time with preschool children. Take a look at the table below, which is based on the most reliable data available (U.S. Bureau of Labor Statistics). This means that 59% of families with preschool children have a primary caretaker at home. In certain racial groups, such as whites, this percentage is higher yet.

So where does the figure of 7% come from? It comes from using the oldest of statistical manipulations – by shifting the basis of comparison. Instead of comparing "traditional" families to other families *with children*, the "7 percenters" compare traditional families against *all other* families (families headed by grandparents, "empty nesters," students rooming together, unmarried adults living alone, newly married couples without children, etc., etc.). This of course greatly distorts the outcome of the derived statistic. Then, as the icing on the cake, the "7 percenters" put all the mothers working part time into the same category as mothers who work full time. The Department of Labor is part of the problem, for it counts the following mothers as working mothers outside the home: any mother who works one hour per week or more, any mother who works seasonally, any mother who works on a family farm without pay, any mother who runs a business out of her home (12 million women are in this category alone), any mother who works flex-time or odd hours, any mother on maternity leave, even those who later decide to stay home. Nevertheless, by these manipulations the misleading, but highly touted, "7 percent" statistic is derived.

As David Blankenhorn points out, this "false and pernicious claim" leads people to believe that the traditional family is dead, a dinosaur from the recent past of one generation ago.[78] The adherents of the delusion seem desperate to believe that parents who stay home to care for their children are old-fashioned and irrelevant. Blankenhorn further points out that all our families need support for their efforts, not merely the "new families," and that we need to strengthen all our families, not pit one type against another.

FAMILIES WITH PRESCHOOL CHILDREN

FAMILY TYPE	PERCENT OF ALL FAMILIES WITH PRESCHOOLERS
"Traditional": Father works, mother at home	33.3
"Working": Both parents work full time	28.8
"Mixed": Married mother works part time	15.8
Single in-labor-force mother head of family	10.1
Single at-home mother head of family	7.3
Married couple, father not in labor force	2.7
Single father head of family	2.0
Total	100.0

Calculated from Bureau of Labor Statistics survey of
March, 1987: Institute for American Values.

There is no doubt there are fewer traditional families now as compared to the 1950s and 60s. Family break-up and no parent at home with the kids are realities in many modern families. But, as the true statistics show, the traditional family is far from irrelevant. In fact, it is still the most common kind of family among those with preschool children. As I will discuss later, some of these families are among the strongest families ever seen in any generation. Their special strength comes from blending the best of old-fashioned values and knowledge with the best of new knowledge on the dynamics of healthy family life and healthy parenting.

Another source of strength for the resurgence of the family can be seen in the small but growing number of fathers who are becoming significantly involved with their children. In the 1950s and 60s, a growing, healthy trend was for fathers to spend more time with their children, but this was later swamped by the obsessive materialism of the 70s and 80s. Now, however, a small but dynamic proportion of fathers are reacting against excessive careerism by putting more time and energy into their children. This slight swing in the pendulum is hopefully a harbinger. The resurgence of the family cannot, will not, work as a solely female phenomenon. It will happen only when fathers put their time, energy, thoughtfulness and support into it. Fathers must realize how important they are to child development and how devastating are the effects of father-abandonment. A new ideal for fathers is called for, one that takes into full account the importance of fathering to children (as well as to the father). The small but growing number of new, devoted fathers is a requisite step to strengthening our families.

Another source of strength can be seen in the growing awareness that our sorry, regressed values of the past few decades have caused great harm to our children and families. The 90s will see an even greater recognition of this fact.

The current obsessions with materialism and hedonism can lessen as quickly as they came. They are primitivistic and false values, and false values readily collapse once seen for what they are, provided there is a countervailing positive idealism to believe in. The cynicism generated by the 20th Century Myth must first be replaced with positive ideals.

It is ironic that over the past quarter of a century when our families have been disrupted by false values, the work on what makes a healthy family has proceeded apace. We now know more than ever about those ingredients that make up healthy families. Some families have searched this knowledge out and put it to use while others seem to apply it with an almost instinctive awareness of the critical ingredients.

As noted earlier, buried under the current anxiety over the state of the family is a small proportion of families that may be the best, the healthiest families ever. They can provide a model for others who seek to blend the best of the old with the best of the new in family life. Hopefully, we are in the first stages of an Hegelian process of change for the better in family life. It is common to hear today's social critics claim that all forms of families are equal. This, again, is nonsense. All families, and all family forms, are not equal in providing the security, stability, protection, quality of love, supervision and thoughtful discipline children need for healthy growth.

Some folks look upon the sudden deterioration in family life and call for government to step in and compensate for the new deficiencies. This response is yet a further application of the 20th Century Myth, that is, turning to government to solve human relationship problems (especially ironic when the problems were exacerbated in the first place by application of the New Myth). As Elaine Kamarck and William Galston of the Progressive Policy Institute state in their report, *Putting Children First*, "Public programs cannot substitute for healthy families and should not try... Given all the money in the world, government programs will not be able to instill self-esteem, good study habits, advanced language skills or sound moral values in children as effectively as can strong families."

The crisis in today's families is a crisis in values. A shadowy, self-seeking materialism has temporarily replaced higher values, and there is little our government can do about the values of individual citizens. This area is the province of the family, the schools, and the churches, with government a distant fourth as a viable values-producing institution. And the dangers of government approaches are great. Witness Sweden, where government has been highly involved in family matters, and where nearly every child is in a government-controlled day-care center and half of all births are now illegitimate.

It is time to look at another area influenced by the 20th Century Myth which has had a major impact on the family – the relationship between the sexes.

Summary

American families have been corrupted by a variety of infections spawned by the 20th Century Myth. These infections, themselves myths, have created a family unit where it's permissible for adult members to "do their own thing" regardless of the consequences for other family members – often the children.

Divorce has become a primary remedy for familial difficulties, further reinforcing the need to "do one's own thing" to be happy. This leads to Modern Myth #1, itself an offspring of the 20th Century Myth – Children are improved by divorce in contrast to staying in an unhappy home. This provides a convenient excuse for running away from marital difficulties. More often than not, broken homes lead to broken children – a condition that's extremely hard to remedy.

This leads directly into Modern Myth #2 – Although the children may be harmed, at least the adults are better off after divorce. That may be true in some circumstances, false in others. In any event, parents bring children into the world; taking responsibility for the welfare of their offspring is a paramount value in a healthy society.

Modern Myth #3 further promotes stress on the family unit with the declaration that both parents have to work full-time for the family to survive financially. In reality, today's purchasing power is similar to that of earlier decades, when most families only had one full-time working member. The chief difference today is materialistic expectations that create a need for dual incomes.

Dual wage-earners create Modern Myth #4 – It's okay to have someone else care for children as long as there's "quality time." Other than convenient justification, there's no solid evidence that quality time replaces the need for quantity time in child rearing. Both are needed.

This all dovetails into Modern Myth #5 – Only 7% of today's families fit the old-fashioned model of breadwinner father and homemaker mother. In fact, Bureau of Labor statistics show that the traditional family is still the most common form found among families with young children, though barely holding its own. It is, as it should be, up to each family to decide on the specifics of how they will provide home care, training and education for their own children. The main message to young families is not to allow themselves to be swallowed up by the above five myths, for the fact is that the majority of families today still have the degrees of freedom required to make choices on child care and family direction, including the hard choices.

It is clear from the research that it is children, not adults, who pay the biggest price for the deterioration often found in today's families. False values, products of the 20th Century Myth, are mainly responsible for this deterioration. Hard choices, inspired by higher values, are the only reliable antidote to this deterioration.

Chapter Five

The Sexes
Women: From Behind the Scenes to Making the Scene

The 20th Century is the Century of Woman. No time in human history compares with it in bringing about changes in the status of womankind. A few women in previous centuries attained political or even military power (Queen Elizabeth I, Joan of Arc). And there were remarkable women who affected the course of human events, though usually in quiet and subtle ways. Women have always held more sway in the domain of family life than publicly acknowledged, and it has been forever true that "the hand that rocks the cradle controls the destiny" of the next generation. But in the latter half of the 20th Century a whole new phenomenon occurred. For the first time women entered traditional male fields in unprecedented numbers and assumed a leadership role in much of the public agenda as well. What used to be regarded as "women's issues," relegated to the women's sections of newspapers (now, interestingly, called *Life* sections), are today's primary topics on the public-political agenda: childcare, child development, abortion, public education, women in the job-market, the economic strength of women, the consumer habits of women, to name a few. Two factors make this dramatic change in public priorities all the more remarkable. First is the fact that this change in the status of women and women's issues occurred so quickly. Second is the fact that this change occurred most rapidly and dramatically in the so-called leading societies rather than in isolated or backward cultures.

These and many related changes were fostered by the new feminism that came out of the 1960s. The new ideology required that society be rebuilt so that equal opportunity in all arenas would become a reality. Central to modern feminism's ideal was the assumption that equality between the sexes was attainable only when we understood that the sexes were essentially the same in their needs, drives and natures. The readily observed differences between males and females were explained away as the products of differential cultural conditioning. Girls were trained to act like girls and boys were trained to behave like boys. But all this had to change if we were to attain equality. Equality was defined as sameness, hence a totally equal division of labor in all fields would follow once we threw off the social ties that bound us. That was the ideal. The reality has proven to be quite different. Indeed, current scientific evidence overwhelmingly points to the conclusion that most of the differences between males and females have a genetic-biological basis as much or more than an environmental basis. And this fact means that the most primary assumptions underlying modern feminism are erroneous. Equality cannot be defined as sameness. Feminism, with all its ramifications for self-development and family life, must be rethought from top to bottom. We'll look first at the scientific data that brought this situation about.

The Research on Sex Differences — Born or Inbred?

Feminists in the 60s and 70s took as one of their basic assumptions an attitude about human nature borrowed from modern psychology. This attitude stated simply that all sex differences were the products of social conditioning. It was said that all differences between boys and girls, and later on men and women, were due to the different ways in which they were taught to act and think by their "culture" (their parents, schools, the media, etc.). It was commonplace in the 70s to hear such comments as "the only difference between men and women is in their plumbing; all other differences are the result of differential social training."

This assumption that all sex differences are due to differences in cultural training has a respectable lineage. In this century it can be traced to the earliest leaders of American behaviorist psychology: John Watson and B.F. Skinner. Watson and Skinner were the two leading proponents of the vigorous American branch of psychology that broke away from the Freudians, neo-Freudians, and Piagetians of Europe. Their uniquely American school of thought experienced its heyday from the 1920s through the 1960s. Their basic assumption was this: that all behavior was due to and controlled by the principles of environmental conditioning. B.F. Skinner went so far as to write a Utopian novel describing a society in which conditioning principles were used to manipulate the environment so that human beings could enjoy the best possible life. Skinner, of Harvard, was an archetypical 19th – early 20th Century intellectual. He believed that man, through application of his own thought and science, could create heaven on earth. The gods were no longer needed. The social-environmental manipulations described by Skinner in his book were repugnant to many of its readers. Nevertheless, the book had to be taken seriously because in many ways it represented the apex of early 20th Century psychological thought in America.

Many European psychologists disagreed with their American counterparts. They took the position that human behavior was more complexly determined by an interaction of social environmental factors with other factors that were, in varying degrees, genetically determined. Time has proven the European psychologists to have been more correct on this issue than most of their American counterparts.

It is understandable, though, why feminists used the framework provided by the social conditioning theories of American psychologists and sociologists. It was a concept many of them had been exposed to in college and it fit perfectly with their own ideology and social program. What feminists didn't know was that deep in the groves of academe American psychology was changing dramatically. By the 1970s most American psychologists, especially those involved in research, had already dismissed the earlier behaviorism as entirely too simplistic to explain complex human behavior. There was a growing appreciation for the significant contributions of human physiology, neurology and biochemistry to our understanding of the causes of human behavior. It was beginning to be understood that all behavior is the product of a complex interaction between social/environmental factors on the one hand and genetic/physiological factors on the other hand. Everything we do, say, think or feel is the result of a continuous interplay among these many sets of variables. Some of these variables have been brought about by cultural conditioning while others are brought into play by genetically influenced neurophysiological and biochemical factors. Psychology is only beginning to understand the nature and complexity of these interactions among different variables that bring about what we see in everyday life as "human nature."

Sex differences are manifestations of human behavior. To try to claim that sex differences are exempt from the same laws of interaction that govern all other forms of behavior is not a defensible posture. Sex differences therefore follow the same principles of causation as all other forms of human behavior, and thus they are the product of a complex interaction between both environmental and genetic/physiological factors.

One thing is for certain – there are plenty of sex differences. There have been many books and articles published in recent decades attempting to catalogue the many forms of sex differences observed by scientists of various disciplines. And many of the leaders in this field of research are female scientists. These lists are always in a state of change and revision, as they should be, since the findings of science are themselves always in a state of change. It is not my purpose here to review these lists, but it might be helpful to look at one area of research that has helped to put the death knell on the earlier, simplistic assumptions about male-female differences being due strictly to social conditioning. We'll take a look at the research of the past twenty years that has investigated the different ways in which male and female hormones act upon the brain and subsequent behavior.

Estrogen is often thought of as the primary female sex hormone. This statement is not altogether valid, however, because women have a greater variety of sex hormones since the female reproductive system is so much more complex than that of the male. These endocrine hormones are intimately involved with the regulation and monitoring of the various functions of the female reproductive system. Estrogen helps to feminize a young girl's body upon the onset of puberty; for example, it stimulates the growth of fatty tissues in the breasts and buttocks, thus helping to bring about the female form.

Testosterone performs a comparable function for males. Testosterone is produced in the male testes and in the adrenal glands. Females, therefore, have some testosterone in their bodies produced by their adrenals. One of the many jobs of testosterone is to stimulate the development of muscle tissue.[1] When boys enter puberty this growth in muscle tissue is especially noticeable in the upper body, thus helping to produce the male physique.

Though males and females produce opposite sex hormones, it is generally true that females produce more female hormones and males produce more male hormones. A post-puberal male, for example, is likely to have twenty times more testosterone coursing through his blood (and brain) than a post-puberal female. But as in all matters pertaining to sex differences there are exceptions. A few women, for example, naturally produce high levels of testosterone. Their bodies are often unusually muscular. If they then reinforce this inherent tendency with systematic weightlifting (and especially if they elevate their testosterone levels with steroids), they can actually transform their bodies into highly muscular replicas of the male physique. Similarly, a few men have naturally high levels of female hormones. Their bodies are often soft in appearance, especially in comparison to the average male. If these males then augment this natural tendency by taking female hormones (a common practice, for example, among men who work as female impersonators), they can transform their bodies into remarkable imitations of the female form. The average man and woman, however, would find it extremely difficult to cross over to the opposite sex physique without radically altering the composition of their natural sex hormones (a practice fraught with harmful side effects).

Now, these facts have been well established for many decades. What is new is found in those studies that have attempted to find correlations between sex hormones and behavior tendencies. For example, many studies over the past thirty years have reported correlations between testosterone, the male hormone, and tendencies toward various forms of physical aggressivity, sexual activity and even outbreaks of physical violence. Of course, farmers and ranchers have known for centuries that if it becomes necessary to pacify a male animal, to make him less physically or sexually aggressive, you castrate him (thereby eliminating his main source of testosterone). In recent years research on these matters has become considerably more sophisticated. Some investigators have reported "critical periods of development" in brain formation as influenced by sex hormones. By carefully timing injections of the opposite sex hormone into the fetus, the subsequent behavior patterns after birth are changed so that they resemble the behaviors of the opposite sex. For example, in unborn female rhesus monkeys, testosterone can be injected at a critical period into the embryonic female. After birth, she exhibits behavior patterns commonly observed in male monkeys: mounting females while they are in heat and engaging in roughhouse play with male monkeys. Thus, female monkeys who receive testosterone during a critical period of fetal brain development subsequently act more like male monkeys than female monkeys. Similarly, unborn male monkeys can be feminized in their subsequent behavior patterns by receiving injections of female hormones during the critical period of brain development *in utero*. There is a growing body of evidence indicating that brain functions respond selectively to the different effects of male and female hormones. And, there is a growing body of evidence indicating that there are measurable, structural differences in certain subsections of human male and female brains, and these areas appear to respond selectively to male and female hormones.[79]

There have been a large number of studies over the past two decades on a wide range of mammalian species, including humans, indicating these same effects. We can now state that the hypothalamus in the male brain is measurably different (thicker with more neurons) than in the female brain. The hypothalamus is a major brain center for sexual and aggressive behaviors. Increased levels of testosterone flowing through the blood brain barrier and bathing the hypothalamus increase the individual's receptivity to sexual or aggressive stimuli. This effect is heightened if the person's hypothalamus has been "prepared", *in utero*, to be highly receptive to testosterone – an effect much more likely to have occurred in males than in females. It has been demonstrated that these and other sex differences in male and female brains are present before birth, before social conditioning can occur.[80]

Interestingly, these data indicate that both males and females are affected more by "raging hormones" than most care to admit. About 20 to 25% of human females, for example, experience significant depression or irritability or both as the result of changed hormonal influences during the menstrual cycle (PMS). And many males have problems with temper outbursts and/or obsession with sexual stimuli due in part to heightened levels of testosterone. Controlling the influence on our behavior of the endocrine hormones is a different challenge for men and women, and no easy task for either sex.

Another reliable finding has been that the corpus collosum, the brain tissue that connects the two hemispheres of the brain, is more thickly interwoven in women than in men.[81] Females are thus able to use both of their hemispheres somewhat more effectively than males. Most males are more efficient when using their right hemispheres (where, for example, the centers for spatial relationships are located). Most females are more efficient when using their left hemispheres (where many language centers are located). Nevertheless, females can utilize both hemispheres more readily than males thanks to their inherent advantage in the corpus collosum. Males injured in the language centers of the left brain may never regain the use of language. Females with the same injury are much more likely to regain facility in language because their brains can more readily "tap into" language centers in other parts of the two brain hemispheres.

Human females are more sensitive than males to auditory stimuli, touch and smell. Males, however, are inherently more dominated by the visual sense.

Two-day-old baby girls have been shown to be much more responsive to human faces than baby boys. The boys are more responsive to physical objects and geometric designs. This is merely the first indicator of one of the more reliably reported sex differences – that females are more responsive to interpersonal and human relationship stimuli, whereas males spend more time analyzing and manipulating the physical environment.

Male brains and female brains are morphologically different. These structural differences are reliable, significant and well-documented. And these brain differences correlate with many of the more commonly observed sex differences in behavior. From what we now know about the human male brain and male hormones, we can predict that, *on average*, males will be more physically aggressive than females, more violence-prone, have a heightened preoccupation with sexual stimuli, a greater physical activity level, be more responsive to visual stimuli, and have better spatial abilities (the abilities critical to success in such fields as higher mathematics, engineering and architecture). And these predictions can be made strictly on the basis of neurological data. Theories of social conditioning are not required (though they help to flesh out our understanding of the commonly observed sex differences). Similarly, from the same data base we can confidently predict that females, *on average*, will be better than males in language and verbal abilities, they will read, speak and write at an earlier age, they will "read" social cues better than men, be more likely to demonstrate intuition, and will more readily invest time and energy in relationship and interpersonal matters.

The sexes are different, very different. And these differences are rooted at least as much in our biology as in our social conditioning. The data on this last point are ample with more coming in daily. These data stand in contradiction to the most basic assumptions underlying modern feminism. And it has always been true that ideologies based on false assumptions about human nature can cause much mischief until truth is sorted out from error.

We do not yet know if the sex hormones act upon the brain (a) in a more generalized versus local function manner or (b) primarily through a structural differentiation or through a biochemical process or some combination of both; nor do we know the degrees and ways in which the effects of these sex hormones interact with the social conditioning experiences of the individual. One thing is clear: there is a correlation between sex hormones and certain behavior patterns. It is interesting to note that persons who request surgery to change their gender are required to undergo hormonal therapy before surgery occurs. For example, a man who wishes to become a woman (far more common than a woman asking to become a man) undergoes extensive injections of female hormones for months prior to the castration and associated surgery required to feminize his body. The massive injections of female hormones help to feminize his secondary sex characteristics prior to the surgery. His body may even take on something of a feminine form as he begins to develop fatty deposits on the buttocks and chest areas. These men report that they begin to "feel and think more like a woman" as the hormonal therapy continues. Is this change in thinking and feeling merely self-induced, a form of self-fulfilling prophecy? Or is it in part due to changes occurring both neurologically and biochemically within the person?

In this respect it is interesting to note some of the recent research on fetal development. Studies over the past few decades indicate that all fetuses, in a sense, start out female.[82] About six weeks after conception, however, provided that the fetus is XY (male) rather than XX (female), the Y chromosome kicks in the production of testosterone which then masculinizes the fetus over the next several months. Testosterone is the catalyst that remakes the female fetus into a male fetus. And, as noted above, this masculinization of the fetus also involves masculinization of the brain.

These observations on fetal development have led to speculation that the greater incidences of miscarriage and birth defects among male fetuses may be due to the fact that it is harder for nature to make a male than to make a female. Simply put, there seem to be more things that can go wrong with a male fetus than with a female fetus since the male fetus is in a sense a complex "overlay" of the underlying female structure. This process may also help to explain the appearance of "feminine men" as well as the universally observed higher incidence of homosexuality among males. Such men may be in part the result of a process that was not altogether completed *in utero*. Similarly, some studies suggest that women thought of as "masculine" were the recipients of a larger than normal amount of testosterone while *in utero*. The complex sexual differentiation that occurs while the fetus is still in the womb no doubt occurs in different parts of the body and brain at different points in time during the pregnancy. The process occurs at different stages. The possible permutations of these different effects are mind-boggling and no doubt account to some degree for the fascinating variety of human behaviors and tendencies observed among males and females. Our ignorance on these matters is great. We have barely started on a long, long path towards understanding this complex process of male-female differentiation. But it is already clear that the old Biblical stories about Adam and Eve may have had matters backwards. Apparently it was not the case that Eve was derived from Adam's rib. If it is true that one was made from the other, then evidently Adam was made from Eve.

It has been said that men and women seem like two different species who happen to live on the same planet. Most men and women have enough dissimilarities to keep them busy for a lifetime of misunderstandings. One of modern feminism's goals was to improve understanding between the sexes. But in staking itself to the equality-must-be-based-on-sameness doctrine, feminism hindered its capacity to help both males and females to better understand each other. Indeed, while the changes in woman's status have been exhilarating for many women, others are downright bewildered by the ever-shifting expectations and roles. In a world in which moral and social relativism is the predominant theme and in which "anything goes," it is hard to find anchors. A few women handle this by retreating into a simplistic feminist ideology which concludes that all of woman's problems, both past and present, are due to man victimizing woman. In this way, they avoid the pain involved in confronting their own contributions to these problems, thereby denying themselves the opportunity to learn from their mistakes. As is true of all ideologies, feminism can be used as the "answer for everything." When this happens, the ideologue becomes entrapped by her own self-definitions and fails to recognize the alternative explanations for the problems in her life. Most women today, not settling for such pat explanations, muddle through as best they can while often feeling confused. And men are at least as confused as women. On some issues, which we will discuss later, today's men are more confused than today's women.

The Rise and Fall of Patriarchy

The dramatic change in the status of women in the second half of the 20th Century is even more remarkable when placed against the background of the dominant patriarchal nature of the first half of the century. In some ways the patriarchal family reached its zenith in the first half of the 20th Century. Then, seemingly overnight, it began to crumble and fall, especially in the Western nations. It is not surprising, though, that patriarchy appeared to be at its strongest immediately before its decline since this is often true of social phenomena. In the middle of the 20th Century, for example, Communism was the rising movement of the day and appeared inexorable in its worldwide spread and influence. Now, only three decades later, Communism is in decline and disgrace, in many ways the biggest fiasco of the century. When social movements are based on assumptions that contain too many half-truths about human nature, they can disappear as quickly as they arose.

In the first half of the 20th Century, the "battle of the sexes" was often treated as a humorous topic. Most humor depends on setting the observer up to expect one thing and then delivering the unexpected. Much of the humor of the battle of the sexes thus depended on setting the man or woman up to do the expected male or female thing, then breaking the expectation. In the once popular comic strip of "Dagwood and Blondie" it was Blondie who in situation after situation rescued Dagwood or told him what to do. It was clear to everyone that Blondie was in fact the head of the family. This struck readers as funny in a time when it was generally assumed that the man would always be the head of the family.

Popular radio and TV sitcoms such as "Ozzie and Harriet," "Father Knows Best" and many others portrayed family life in an idealized manner. Although these comedies made sly references to the underlying power of the woman in the family, it was generally assumed that not only did the man of the house have the ultimate say, but that this was right and proper because, after all, he was the primary breadwinner. *He* brought in most of the money, if not all the money. His work was therefore more important than that of the woman and what he said carried more weight. He worked in the "real" world of money-making and commerce while she worked in the "protected" realm of home-making and childcare. He who brought in the money had the power and the say. Money, the making of money, the controlling of money, was the root value in defining power in the patriarchal family system. Woman's work was thought of as secondary in value. And this values distinction was the foundation for patriarchy.

False values give way, no matter how strong and unyielding they appear to be in a given time. Once women began to enter the so-called real world and make money just like men, the assumptions underlying patriarchy were suddenly out of date, no longer viable in the modern world. However, the short-comings of the patriarchal system did not disappear so easily. The value placed on traditional woman's work – as opposed to making money – remained low on the scale. Our failure to correct this latter aspect of the patriarchal equation, as we shall see, is a major cause in the current problems found between the sexes and within our families.

If false values, especially the devaluation of woman and the materialism engendered, were the downside of patriarchy, the upside was that the man of the house was often deeply invested in his family: in its protection, in its welfare and in its continuance from one generation to the next. It was *his* family. A patriarchy may not ensure that the best values go forward from one generation to the next, but it does ensure that the man of the house will normally take a strong interest in the maintenance and enhancement of the family group.

As late as the 1950s the patriarchal family was dominant virtually worldwide. In America the ideal was understood by everyone: the man works hard to support his family and be a good father to his children; the woman works hard at developing and maintaining a home environment in which the family can prosper and in which the children can grow into healthy adults. Also, depending in part on the family's socioeconomic level, the woman was expected to contribute her time to work for good causes both through the community at large and/or through her family's church. Indeed, much was expected of the woman in this traditional role. James Michener wrote in the 1950s that American women worked harder than their sisters of comparable socioeconomic status in most other countries. He had observed in his travels that middle- and upper-class women in other cultures were provided with hired hands to help with the housework and the rearing of children. American women, by contrast, did both these jobs singlehandedly while also being pillars of the community through church and volunteer work. Further, they were always supposed to look good while doing all these things. Sound familiar? Michener marveled at how well American women performed all these different functions. He must be reeling upon seeing what is expected of women today!

All in all, the American family seemed well-established in its ways by the beginning of the 1960s. Everyone knew what the ideal was and many people were trying to live up to that ideal, at least to some reasonable degree. I remember reading an article by a "prediction expert" in 1959. After going on and on about the wonderful and significant changes that were going to occur between 1960 and 1999 (and he was right on some of them), he concluded by stating that the one thing that would not change significantly over the remaining half of the 20th Century was the role of woman. Prediction has always been a shaky business.

Family life in the first half of the 20th Century reflected the nature of the world at large. Patriarchy was the dominant mode in nearly all realms of life. The first half of the 20th Century saw the rise of the gigantic, powerful state, always led by a powerful male figure. Mussolini, Hitler, Stalin and a thousand other smaller-time gangsters rose up to lead a great many of the world's nations. On a much more benign level, strong father figures such as Roosevelt and Churchill led the world's leading democracies. In fact, the generation of leaders who held sway on the world's stage between the 1920s and the 1950s was one of the most impressive groups of dynamic leaders the world has ever seen. Some were tyrants while others were highly effective diplomats and statesmen. In all cases, they were unusually dynamic, forceful and effective. It was a period of time that gave credence to the theory that history is made to happen by great men who change the world by the force of their personalities. When we see the impact of Hitler on Germany, Stalin on the USSR and Mussolini on Italy, in combination with such men as Truman, Eisenhower and Roosevelt in the United States, Churchill in England, DeGaulle in France, Mao in China, Gandhi in India, Adenauer in post-World War II Germany, and many others, it is evident that this was a remarkable generation of patriarchal leaders. The current generation of leaders pales in comparison. From the 1920s to about 1965 the world's stage was dominated by seeming giants. They moved mountains and rivers, literally, while at the same time they remade whole cultures in whatever image they espoused. It was clear that the world was run by men, powerful men, and that the fruits of patriarchy, both good and bad, pervaded all human society.

Religious dogma has long served as the bulwark to the teaching that patriarchy is the ideal foundation both for the family and for the state. Many of the world's major religions have taught that families should be headed by men and that women should be subordinate to men. Certainly the Jewish, Christian and Islamic religions espoused this position for centuries. The Bible was written in epochs when patriarchy was in the full bloom of power, and it reflects this cultural and historical state of affairs.

At some point prior to Biblical times, the primary family unit had passed from its initial matriarchal beginnings to a patriarchy. The primitive family grew out of the bonding of mother and child, and was inevitably a mother-family.[83] While man hunted for fresh meat, often in organized groups, woman took care of her offspring while experiencing endless pregnancies. Whenever possible she grew simple crops so that she and her young had a food supply, rather than depend totally on passing males to provide meat. There's good reason to believe that women were the first agrarians, the first real farmers.[84] There's no good reason to believe that primitive human beings knew of the connection between sexual intercourse and the subsequent birth of a child. Early man and woman often believed that a woman became pregnant by being entered by a spirit, or ghost, or breath, or sunlight, or many other suspected factors. Human beings began to understand the real cause of pregnancy at about the same time that man took up herding in place of hunting as his primary activity and thereby gained greater control of the chief food supply. In time, man also took over the primary responsibility for growing crops, no doubt applying to this endeavor the organizational skills learned on the group hunt, thus increasing his productivity and gaining further control over his world. With the occurrence of these events, the mother-family disappeared almost entirely since it could not compete with the father-family as a means to survival. Patriarchy was born. Woman gave up the headship of her own family, but in exchange gained protection for herself and her children and a much more reliable source of food.

The father-family was well-ensconced by the time the Bible was written. It certainly would have seemed the natural, God-given way of things to the writers of the Bible. It is interesting to note, however, that Jesus never taught that patriarchy is a God-ordained plan. He certainly never taught that women should be subjugated to men. He taught, instead, that women stand equal with men before God. By contrast, the principles of patriarchy espoused in the Bible are primarily found in the Old Testament and in some of the writings of Paul, whose views on women and sexuality have always seemed unduly harsh to many people.

In the 20th Century these Biblical tenets were viewed with increasing skepticism in the Western world. The main group still holding tightly to these beliefs were the religious fundamentalists, who stood firm in their literal interpretation of the Bible as God's absolute Word, with no exceptions and little consideration for the times and culture in which the books of the Bible were written. But by the 60s and 70s religious fundamentalists, while often the most vocal of religionists, were a clear minority in many of their beliefs. The majority of Americans and Europeans simply no longer believed that the old religious tenets were relevant to modern realities. Patriarchy lost its religious underpinnings in the minds of many people. The pronouncements of the Bible on patriarchy seemed so out of whack with the realities of modern life that they provided yet one more reason for people to question the dogmas of conventional religion.

Patriarchy thus lost its religious justifications and its economic rationale at about the same time. Ironically, the very basis of patriarchy, the economic superiority of man to woman, was its undoing. The unraveling occurred when both men and women exhorted women to enter into the money-making jobs of the marketplace on a sexually undifferentiated, equal basis with men. This was a radical departure of the first magnitude from all previous human cultures and times. When such a radical change occurs so rapidly the culture inevitably goes through a period of shock and confusion as basic values are in disarray. Societies rise and fall on the basis of how they deal with radical changes in their values. Those cultures that manage to sort out and encourage the positive effects of change, while minimizing the negative ramifications, are those that endure and even grow stronger. Cultures that fail to do this falter and may eventually disappear.

The decline in patriarchy has brought about a crisis in family life. One response has been a regression to a modern version of the earlier, more primitive form of family life – the mother-family. With the precipitous rise in the divorce rate and the number of illegitimate children that began in the late 60s, the number of children who live in mother-only homes has risen astonishingly. Among American Blacks the mother-family has become virtually a majority. No one would argue that the return to the mother-family is a sign of healthy progress. This is a form of regression, not progression, in human affairs. We need, therefore, to look at the problems raised by the fall of patriarchy. In certain ways patriarchy served human society well for thousands of years. Its precipitous decline has inevitably caused new problems and a great many unintended consequences.

The Loss of Manly Idealism

The Law of Unintended Consequences is at work in the effects of feminism as in all other social movements. The faster social change occurs, the more likely that unintentional consequences will ensue. One such consequence has been a decline in manly idealism. Occasionally a boy will handle this loss by a show of exaggerated masculinity, or "machismo," but it is more common today to see boys who simply aren't sure of what it means to be manly. In working with thousands of young people over the past quarter century, I have seen a growing ambiguity among boys in their attitudes toward themselves as young men (often coupled with an increased hostility toward females). Since boys in some ways are more difficult to socialize than girls – they are more prone to physical aggression and, as adults, to abandon their families – this growing antipathy among boys is cause for concern. Boys are at their best when they have a positive rationale for controlling their sexual and aggressive tendencies. This need for a positive ideal to govern male impulses is part and parcel of the "search for the holy grail" that has enticed males forever, but only when they believe there is something to search for, to believe in, so the "sacrifice" of their natural tendencies is worthwhile.

As recently as the mid-20th Century, most boys had a good sense of what was expected of them as men. A man was someone who worked hard to provide for his family and protect them. A real man always defended and protected those who were weaker. He was especially respectful toward and concerned for the safety of women and children. Men of high status and accomplishment were "gentle men."

This set of values, this "manly idealism," was all around us as boys growing up in the forties and fifties. It did not always achieve the desired results, but it was always there. Most of us were fortunate to have fathers in the home who set examples of these ideals on an everyday basis. Our parents drilled into us that a boy never hits a girl. We read and heard on the radio and later on television the fast-paced, highly idealistic adventure stories that portrayed this idealism for us. The Lone Ranger, Tarzan, Superman, Batman, Zorro, Roy Rogers, Captain Marvel, Jack Armstrong, Sky King, et al, were heroes who defended those who were weaker and stood up for the ideals of honor and justice. As we matured we were taught both at home and in church that a boy should never force sexual relations on a girl since it was she who must carry the child through pregnancy and deal with the consequences. This latter teaching was a tough pill to swallow once the hormones kicked in in adolescence, but most boys respected the tacit "gentlemen's understanding" that the girl always had the final say on whether or not the couple had sexual intercourse.

In Latin cultures the term *macho* referred to this same sort of manly idealism. To be called *macho* was to receive a high compliment; it meant that you were a man who took good care of his family and protected its honor. But the true meaning of *macho* was ignored by early feminists who early on redefined the word to include only the exaggerated forms of aggressiveness and use of force by men against others. In this more restricted sense *macho* was bad, a form of devilism, and had to be destroyed. There is no doubt that the extreme expressions of *macho* deserve eradication, but the beneficial aspects of machismo were thrown out along with the bad aspects. This was all part of the rush to throw out all forms of sex role differentiation. The sexes, overnight, had to be equal in the only way acceptable to the ideologues – equality must mean sameness. Machismo, as quickly redefined, was to be the first casualty of this all-out, immediate change between the sexes. And it was. *Macho* became a term of denigration implying only the thoughtless use of force.

One of the byproducts of this sudden change in mores was that the notion of *manly idealism* was ripped away from the next generation of young boys. For these boys, the young men of today, machismo and manliness were portrayed as old-fashioned concepts that society had suddenly outgrown, something to poke fun at. It was wrong for men to protect women. The new woman was as strong and as forceful as any man. The old heroes of the Superman ilk disappeared, only to be seen again in the occasional nostalgia movie (a harking back, it was said, to simpler times). The new ideal was egalitarianism between the sexes based on the modern humanistic notion that the only way to define and measure equality is through sameness: sameness of function, sameness of role, sameness of output, sameness of result.

This new idealism has little appeal to most boys. It provides no special role or function for young boys to look forward to. It fails to address both their sexual and aggressive tendencies, which are different in important ways from the same tendencies in girls. Societies that fail to provide socially constructive outlets for the sexual and aggressive energies of their young males will find their social mores deteriorating to primitivistic levels. As Jungian scholar Anthony Stevens notes,

> Since our elders – in accordance with the general crisis of confidence in our culture and our collective loss of respect for traditional symbols and beliefs – no longer initiate the young (for they have little idea what they would be initiating them for), adolescents are forced to turn elsewhere. If they are unable to undergo a 'Jungian' initiation through an inner relationship to the Self, they will seek initiation through the achievement of economic or intellectual status by joining a hierarchically structured organization like the Army (which still formally initiates its recruits) or through informal initiation into a less structured group, whether it be a sporting team, 'drug culture' or delinquent gang. The problem with these less formal alternatives is that the aggressive masculine energies which are traditionally channelled through initiation into the service of society can now flow into forms of group behaviour which are socially disruptive; and instead of producing mature males inspired with the ideals of the community, we are in danger of fostering large populations of morally and sexually ambivalent men in whom the masculine principle is only imperfectly actualized.[85]

Many feminists, rightly repulsed by the increased physical violence committed against women and children by men, have called for an increased effort to obliterate all aspects of traditional roles for men and women. Only in this way, they contend, can man be rid of his propensity for using physical aggression toward those who are weaker than he. This line of thought may be a classic example of the ideologue trapped inside her own dogma. For it was these same traditional roles that in the past usually protected women and children from violence by men. These norms were never guarantees, but they established tendencies because they appealed to the ideals of manly idealism already implanted in most boys. We move young males when we appeal to their desire to regard themselves as manly boys becoming men. When we fail to do this, unmanly, cowardly, self-serving behaviors inevitably increase in frequency. Men had been raping women for thousands of years until the concept of chivalry curbed these tendencies by teaching young men that in their relations with women physical might did *not* make right, that they had no inherent right to take physical advantage. In short, chivalry took an inherent difference between the sexes, the physical superiority of males, and turned it from a negative (a basis for maltreatment of females) into a positive (a basis for protection of and respect for females). If this ideal is precipitously removed with no adequate substitute to take its place, then much harm is sure to follow.

Ironically, the decline of manly idealism leads to an increased tendency for boys to view girls as sex objects. Ironic, because one of the chief aims of feminism was to eliminate the notion of females as sex objects. But appeals to idealism based on sameness are a weak controller of the sexual tendencies of young men. If a girl is to be treated the same as a boy, then in the boy's mind she should have the same sexual needs he has and should happily share his drives and fantasies. His manhood, such as it may be, is served when she responds to his sexual needs. This has always been a difficult arena for men and women to deal with, but chivalry provided a built-in hedge, a set of values that both boys and girls could appeal to when the affair became too hot to handle. Any society that denies manliness as a valid goal for its young males is likely to see an increased emphasis on the sexuality of its females as young males cast about for avenues by which to express their sexual and aggressive drives. By denigrating manly idealism, which contained many positive expressions for manliness, feminism unwittingly counteracted one of its chief aims: it increased, instead of decreased, the value of woman as sex object.

And here we find an irony within an irony. By encouraging women to be as sexually free as men, feminism devalued women in general. Woman's availability as a sex object increased while at the same time her value as a treasured life partner declined. Sex has always been the special means by which man and woman consummate their bonding together as life partners. In the past, the relative chasteness of woman increased her overall value to the specific man who wooed and won her. Virtually all human societies promoted double standards regarding sexual behavior. These old double standards provided certain reassurances to a man contemplating a lifelong commitment to a woman. For example, if she had been chaste, then he could be sure that any offspring were truly his, and he also had a sound basis on which to predict her future sexual conduct. Woman's chasteness in olden days thus increased her value as a life partner. When feminism stripped this old ethic away, asserting that women should have equal, meaning the *same*, sexual conduct as men, it decreased woman's overall value while at the same moment it increased her availability as a sex object. This irony of ironies has never been honestly dealt with by those who advocate the new morality, for it shows all too painfully the difficulty of defining equality of the sexes on the basis of sameness of the sexes. It also points out again the difficulty in dropping an old ethic too quickly when the new ideology to take its place is simplistically formulated and possibly based on erroneous assumptions about human nature.

Women used to be smarter than they are now. As Mona Charen notes,

> There was a time when women understood men better. They looked with good humored skepticism upon the initial blandishments of a suitor, and waited to determine whether his intentions were honorable.
>
> The modern woman rejects the protections of the old morality but then is constantly astonished when men fail to behave like gentlemen.[86]

Adolescent girls and adult women now go to bed with prospective suitors much more quickly then they used to. Why not – aren't their needs the same as men's? Girls and women then find themselves hurt and frustrated with males when the affair doesn't work out. The woman felt that a commitment had been made. The man felt his hormones at work. Both were badly misled by the modern ideology that fails to recognize inherent differences between the sexes while insisting that all value judgements are relative to the individual's need and perspective.

There are no easy answers in this arena, especially if we acknowledge male-female differences in sex drive and in the consequences of sex. Only if we insist that there are no gender differences in sexuality can we attempt to abolish double standards on the basis of equality as sameness. If we adopt this awkward belief, then it probably would be more functional to promote the feminine ideal of chastity rather than the masculine ideal of free sex. Interestingly, while promoting sameness of the sexes as the basis for equality, modern feminists have often shown a bias toward women adopting male standards of behavior instead of vice-versa. Sameness for all usually meant maleness for all. The disdain for the feminine has been one of the more striking features of the feminism that came out of the 1960s (in contrast, for example, to the black civil rights movement where Black Pride was a major thrust).

For boys and young men the concept of equality based on sameness is at worst pallid and at best confusing, engendering ambiguities at every turn. It does not appeal to the emotions, the yearning for adventure, of the young boy, or of the young girl either. It offers no heroes who draw from that river of mythological themes that have served to inspire human beings for eons. It offers instead an idealism that is strictly intellectual, and which, by definition, offers no specialized role for the young man; no dragons to slay, no fair maidens to rescue. Take away these features from youthful idealism and you cut out its heart, for these are not mere fairy tales for children – they teach the young that the hero is always willing to put his or her own life on line for another. They arouse the imagination while teaching the value of non-selfishness, of reaching beyond our natural self-centeredness to a value, an action bigger than ourselves. They inspire and thrill at the same time. They always teach that "might makes right" is inherently evil and that the stronger should always defend the weaker. Strip away these concepts and a values vacuum is created that is too readily filled with negative alternatives. This may take the form of shutting down meaningful communication with others (a common male response), or eliminating shows of tenderness and affection toward others, or it can even result in outbursts of violence. Males function socially in terms of their manhood, no matter how equivocated, or they do not function socially at all. A society that fails to provide its young males with a viable "male ideal" is a society creating serious problems for itself.

The new ideal that equality must mean sameness not only fails to inspire but also adds to confusion by ignoring another basic fact of human culture. Women and men have always entered into parenting and homemaking from significantly different perspectives. Woman, unlike man, has a *built-in*, specialized function in the family. Only she can give birth. She carries the child, and after giving birth, she shows the same tendencies of quick bonding and resultant need to nurture her young that all other mammalian females display. Call it instinct or call it whatever. It was no accident that the first families were mother-only families. The mother-child bond is a fact of nature and, though it can be distorted by circumstances, it will not go away. It is required for the survival of the species. It is a rare woman who will abandon her children, especially when they are small and helpless.

Men, however, have been abandoning their children since time immemorial. It takes most men longer to bond to their children. Even then, many men can be readily pulled away from their children by the lures of new adventures, new sources of stimulation. Man, unlike woman, must be provided with a specialized role in the family. The surest way to bond a man to his family is through inculcating him, as a young boy, with an idealism that provides him with a specialized role in his family to come. If he sees in his own home some of these features modeled daily by his father, then all the better still.

Men have always had to be enticed into family life. And women have always struggled with this issue. They have always been hard workers so as to make themselves useful to man. They have spent an infinity of hours on their physical appearance. They have often made themselves alluring and charming. Today they read copious women's magazine articles that tell them how to catch a man and then how to hold onto him. Man has always been the more reluctant partner to family life. He wanted woman's sexual favors but was skeptical about his degree of involvement with the consequences of sex. Woman has always found this disparity between the sexes exasperating and often resented it. Kinsey, after a lifetime of study of sexual behavior, stated that most men would be sexually promiscuous throughout their lifetimes if there were no social sanctions against it. Marriage based on monogamy is not natural to the male of the species.

Although it's unlikely this difference will ever disappear, women and men had been making slow progress on this issue in recent centuries. Patriarchy, in some cultures, had produced an idealism in which sons were taught that a real man, a good man, takes care of his family and fulfills his commitments to them. Take away this vital element of the manly ideal and a vicious cycle is set into motion: men leave their families in increasing numbers, thus more sons are reared in fatherless homes so they are not exposed to committed male models, thus the next generation of fathers is even less likely to be dedicated to its families.

Feminism was on firm ground when it demanded equal opportunity, equal pay and equal respect for women vis a vis men. But it stumbled onto shaky ground when it demanded that all of society by remade on the basis of sexual sameness. In this respect feminism acted like a typical social movement of the 20th Century. Not content to liberate individuals so they could exercise more free will and choice in their lives, feminism instead insisted that society be remade overnight into an homogenized image based on unproven, ideological assumptions about human nature. Along with this unfortunate emphasis came the attempt to make others' thoughts conform to the ideals of the ideology. Ideologues of all stripes, humanistic or religious, always generate "thought police." In the case of feminism, this usually takes the form of "language police." Operating on the assumption that language dictates thought, some feminists work long and hard at telling society how to speak, that is, how to talk correctly about women and men. Correct speech patterns are defined as those that are congruent with current feminist ideology. Sometimes the self-appointed language police make good points, but as often as not they are carried away by the ramifications of their ideology; they become dogmatic and punitive, and end up unduly restricting individuals' freedom of speech in the process. And feminists have not been reluctant to use pressure, including governmental power, to try to force this homogenized image onto the rest of society.

In these various ways feminism counteracted one of its main goals, which was to place female-male relationships on a healthier basis. Male hostility toward women has apparently increased since the 1960s. Acts of violence by men toward women have increased over this same period of time. The *reporting* of such violence has increased significantly, though it's impossible to determine if the frequency of actual events has truly increased. In discussing these issues with groups of girls and women, my impression is that women are angrier with men than ever before. This perception is supported by a 1990 Roper poll that compared women's attitudes toward men to those of a similar 1970 poll.[2] In 1970 two-thirds of the women stated that "most men are basically kind, gentle and thoughtful." In 1990 only half of the women agreed. On every question asked, women in 1990 were more negative toward men than in 1970. Men in 1990 were seen as more sexist, more selfish, more insensitive to women's needs, more concerned with their own ego needs and more interested in women as sex objects than in 1970. Yet, it is over this same 20-year period that feminists have pushed hardest to change men by eliminating these same aspects in men.

Too often, feminists have tried to build up femaleness by tearing down maleness – an approach that always causes more negative than positive outcomes in the long run. By trying to cram both men and women into the same bottle, with no tolerance for inherent differences and no support for the positive aspects of those differences, feminism has increased, not decreased, hostility and misunderstanding between the sexes.

The Sexes: Equality or Equal Quality?

The above issue is symptomatic of a deeper issue men and women are struggling with. Namely, is there such a thing as women's rights versus men's rights? If we accept the notion that equality between the sexes means complementarity rather than sameness it follows that there must be certain areas where women or men receive special consideration. Maternity leaves for women and military combat duty for men are two obvious issues that relate to this point, but virtually all areas of male-female interactions sooner or later come to this question. The fact that pregnancy must now be defined by employers as an "illness" that leads to "sick leave" is an interesting example of how the "equality must be sameness" doctrine results in a corrupted view of female-male differences.

Intelligent discussion of male-female differences and women's versus men's rights is hard to come by without considering the fact of overlapping distributions. "Overlapping distribution" is a statistical term referring to a simple observation. Namely, there is always some overlap between the sexes even though the ability or trait being measured shows otherwise reliable differences between the sexes. It is often difficult to understand another person's position on a matter of sex difference unless you know the segment of the male-female distribution on which he or she is focusing. As an example, let's use a male-female difference so reliable and clearcut that virtually no one would care to dispute it – upper body physical strength. Males, on the average, have greater upper body strength than females. If we were to take a sample of 1000 males and 1000 females of, say, 21 years of age each, and have these 2000 people take standardized tests of arm and shoulder strength, it is a safe bet that, on average, males would score stronger than females. But would all males score stronger than all females? Probably not. It is probable that the average difference between the males and females in this study would be sizable and reliable. This average difference would be large enough to meet the tests of statistical inference and thus be termed "statistically significant" by the investigating scientists. When scientists term the findings of a study "statistically significant" they are bestowing high praise. They mean to say that the observed differences are both reliable and sizable enough to afford us a degree of predictability in dealing with this aspect of nature in the future. But does this average difference mean that all males are stronger than all females? Of course not. In the above study we would probably find some females scoring stronger than some of the weaker males. We might find a few females scoring as strong as average males. We might even find a few females who would score stronger than the average male. In short, we would find some overlap in the distribution of upper body strength in our comparison of the two sexes.

Now, admittedly, this point of overlap between the sexes seems so obvious why bother mentioning it. It may be obvious once we stop to think about it, but it is remarkable how often we forget to take this fact into account in our everyday conversations on the sexes.

Now let's look at our next example. As long as coeducational schooling has been around, it's been noted that girls score better than boys on measures of reading and spelling, whereas boys score higher than girls on measures of mathematics. We can argue endlessly about the causes of these sex differences, but the fact remains that they exist and have proven to be highly consistent. When we look only at the *average* difference between the sexes on these characteristics, we see differences of relatively small magnitude. These sex differences, however, are highly reliable. They occur over and over regardless of the investigator, the population sample, or era of the study. Now, do we focus on the reliability of these differences or on the smallness of the average? If we focus on the average difference can we then justify the expenditure of public funds to provide special teaching for males in reading and spelling? After all, when was the last time a boy won the spelling bee in your child's school? Or, should we expend public funds to provide special education for girls so they can catch up with and be equal to boys in mathematics? If we expend these considerable funds, can we be guaranteed success since we do not know the degree to which these sex differences are innate versus environmental? Are these sex differences large enough in magnitude even to bother with? After all, there are many boys who read better than the average girl. And there are many girls who are better at mathematics than the average boy. The degree of overlap between the sexes on these two characteristics is fairly extensive. So what do we focus on, if anything? At this point, feminists may rightly point out that since fewer females than males score at the highest levels of math achievement, this limits the number of women who gain entrance into professions based on higher mathematics, such as physics and engineering. But at what point does this difference become large enough to warrant ameliorative attempts? It is difficult to discuss these issues with any hope of resolution until we determine (1) the degree of overlap between the sexes, (2) the size and reliability of the average differences, and (3) how far each sex extends its distribution onto the distribution of the other sex. It would also help to know the degree to which these differences are genetic versus environmental. Unless we have this information, discussion of sex differences, much less the respective rights of the sexes, is not very meaningful.

Let's consider one more example, but one vastly different from those above.

This next sex difference shows hardly any overlap. Nevertheless, it has ramifications for current policy-making. With the increase in numbers of women in the US military, there has been considerable discussion on the justification for barring women from combat duty. Some women in the military feel they should have access to combat roles and they have pushed hard for equal access with men to these "opportunities." They opine that promotion in the military can be limited unless one has access to combat duty. One way to look at these deliberations is to take the historical view: to look at what past and present societies have done on this issue. The USSR in World War II had a small number of women who flew combat aircraft, but immediately after the war the Soviet Union excluded women from all branches of military service. Israel used a small number of women in its revolutionary war of the late 1940s. Israel still conscripts women as well as men for military duty, but females are now assigned strictly to support rather than combat roles. Looking at primitive or past human societies we find that the exclusion of women from combat is virtually universal.

Now let's picture a high ranking Army officer testifying before a Congressional committee on why the military does not sanction women in combat. He would probably focus more on average differences between the sexes, rather than on their overlap in their distributions of abilities. He may point out the significant average difference between the sexes in physical strength and the relevance of this fact for combat infantry since they often have to hike long distances carrying 80 pounds or more of equipment on their backs. Even more relevant would be the fact that combat soldiers, even in this high-tech age, can be confronted with life-or-death situations involving hand-to-hand combat. Our hypothetical officer might also argue that sex-difference data indicate males are far more inclined than females to engage in physical violence toward others. The officer might then conclude his argument by stating that from the standpoint of a cost-benefit analysis it would not be cost effective to train women for combat duty on an equal basis with men. He would hopefully qualify his conclusion by noting that some proportion of young females could be trained to be effective combat soldiers, but he would not know the size of this proportion, i.e., the size of the overlap between the sexes. And without this information it is hard to derive sound policy. Then there are other considerations. Sexual relations would of course occur between male and female soldiers living together under close, combat conditions. How does this affect the morale of the fighting unit? How does this affect the leadership capability of a lieutenant who is sleeping with a rank-and-file soldier? How would pregnancies be treated? Is it fair to male soldiers to allow time off to pregnant comrades-in-arms who are supposed to be treated on an equal (same) basis with males? Who would rear the children – the government? In short, is it really possible *always* to treat males and females on a sameness basis with equal (identical) rights and equal (identical) responsibilities? The answer is obvious and the answer is no.

Plato dealt with this issue when he argued that the only way women and men could be truly equal would be if women handed child rearing over to the state and fought alongside men in combat on an equal (same) basis. He went on to state that men and women would need to work out together in the nude so they could better function together as co-equals. This latter proposition is one of many awkward positions advocates of the "equality equals sameness" concept find themselves in as they attempt to deal with the basic facts of human nature. Of greater interest here is the fact that this was one of the few times Plato took a position that placed him at odds with a universal archetype. The concept of archetypes seems to have originated with Plato, and one of the most universal and basic of archetypes is that of Woman as Giver of Life, Nurturer of Life. Fertility, that is, New Life, and Woman have been inextricably woven together in all cultures, in all times. Yet, in recommending woman for combat duty we recommend that she engage in premeditated murder, that she become a destroyer of life. Societies that blatantly go against archetypes are usually playing with fire. It is clear that women were exempted from combat, virtually worldwide, a long, long time ago. By returning women to combat duty, in the name of equal opportunity, we engage in a common practice of the 20th Century – regression to earlier, more primitive mores under the heading of progress.

When we define equality as sameness, our job is relatively simple – cram everyone into the same package and divide down the middle. However, when we define equality in terms of complementary factors, then our job is much more complex. When are women's rights and responsibilities identical with men's, and when are they different? How are they different? Under what conditions? What will be the different effects of different treatment, when such is called for? We can hardly blame the feminists of the 60s and 70s for wanting equality defined as sameness. It was so simple, and it was a shortcut to equality. Typical, though, of shortcuts to higher values and goals, too many negative consequences were spun out. We now turn to the most destructive of those unintended consequences.

The Gender Gap: Parenting and Dysfunction

In their drive to achieve materialistic equality with men, feminists early on perceived that women could no longer spend so much of their time caring for their children. They accurately saw that the time demands of childcare and child development were the chief impediments to competing with men on an equal basis in the commercial marketplace. It was not going to be possible to serve two masters. Childcare had to be turned over to somebody or something else. Rationalizations, such as the "quality time" notion, had to be quickly found to help people feel better about this sudden, dramatic change in priorities. The more thoughtful feminists were distressed by all this, but could think of nothing else to do. For if women were to be equal with men on materialistic and power terms, there was no other option than to downgrade woman's traditional role as primary caregiver for her children. Other resources had to be found. Only in this way would she be free to compete with men on men's terms. How else could she find the time?

This sudden shift in childcare values and priorities, supported by both men and women, may turn out to be the biggest folly of the 20th Century. It is the single best example of that process which has too often characterized social change in the 20th Century – regression to more primitive mores masquerading as progress. One irony of this sudden regression is that it occurred at a time when woman was finally beginning to enjoy some of the rewards she had been struggling to attain in prior centuries.

By the 17th and 18th Centuries, at least among the middle and upper classes in Europe and America, woman was attaining new respect and new freedoms. She worked hard, but she was increasingly exempted from back-breaking work. She gained more time to be with her children and to do something she had always wanted – to create a home setting for her family that expressed her own desires for charm and grace in living. She gained new respect for her insistence on higher moral standards in society and for her preference for peace, not war. Man showed his new-found appreciation for her special contributions through the acts and manners of chivalry. Perhaps most important of all, woman was becoming more successful at inducing man to become more emotionally involved with his children, his family, and her, through the relatively new concept of romantic love between man and woman as social equals. Woman had always wanted true monogamy and an emotionally committed man beside her, and now she was making progress toward fulfilling her desires. And society was benefiting enormously from her gains, especially in terms of improved home and family life and better relationships between the sexes. As the middle class spread in size among the industrialized Western nations, more and more homes took on these positive characteristics.

By the middle of the 20th Century, these characteristics had succeeded so well they had become the expected way of home life. A growing proportion of men had accepted the new norms well and even wholeheartedly. This was a major triumph for female will, intelligence and spirit, for long-term marriage contains few inherent inducements for most males, who would normally choose to roam, to come and go as they please. But the notion of romantic love was in its heyday and was the predominant topic of the popular media and literature of the time. As silly as some of its aspects were, the idealized concept of romantic love between man and woman spoke to their deepest yearnings for each other. New marriages started out in great and good hopes, in contrast to today's marriages which all too often begin with underlying fear and sarcastic jokes about whether or not the marriage will last beyond the first year. Many men were taking child rearing and child development more seriously. A popular topic of magazine articles in the 1950s described how the new father was less authoritarian than his own father and was spending more time with his children. A catchphrase of the time was that the more modern fathers were learning to be "pals" to their children.

Now, only a few decades later, we have unprecedented numbers of dysfunctional families, unprecedented divorce rates, latchkey children at every turn, infants being nurtured in daycare centers, more distrust between men and women, romantic love is generally regarded as a joke, and women have returned to the unending, impossible work schedules of their mothers' mothers with little time or energy left over for their own families. This is progress? Hardly. This is regression, not progression.

It would be unfair, however, to portray the 1950s as some sort of "golden age" for woman. It is true that she was attaining many of her long-sought goals, but there was a bitter countercurrent to her achievements. She felt the rising tide of materialism as a personal sting, a highly personal rebuke. Increasingly she felt that society did not really value her contributions after all because her particular contributions did not make money. In a society growing increasingly materialistic, work that does not produce money is, after a while, not even seen as work, at least not as "real work." Woman, who had come so far and gained so much, suddenly found herself wanting in the context of society's "new" ethic – self-development and materialism. By the late 60s and early 70s she was fed up with being put down. Many women concluded that the only way to gain respect, including self-respect, was to adopt the masculine ethic – to go into the world to succeed as men did, by striving for money and influence, even at the risk of putting the children on the back burner. This movement coincided, indeed was part of, the accelerating divorce rate (caused primarily by the rising emphasis on self-centeredness fomented by the 20th Century Myth), which left many women with no choice except to enter the marketplace. Marriage could no longer be counted on to provide lifetime security. The new *Zeitgeist* seemed to engulf everyone. In a sense, men "won" the battle of the sexes in the 20th Century after all, for women capitulated and accepted as their own the male ethic, the world as males define it. Women were thus exhorted to adopt and mimic the lifestyles and values of successful men. Many of them did, and feminism was said to be making great progress. And mothering was, by necessity, downgraded in importance.

The mother-child bond is the most successful and most productive human relationship. It certainly is the most basic. Feminism generously opened up new and viable options for women who are not mothers. As a result, women today can define themselves in ways other than motherhood. A woman who chooses not to have children, or who doesn't have children for whatever reason, can enjoy healthy self-esteem much more readily today than in times past. She has other, valued options, which is the way it should be. And this is a major step forward not only for women but for all of society. But in building up alternative, healthy options for women there has been an unfortunate tendency to tear down the value of mothering. The central importance of the mother-child bond, however, cannot be denied for too long for it provides human young with the means to survival: it is through the mother-child bond that the child first learns to receive and then give love. Through this bond the child experiences his most dramatic modeling of what it means to sacrifice something of yourself so that you may serve others. Through this bond the child learns to see the world as a safe, secure place where he can grow up without the hobbling effects of irrational fear. When mother-love is at its best it provides the child with that sense of courage, strength and security (healthy self-concept, we say today) that allows him to stretch and test himself, to discover his potential as a human being. Most important, the mother-child bond, at its best, provides the new human being with his first experience with unconditional love. Somewhere in our lives someone must love us unconditionally if we are ever to become fully functioning human beings. Someone must consider us worthwhile, indeed, precious, no matter what we do or how badly we mess up. Human beings who have not experienced unconditional love are the most pathetic of people and capable of doing great harm to others. Most people experience some degree of unconditional love in their first human relationship – the mother-child bond. They are thus provided with their first injection of belief in themselves. They will need many more such injections to fight the battle of life, but without that first, great injection they are forever handicapped.

And all this has been going on for millions of years. Often in the dark and often unwisely, but it has been going on nevertheless. And human society survived. Not only survived, but slowly, slowly improved. Until now. Now we have decided that parenting isn't so important. Making money is where it's at. Got to have a job. Got to make money. Got to have a house, not an apartment, but a house. Maybe a bigger house. Got to have a new car, not a used car; or maybe a boat! Got to have this, got to have that. Can't wait. Oh, then there's the kid. Love that kid, but he'll be OK in the daycare center, won't he? Sure he will. I'll get in some quality time nearly every day. All the magazines say it's OK. Got to have this, got to have that.

Are we so absorbed by materialism and the need for self-gratification that we can so easily rationalize away the need to care for our own children? Can we so easily throw out a million previous years of human history on the importance of parenting so we may pursue a higher standard of living? Interestingly, a long-range study of graduates of prestigious Barnard College who dropped out of the labor force to be fulltime mothers found that this did not affect their later earnings.[87] The study reported, "Those within a given occupation tended to end up in the same bracket whether or not they had taken time out for children," and, "Overwhelmingly, respondents said staying home with their children was the right thing to do." Nevertheless, we increasingly hand this most important of jobs over to hired hands who barely know our children, minimum-wage workers who nurture and teach our children in institutional settings. Social regression, masked as progress, is a recurring feature of our times.

It is difficult to determine how much feminism caused this mess in child-care versus how much the movement itself was picked up and carried along by the rising tide of thoughtless materialism. Certainly, women should have the option to pursue their job and career development as they see fit. And most people want the best for their children. They want to provide optimal conditions. But as each succeeding generation came on stage in the 20th Century, it became easier and easier to accept, unthinkingly, materialism and the pursuit of self-gratification as the chief goals of life. Increasingly, there seemed to be no other way, no other viable options. The last flourish of idealism, of reaching out for higher values, was exhibited by the kids of the 60s. But this last gasp of idealism was thoroughly humanistic in its foundations and was born of immature minds. It quickly lost its impetus and receded into selfishness. Modern feminism erupted onto the scene just as the last glow of the 60s faded. And materialism, the drive for more goods and pleasure enshrouded by the "new" ethic of self-realization and self-enhancement, imbued feminism with both a goal and a rationale.

What Does Woman Want? What Does Man Want?

When the eternal question is posed – "What Does Woman Want?" – most men readily reply that they haven't a clue. This ignorance is partly due to the fact that few men spend much time studying the psychology of women. They spend considerable time studying the body parts of women and have little time left over for the study of woman *per se*. Women, on the other hand, have always spent great amounts of time studying men, analyzing their attitudes and reactions. They often believe they know exactly What Man Wants. Despite all the time and energy that some women put into the study of the male animal, it is rare to find a woman who truly understands what men are about. Throughout the ages, men have tended to look upon women as sometimes frightening, often weird creatures. Women, meanwhile, have studied men so they can better cope with them, only to find themselves baffled and bewildered by the response of a man they thought they knew well.

We should not let these sex differences in perspective, reaction, and attitude dishearten us. Men and women have been evolving along separate lines of ability, tendency and reaction for at least one million years. Sexual differentiation of roles and jobs is among the most universal traits found in all human societies, both primitive and modern. It is only in the last few decades that this has begun to change. What would be surprising would be to find no intrinsic differences between the sexes.

So what does woman want in these rapidly changing times? In posing that question to some female friends with whom I played mixed doubles in tennis, I got this response: What Woman Wants is a Big Serve (just like a man's!). While their answer would have pleased Freud, it was no more enlightening than Freud's own entangled response to the same question. It is most likely that what woman wants is what she has always wanted – loving intimacy with a man of her own (and an emotionally and financially secure future with him). And most women still want children and family. So far, so good, and nothing new. But now the problem begins because woman, for the first time, can have much, much more. She can have it all. Or so it seems. And many women want it all: a satisfying, well-paying career; a husband with whom she can share intimacy; beautiful, healthy children; a fine house stocked with pretty things; all the things that make up the "good life." But can any of us "have it all?" Is there enough time in a day, or energy left over, to do and have it all? Does something have to give somewhere? If I focus on my career, does that mean I inevitably shortchange my children along the way? If I focus on meeting my spouse's needs does the development of my own self-potential fall by the wayside? These are questions that women, and men, struggle with every day.

And What Does Man Want? Man wants endless adventure, the Viking Ideal. New adventures unfettered by 9-to-5 routines. Adventures that stretch his physical as well as his mental abilities. There must be something to conquer. For some men, at least a modest threat to life or limb is called for to make the adventure meaningful. For many men the prospect of a sexual dalliance with a new, attractive female is the spice that makes the adventure worthy of time and effort. Of course men want home and family too. But, true to the Viking Ideal, they want to be able to leave the wife and kids from time to time to go off on new adventures (which contain the potential for non-binding encounters with titillating new females). Most men really mean it when they say they had every intention of returning to hearth and home. It's just that it doesn't always work out that way.

Most men are reluctant to talk honestly about this "male dream" with women, not because of the supposed male reluctance to express one's innermost thoughts, but because men know how boyish and irresponsible it all sounds. It's embarrassing. But for the majority of men, and especially highly masculine (high testosterone) men, this "dream" is very, very real. Its re-emergence is nearly always the catalyst to the midlife crisis of the male.

Men are also reluctant to discuss these thoughts because they know women won't stand for them. Clearly, What Woman Wants – passionate commitment and true monogamy – and What Man Wants – clash on several key points. Most men conclude early on that it's best to keep such dangerous thoughts to themselves; especially if the woman in his life no longer excites him sexually as she once did, for now guilt enters the picture, driving his inner thoughts deeper, deeper still. Some men deal with these feelings of guilt (she rarely excites me anymore, but she's a nice person and the mother of my children!) by developing a protective shell expressed as flat affect while with their wives. Passion is gone. Everything must be rational and businesslike. Other men, with different personalities, remain affectionate to their wives while leading a second, secret life in which their sexual desires and fantasies are acted out in a number of ways.

The double-life syndrome of course leads to more guilt and fear, even to projected feelings of being unduly controlled and intimidated by woman.[3] Men in this situation often come to feel that their wives embody a higher set of morals than their own. "The wife" begins to represent the need to follow through on one's commitments to one's family, or more simply, she becomes "the old ball and chain" in the man's mind. As the woman comes to represent a higher moral authority (a fact she is often unaware of), she becomes "She Who Must Be Obeyed" (see the works of H. Rider Haggard and Carl Jung for more detailed discussions of this aspect of the archetype of Woman). The woman, however, is usually less interested in commanding moral obedience than she is hopeful that her man will come to feel about these matters as she does. And she is further conflicted because she often feels so bonded to her children that she is circumscribed by them. For her, there is no escape from her maternal duties, but she suspects that her man may not feel nearly as bound as she. Yet, it is this very dedication to duty that imbues woman with a moral authority that often intimidates man (at least for a while). Needless to say, this subject rarely inspires honest communication between women and men.

Woman's best hopes that man will come naturally to feel as she does on these matters are rarely met, thus the ongoing tension between man and woman continues with only brief periods of respite between storms.

Modern feminists have tried to deal with this essential tension between the sexes by advocating an equality based on sameness – a sameness that cuts it both ways for woman while attempting to redress all her grievances in one fell swoop. In this new scheme of things, man is called upon to develop the same emotional responsivity and capacity for monogamous commitment as woman, while freeing her to engage in all the same adventures as man. Such an ambitious and radical program naturally has spun off an abundance of unintended consequences.

An American Perspective as Noted by a Frenchman

It is always good to go back and recapture historical perspective, and this is especially true for baby boomers who have always believed that history began with them. In the 1830's Alexis De Tocqueville came to America from France to study the exciting, dynamic culture being created in the new world. America was an endless source of fascination to Europeans. His sharp observations have in most cases stood the test of time. He predicted very well the major routes of development in American society from the importance we bestow on our legal system to our problems in race relations. His work is generally credited as the best study of America ever done by a foreigner.

In observing the sexes, he was awed by the equality he observed between men and women in America. Women, he noted, were highly esteemed by men and treated as equals, but had different roles and functions. In his 1835 book, he humorously contrasted the American attitude on these matters with what he had seen in the upper levels of European society:[88]

> There are people in Europe who, confounding together the different characteristics of the sexes, would make man and woman into beings not only equal, but alike. They would give to both the same functions, impose on both the same duties, and grant to both the same rights; they would mix them in all things – their occupations, their pleasures, their business. It may readily be conceived, that, … from so preposterous a medley of the works of natures, nothing could ever result but weak men and disorderly women.
>
> It has often been remarked that, in Europe, a certain degree of contempt lurks even in the flattery which men lavish upon women: although a European frequently affects to be the slave of women, it may be seen that he never sincerely thinks her his equal. In the United States, men seldom compliment women, but they daily show how much they esteem them. They constantly display an entire confidence in the understanding of a wife, and a profound respect for her freedom; they have decided that her mind is just as fitted as that of a man to discover the plain truth, and her heart just as firm to embrace it; and they have never sought to place her virtue, any more than his, under the shelter of prejudice, ignorance and fear.

He was also impressed by the high moral standards he observed in the daily lives of the people:

> Although the travelers who have visited North America differ on many points, they all agree in remarking that morals are far more strict there than elswhere.
>
> No free communities ever existed without morals; and, as I observed in the former part of this work, morals are often the result of women. Consequently, whatever affects the condition of women, their habits and their opinions, has great political importance in my eyes.

He concluded that this great positive influence of women on American life was due to their being regarded as equals by their men:

Thus, the Americans do not think that man and woman have either the duty or the right to perform the same offices, but they show an equal regard for both their repective parts; and though their lot is different, they consider both of them as beings of equal value. ... I have nowhere seen woman occupying a loftier position; and if I were asked, now that I am drawing to the close of this work, in which I have spoken of so many important things done by the Americans, to what the singular prosperity and growing strength of that people ought mainly to be attributed, I should reply, to the superiority of their women.

What would De Tocqueville say today? He accurately noted that the only valid way to measure the impact of a social movement is to register its effects on society's basic institutions, its families, its children, its schools, its morals. Has the feminism of the past two decades helped or hurt these institutions? Clearly it has done both. Our job is to learn from the mistakes made and move forward with more wisdom than has been displayed to date.

Toward Womanliness, Manliness and Family-ness

In modern times, girls are still brought up to be women, but upon reaching adulthood they must also be "men." The inherent difficulties of this dilemma are being recognized by a new school of thought among feminists. They are moving away from the earlier position that the two sexes must be treated the same in all respects. This new movement asserts that women require a "psychology for women" that fully recognizes the essential differences between males and females. It is still difficult for many of the new wave feminists to acknowledge that gender differences are partly genetic and thus partly natural, but the force of current research findings is nudging them in this direction.

They posit that certain traits are more characteristic of women, such as greater emphasis on relationship-building, on a more conciliatory and less hierarchical approach to group and work efforts, on verbal communication to solve problems (including different male-female language patterns), on a greater use of gestalt cognitive styles, on a heightened sensitivity to one's own emotionality, and on responsivity to other people's needs in order to nurture them and help them nurture themselves better. These women "...no longer measure themselves with a male yardstick. Instead, these women are saying that feminine truths – no matter how different – are equally valid..."[89] These women appear to be giving themselves permission to be women. If this new feminism continues to respect the inherent differences between men and women, and pursues a less materialistic definition of equality, then a celebration of both womanliness and manliness becomes a more likely possibility.

Sometimes, though, the new feminists seem to be saying that womanly traits are superior to manly traits. This attitude, however, is more defensive than offensive in nature, for these new feminists know they are treading on dangerous grounds. They dread the idea that, in admitting to real and important differences between men and women, these differences will then be used as a basis to regard woman as once again inferior to man. And their fears have a basis in reality as long as society places extraordinary emphasis on external achievement, disregard for the inner life, and material gain instead of relationship-building as the primary routes to happiness and esteem.

This new feminism, still struggling in its infancy, is closer to the truth than the feminism of the past three decades. Woman cannot emancipate herself until she asserts that womanliness is good and valuable in its own right and stands equal to manliness in its value to society. Woman cannot emancipate herself by claiming to be the same as man and by mimicking male lifestyles and values. When woman does this she merely exchanges her old master for a new master. As Jungian E. Whitmont notes,

> Self-affirmation for women means, first and foremost, acceptance of their difference from men, rather than identification, imitation and competitiveness with them by androlatric standards. Only by first finding this basic feminine stance can they also claim their Yang element and give expression to their masculine drives and capacities, in their own ways, as women.[90]

When a woman regards her womanliness with value, she frees herself to deal with her masculine side (her *animus*, as Jung called it) in a more healthy, less neurotic manner. This is, for example, especially difficult for a woman who as a girl repeatedly saw her mother ridiculed or in other ways denigrated by her father. And this is further exacerbated if she were reared in a religion that relegates females to second class citizens. If she then lacks a sense of the intrinsic value of her own femininity, then her *animus* can readily dominate her female ego, thus causing a myriad of problems for her and her loved ones. It is then that her animus becomes part of the dark "shadow side" of her personality rather than what it was intended to be – a masculine counterweight to modify and balance her essential femininity.

Similarly, men cannot define their manliness on a positive basis unless they deal effectively with their feminine side (the *anima*, as Jung called it). A man who fails to do this is out of balance and will find himself embroiled in and confused by relationship problems. These problems are exacerbated today by the fact of the growing numbers of boys growing up without fathers and by the often bitter assault in recent decades on traditional manliness. Fewer men today feel good about or comfortable with their own sense of essential masculinity. Without this sense of value their ability to deal with their feminine side, their *anima*, is distorted or even blocked altogether. The outcome is an exaggerated show of masculinity, or, at the other extreme, a sense of confusion that leads to ineffectualness characterized by an inability to follow through on one's commitments to others. These ineffectual males, much less the ones prone to violence, cause severe problems for themselves and the other people in their lives.

These difficulties can be resolved by first recognizing the important differences between the sexes and then moving to the critical second step – the recognition of the equal value of womanliness and manliness. A woman must feel and know the value of her essential womanliness. A man must feel and know the value of his essential manliness. On this basis a man and a woman can then learn to deal effectively with his *anima* and her *animus*. A sense of balance in one's personality is then attainable. Paradoxically, women and men cannot deal healthily with their opposite-sex sides until they first accept and value their same- sex sides. It is in coming to terms with this paradox that men and women learn to give each other the benefit of the doubt and thereby grow in appreciation of their common humanity.

> The antagonism between the sexes is largely a projection of the unconscious struggle within the person, between his or her masculine and feminine components. To make peace between the sexes, make peace within the person.
>
> Abraham Maslow

As we draw near the end of the 20th Century, there seems to be a growing awareness that rather than trying to enforce sameness it is preferable to find ways in which the two sexes may complement each other. We are moving on to the more complex, more demanding concept of *complementarity of the sexes*. Of course, the sexes have always worked to complement each other. But in the past this complementarity was rarely achieved on the basis of equality between the male and female partners. As we move forward, complementarity must be based on equal appreciation of both partners' roles, both at home and at work, or it simply will not work. We have come too far to regress to complementarity without equality. And this equality, a reality-based equality, is not attainable unless womanliness and manliness are esteemed as equal in value.

Whether males and females can attain equality in the workplace is problematical. When we go back to the scientific data on sex differences, it is clear that males have many inherent advantages in the workplace. They are more aggressive, more often driven toward positions of dominance, more fascinated with technology and the physical world (99% of all new patents are applied for by males), and far less circumscribed by the demands of childcare. This is no argument for gender discrimination in the workplace. Equal opportunity is a value well worth fighting for. But equal outcomes are probably unrealistic. The continuing disparities will matter mainly to those men and women who remain heavily influenced by materialistic values and goals. No doubt, women will continue to influence the workplace in numerous ways even though they may not dominate it. Men who aspire to positions of dominance, for example, will learn to better develop their *anima* – they will become better at relationship-building and less overt in their use of hierarchical power, for such changes will help them in their quest of job dominance. Regardless of what happens in the workplace, women and men must attain equality on the home front, which is where society is ultimately made.

Feminism was unduly influenced by this icon of the 20th Century Myth – that equality is real only when defined as identicality, sameness, equal outcome. Feminism has been at its best, however, when encouraging this value of traditional liberalism – that each person's development is a personal affair, not to be unduly constricted by someone else's preordained rules.

With the rise of feminism, we have entered the third major era in the evolution of family structure. The original family was the mother-headed, mother-child-only family. Then came the father-headed family. These patriarchies, in addition to their obvious economic gains, provided two other major advantages over the more primitive, mother-only families: they were more effective at socializing the young (especially the more aggressive boys) into the increasingly complex duties and expectations of their societies. And, the father was bonded to his family, which in most cases benefited both him and other family members. Patriarchies, though, are now in decline. A new model is required. But this new model must build on the advances wrought by patriarchy, not tear them down.

We are now passing from the patriarchal family to the dual-headed family where the father and the mother stand on equal footing as the two heads of the family. This new family has the potential to be a major step forward in human evolution. When the different abilities of men and women are brought together on a mutually respectful basis, then the inherent and great strength of the female-male partnership can be seen in all its splendor. The long overdue recognition of the unique capabilities and sensitivities of woman can finally be a reality. But these new ideals can be successful only if womanliness and manliness are seen as equal in value and complementary to each other. They cannot succeed if power (and thus value) is based on who brings home the paycheck, or the bigger paycheck. That was the basic fault and great weakness of the patriarchal family and too easily led to a devaluation of woman's contributions both to the family and to society at large. It was this very devaluation of woman that early feminists reacted against. Unfortunately, feminism went off track when in its reaction it adopted, as its own, the same materialistic standard that had instigated the devaluation of woman in the first place. The new family, where man and woman stand as equals, will fail if it repeats the mistake of basing control and authority on money-making capacity. This point is critical. If we fail to address this issue, we will regress in childcare and then try to call it progress, as can already be seen in the childcare habits of far too many two-career families of today.

In the new family, sex roles and gender expectations will be defined more freely. However,this flexibility and tolerance for variability will be conditioned by the differing inherent tendencies of the sexes. Males and females, as we've seen, have enough inherent differences that no one need fear (or hope) that this new tolerance will result in the disappearance of sexual differentiations. It *will* result in more tolerance and support for those people who are on the *overlap* of the various dimensions of sex differences.

Women will be women, and proud of it; men will be men, and proud of it. No longer will the finer features of men's and women's natural tendencies be ridiculed. Both women and men will find that they can integrate these roles in a complementary fashion, without losing their sense of self or self-worth, while working together to create far stronger family units than most that exist today. But this desirable goal will never be attained on the presumption of equality as sameness, for this false concept is destined to drive the sexes farther apart.

The new families where men and women serve as co-heads as well as co-founders will advance society in two critically important ways: the value of woman will be enhanced without being based on artificial materialistic standards; and these families will be better positioned to provide optimal, not merely minimal, conditions for child development, which is the sure mark of an advanced and advancing culture.

Summary

In response to the "almighty" patriarchal society which engulfed the planet until well into the 20th Century, feminism arose to champion the rights and opportunities of women. This modern feminism, though, was enshrouded and distorted by the 20th Century Myth: self-centeredness, dolled up as self-development, and money- and power-seeking quickly became its chief values while traditional feminine values were denigrated.

In challenging man's upper hand, the feminist movement fought for sameness of opportunity and outcome rather than for complementary opportunity and outcome. The difference is critical, and it shows up consistently in three areas where feminists have made mistakes.

First, feminism has hurt the family with its devaluation of the importance of parenting and personalized childcare. Second, it has too often promoted materialism and self-centeredness. Third, it has increased hostility between the sexes. In short, feminists have committed the same mistakes as the patriarchs before them – only this time from a female perspective.

While some objectives of feminism have worked to the disadvantage of women and men and, most of all, their children – some of the many positives are that women have been encouraged to see themselves as empowered individuals, to see femaleness as good and healthy, and to regard motherhood as a matter of personal choice rather than as a social requirement. The fact that women today can exercise far more options on values, lifestyles and career options is feminism's greatest accomplishment.

Feminism is probably the most important social change movement of the 20th Century. Its impact on the family, as the basic unit of society, and male-female relationships is profound. But the hoped for positive outcome for society as a whole will not be realized until feminism sheds its involvement with the 20th Century Myth. This means shedding its focus on materialistic, here-and-now values and its emphasis on equality of the sexes defined as sameness of the sexes. There are now ample scientific data indicating the inherent differences of the sexes. Sameness as the basis for equality is not possible. Instead, a new basis for feminism is needed, one that encourages complementarity of the sexes and insists that both womanliness and manliness are equal in value to human society. Only then can there be a healthy foundation on which to build the new family where men and women serve as equals.

---

[1] Steroids (anabolic-androgenic type) are synthetic copies of the male hormone testosterone. Steroids thus generate muscle tissue (as well as many other effects, both good and bad) when taken by men or women.

[2] The pollsters stated that the increased hostility of women toward men "undoubtedly" is due to the "rising expectations of women." This politically correct answer ignores the more parsimonious observation that women are reporting real changes in men's attitudes toward women and that the cause of these changes is in addition to a mere change in women's perceptions.

[3] Especially since this conflict typically doesn't occur until the Power Struggle era of the marriage begins (discussed in the next chapter).

Chapter Six

Toward the New Family
Principles of Effective Male-Female and Family Relationships

Marriage and family life bring out the worst in us. They hopefully also bring out the best in us, but that result usually comes later in the evolution of a healthy marriage. First comes the time of trial, which can last for a few years or several decades. It can lead to divorce if handled unwisely or it can result in great personal growth. How the couple handles this time of trial makes or breaks their attempt to create a family.

The great intimacy demanded of us by marriage pulls out our worst fears about ourselves and others, thereby setting the stage for resentments to develop, fester, then one day explode. Strangely, this occurs in the context of what is often selfless love for the other. To paraphrase Dickens, family life is the best of relationships and the worst of relationships. No one can disappoint us more intensely, or frustrate us more maddeningly, than our spouse or child. We have so much of *our selves* invested in these persons that when they fail us, or seem to fail us, we feel our reactions with an intensity multiplied many times over. In such times it is hard for us to stop and see that it is usually our own selfness that's been wounded, that is, our own hopes for the future and needs of the present. Instead of seeing the problem as a thwarting of our own desires and hopes, we infer that the other has chosen to hurt us and thus deserves blame, judgment and punishment. The resentments grow, whether expressed at the moment or not. And all this is a perfectly normal course of events when two people embark on family-building. For now two egos, both still infantile in many ways, must learn to give up something of their precious parts so they can work together effectively. There is no harder task for most people than this.

Carl Jung stated that marriage and parenting bring out the "shadows" of our personalities (our fears, our prejudices, our character defects) more so than other human experiences. He stated that these experiences contain great potential for personal and spiritual growth. They bring forth our weakest parts, so we can see them in their rawest state. We can then know our own "Achilles heels," those areas of self-centeredness that will destroy our most intimate relationships with others unless we heal ourselves. But this self-confrontation takes great courage, for it is much easier and more pleasant in the short run to lie to ourselves about these unpleasant facts, or, more simply, to deny responsibility and quickly put the blame on the other person. Growth involves pain, and few of us deal well with the pain caused by self-knowledge. Yet until we come to terms with this pain, our capacity to enjoy enduring relationships with others remains forever stunted.

The question is this: what do we need to know to help us grow out of our

118

normal self-centeredness so we may enjoy and benefit from intimate relationships? We'll first look at some basic factors that help establish fertile ground for growing out of self-centeredness. Then we'll discuss the five processes that each partner in a marriage must deal with effectively for marital maturation to occur. We'll conclude with a discussion of the seven principles of healthy parenting.

Establishing Fertile Ground

A prime consideration is *age* at the time of marriage. It is extremely difficult to discover healthy marriages where the two partners were under 21 when first married. *The older the two partners when first married, the greater their chances for success.* This factor has been demonstrated time and time again in studies over the last 50 years. Nevertheless, people still marry, and even have children, while still in their teens and early twenties. Of course, some people still take up cigarette smoking, too.

A second factor is that of *equal and strong commitment* to the marriage. When both persons enter into marriage with the idea that it is "forever," they seem to do better over the long haul. This may be the main reason why marriages endure better when both partners are strongly committed to spiritual ideals.[91] Studies from 1939 to the present have consistently found that the spiritually-involved show lower divorce rates and report greater marital happiness than the non-religious. This factor is apparently the main reason underlying the consistent finding that couples who do not live together before marriage have lower subsequent divorce rates than couples who do live together before marriage. Couples who abstain from living together before marriage are usually more religiously involved than those who do live together before marriage. When *both* partners are spiritually committed they often have an additional source of strength to appeal to in times of marital crisis. When this is true, they can more readily forgive themselves, and the other, so that healing of the relationship can occur. If, however, only one of the partners is committed to this ideal, then the power for good of the committed partner is diminished, though not altogether eliminated.

In my experience, the most difficult couples to counsel while in marital crisis are those who have no shared higher values to appeal to in each other when under stress. They may be delightful people, but they are easily distracted from their commitments to others if their values are fixated at the level of "I'll scratch your back if you scratch mine." As always, the values which underlie our actions are the keys that lock or unlock our relationships with others. As Stephen Covey (in his work on the characteristics of effective, successful persons) notes:

I believe that a life of integrity is the most fundamental source of personal worth. I do not agree with the popular success literature that says that self-esteem is primarily a matter of mind-set, of attitude – that you can psyche yourself into peace of mind.

Peace of mind comes when your life is in harmony with true principles and values and in no other way.[92]

Couples who marry later and share a mutual commitment to spiritual values greatly increase their chances for a lasting marriage and a happy marriage. But of course, there are couples with both of these factors working for them who nevertheless struggle along in less than satisfactory relationships, and this brings us to our third factor – *knowledge*. In healthy families the partners grow in their knowledge of themselves and the other, and in their understanding of the different personalities of their children where children are involved. As mentioned earlier, our knowledge of what makes a healthy family has grown significantly over the past few decades. Most of this knowledge is a rediscovery of what wise people have known in every generation. This knowledge, however, can now be put into an easy-to-understand, systematic format. The more people avail themselves of this knowledge, the better their chances of developing a healthy marriage, especially if they have the first two factors in their favor.

Just as "nice girls" are not all sugar and spice, neither are healthy families all joy and happiness. Healthy families experience most of the same conflicts and problems as unhealthy families. Healthy families, however, deal with these tensions more effectively and bounce back faster from difficulties. I have never seen a healthy family that was not characterized by a sense of humor, which may take many forms depending on the personality styles involved. This humor may be self-deprecating at times but almost never sarcastic toward others. It is marked by *tolerance*, an appreciation for the differing personalities which make up the family. This benign humor, with its sense of the absurd in human relationships, is a great tool for dealing with the everyday irritations caused by living with others.

> Family peace is a humorous affair, of course, because it is something happening between periods of conflict.
>
> Arlene and Buck Weimer

For most of us the development of healthy relationships with others is a lifelong job training program. Often we have to learn the same lessons over and over, though in different contexts, and sometimes the process seems to go on forever. But there is no other way to improve our relationships with others, for there is no magic, although the effect of applying the principles discussed below often seems magical. Let's now turn to the first of the five knowledge principles that underlie healthy marriages.

First Principle: The Paradox of Self-love

A healthy marriage can develop only when each partner is helping the other to develop a sense of self-acceptance, self-forgiveness, self-tolerance, self-respect – *self-love*. Now this seems an odd opening statement in light of earlier comments that the primary cause of divorce is runaway selfishness. Some explanation is needed. A fundamental premise of "pop" psychology since the 1960s has been that we can't love others until we first love ourselves and meet our own needs. This premise appears to contradict the Judeo-Christian ethic, which states that loving others is based on giving to others, placing others first in our thoughts and hearts, losing our preoccupation with our own egos through service to others. What gives here? One premise says, put yourself first, meet your own needs first, then you will be able to love others. The other premise says, put others first, love them, and then you will come to love and accept yourself. Both of these theses cannot be right. One must be wrong. Or can it be that in some paradoxical way they are both valid?

One of the most eloquent expressions of the old ethic is found in the teachings of Jesus, who said that in order to find our lives (find our selves), we must first lose our lives (lose our selves). Throughout history many of the great teachers of mankind have made similar statements. Jesus's teachings, though, at first glance seem to expand the paradox – how does one gain his life by losing his life?

The answer to this riddle goes against the grain of human nature. Self-love that fosters healthy relationships with others *only* occurs when premised on placing others first in our hearts and minds. Placing others first inevitably rebounds back to us in the form of healthy self-love and self-respect provided we exercise some discriminative judgments in *how we go about* placing others before us. A delicate balancing act is called into play on every occasion, for of course our own egos have rights as well as those of other persons. The traditional ethic clearly requires, however, that the fulcrum be tipped in favor of service to others even if at times our own rights are violated. This occasional "turning of the cheek," which occurs when we return another's negative action with a positive action of our own, appears to fly in the face of our natural self-interest. Nevertheless, the traditional view on self-love insists that we can love ourselves and others only when we are willing to sacrifice, or "let go of," some part of our own self-centeredness. And this is a much more ancient wisdom than the contrary view espoused by popular psychology. It has been my repeated experience in working with families in trouble that the ancient view on love and self-love is far more valid than the modern view.

Popular psychology went askew in the 60s when this clause was added to the initial premise – "meet your own needs first." The original statement, "to love others you must love yourself" was essentially correct and little more than a restatement of the Jesusonian principle. (Jesus's teachings on love comprise the most practical psychology ever taught on this mysterious subject.) The error occurred with the interpretation of what loving yourself means in practical terms – *meet your own needs first*. It was at this point that the me-first attitudes fostered by the 20th Century Myth entered into and polluted the teachings of the traditional ethic.

This error initially was based on observations by psychologists that some people give of themselves to others in a sick, seemingly masochistic way. Here we may refer, for example, to the mother who pours herself over her children, smothers them and makes them feel guilty for wanting to emancipate themselves from her. C.S. Lewis captured this form of sickness well in his incisive *Screwtape Letters* when it is said, "She's the sort of woman who lives for others. You can always tell the others by their hunted expression." Or we may speak of the husband who becomes so dependent on his wife for decisions and nurturing that he cannot live without her. Upon her premature death, he takes his own life, leaving their dependent children to fend for themselves. For these people, "giving of themselves" is a form of martyrdom. Their service to others is not based on the desire to help others grow, but instead on a subconscious motive to get their own needs met first. They are doing what the truly selfish do, but covering this over under the socially acceptable mask of doing for others.

The popular recognition of this form of pathology was overdue. Unfortunately, the basic premise was bent out of shape once again, but to a different purpose. Initially, this twisting was done by a few psychologists who were catering to the new movements of the 60s. It suited perfectly the "new" (old) *emphasis* on self-first that came out of the 60s. It coincided with and reinforced all the new emphases on self-development, self-expression, self-fulfillment, self-ness. The new doctrine was thus born: love yourself, expand yourself, explore yourself, develop yourself, meet first your own needs, *then* you will be able to love others and find happiness in life. The old Jesusonian teaching was turned upside down.

The 20th Century Myth validates the regression to self-centeredness, destroys human relationships, nullifies growth in marriage and leaves people utterly confused in their personal ethics. A whole generation bought into this pathetic distortion of the old teaching. Many have paid an enormous price in the deterioration of their intimate human relationships.

Yet there is an element of truth in the new ethic. Our capacity for love and healthy relationships with others *is* based on our ability to be loving with ourselves. Scott Peck, in his brilliant book, *The Road Less Traveled*, goes to the heart of the matter with his definition of love as the "...will to extend one's self for the purpose of nurturing one's own or another's spiritual growth." Gary Smalley speaks to the effectiveness of this definition of love when he notes that happiness comes to us as a byproduct of serving others. But this service for others quickly loses its healthiness when we do it in the secret hope of being rewarded or "paid back" by the other. Then it easily regresses to a somewhat subtle form of that primitive morality, "I'll scratch your back if you'll scratch mine." The ideal form of service for others is that which is done anonymously, where there is little or no chance for the server to be recognized or rewarded for his efforts. This ideal is of course difficult to attain, for it requires that the person grow beyond the "tit for tat" morality of everyday commerce into a higher morality where he is motivated to please and obey the Higher Good for all.

When we seek personal happiness as our primary goal, we end up losing it along the way, for when we search for our own happiness it eludes and frustrates us. Enough is never enough of whatever person, place or thing we've fixated on as the source of our happiness. By contrast, when we seek to help another to attain happiness, we wake up one day and discover *we* are happy, often to our surprise, or as C.S. Lewis put it, we are "surprised by joy."

We cannot have good marriages, and for that matter any good relationships with others, by pursuing our own self-fulfillment first. This is the pivotal error of the ethic that came out of the 60s, which itself was an extension of the 20th Century Myth, into our interpersonal lives. And it is the primary cause of family dysfunction today. If we pursue our own self-development first we never really find it; we even become hateful in the process. Similarly, we do not find happiness by pursuing it for its own sake, but by being of service to others. As more individuals rediscover this ancient wisdom, our marriages and families will be strengthened and renewed. The paradox is not a paradox at all.

Does this mean that we always meet the needs of the other first, that we must stop what we're doing so as to always cater to the other? No, discriminative judgments are called for, which is the process referred to in the ancient teachings when it is said, "be as harmless as a dove but as wise as a serpent." In other words, be aware of the dangers of unwise love. Love cannot be all-tolerant in an imperfect world.

Unwise love can do much harm. Many young people I have seen, now adults, are still irresponsible and self-centered due mainly to parents who loved them deeply but unwisely. These are the parents who rescued their child from every negative consequence. Their love was a mindless love. They got him off with easy probation when he was caught with drugs. They removed him from every teacher who made him uncomfortable. They made excuses for him when he treated their friends rudely. They couldn't bear to take his car away even after repeated violations of his curfew hour. Now they are shocked to find themselves still rescuing a son nearing 30 who can't hold down a job or make any relationships with others last. But, they protest, we "loved our son too much" to allow him to experience the negative consequences of his own foulups. This pandering, unwise love is not what is meant by placing others first.

Sometimes we love the other person best when we confront him with his problems even though we know initially he will be hurt and angry, and we will be anxious and upset. Sometimes we love the other best when we choose to let him go through the pain brought about by his own poor judgment. These are difficult decisions, never easy to make, but in loving others there are occasions when putting the other first means letting him experience the consequences of his self-inflicted pain.

In my work with families, this is an area where I have seen the sexes complement each other beautifully. As a general rule, most mothers have a better understanding of the child's need for unconditional, all-accepting love. Many fathers, however, have a better understanding of the child's need for approval predicated on appropriate performance. *Many mothers give approval too indiscriminately while many fathers give approval too infrequently.* When a woman and a man learn from each other on these matters, they greatly enhance the wisdom of their combined love for the child.

Love, support, tolerance and respect are forces for good to the degree that they are conditioned by wisdom. Wisdom entails being students of the other people in our lives. We put the time and energy into this effort so we have a fair idea of their strengths and weaknesses. We think a lot about their needs — what they need from us versus what they don't need from us. We become increasingly aware of our own needs, and their relative priorities. In other words, *we think*; we put the same effort into this as we put into our jobs or professions. And in order to think accurately about the other, we must first listen to the other. To do this, we must consistently put aside our own autobiography, our own needs, so that we may listen, really listen with respect, to the other. The better we listen, the more we understand. With few exceptions, the more we truly understand the other, the more we love him.

We examine our values and always place our choices within the context of our values. In this manner we grow in the ability to make balanced decisions about when, where and how we serve the other versus serving our own needs. As our ability to serve the other grows, *healthy* self-love inevitably follows, and this is the fundamental building block of healthy marriages.

Couples who practice this principle find their love for each other growing deeper, fonder as the years pass. They have a great capacity to bounce back from the problems and sufferings which affect all families. Some research has suggested that most long-term, happy couples do not develop true intimacy until after 15, 20 or even 25 years of married life together. In my experience, this observation is generally true. Healthy families are continually growing up together. True intimacy with a loving partner is built on years and years of love premised on each habitually placing the other first until, eventually, selflessness is more naturally and freely given by each partner.

By contrast, when we pursue self-love (self-fulfillment, self-respect, etc.) as a goal in and of itself, we doom our efforts to failure. The 60s ethic, "first learn to love and develop yourself, then you can love and develop others," gave us the "me generation," which has suffered terribly for this mistake. I long ago lost count of the marriages I've seen ruined by the application of this ethic. Of all of the mistakes of the 60s, this was the greatest. The 20th Century Myth teachings on love and self-love provided an easy way out of the hard, selfless work required by the ancient teachings. Healthy marriages are based on the old teachings of *wise service to others comes first, then healthy self-love follows.* When both partners practice this ideal, the long-term success of the marriage is virtually guaranteed. The problem, and its solution, reside in our values and how we apply them in everyday life.

Second Principle: The Source of Happiness

The source of happiness in healthy families is found in the *relationship* between wife and husband. The degree to which this relationship is healthy is the degree to which the family is healthy.

Carl Jung said, "Neurosis is always a substitute for legitimate suffering." He did not mean we should wallow in suffering. He meant this – that problems, and thus pain in our relationships, are inevitable given the inherent selfishness of us all. We can learn to deal with this pain constructively or we'll deal with the pain in self-defeating ways. These latter methods of dealing with relationship problems inevitably lead to more hurt and more unhappiness *because the individual seeks to avoid the suffering, the pain that always accompanies personal growth.* We may, for example, deny that a problem exists, or always claim it's the other person's fault, or refuse to open our minds to see the other's viewpoint, or we may always procrastinate and put off the painful confrontation, or medicate ourselves with alcohol or other drugs to alleviate the pain. When we do these things, we set ourselves up to develop neurotic behavior patterns as we try to avoid the pain that accompanies the discovery of our own contributions to our ongoing problems with others. The degree to which we deny, avoid or delay this inevitable suffering is the degree to which we act neurotically, because we deny ourselves the opportunity to learn from our mistakes. Neurosis means self-defeating. When we say someone is acting neurotically, we are saying that his way of dealing with his problems relieves the pain temporarily, but eventually defeats and even destroys his relationships with others.

There is a quick way to determine your degree of neuroticism (we are all neurotic in varying degrees since we are all selfish in varying degrees). Ask yourself this: how good are my intimate relationships with others? Do your relationships start off great but, somehow, always end up blowing up in your face? Can you not get intimate relationships with others going? Do people always, eventually, leave you? Or do you always end up having to leave others because they eventually disappoint you? If you honestly answer "yes" to one or more of these questions, then the chances are great that "the problem" is more with you than with others. We cannot have healthy relationships with others by trying to change others to accommodate us. We first identify the source of our relationship problems *in ourselves*. We identify what *we* are contributing to our continuing difficulties with others. The only way we can hope to improve the relationship is by then changing or removing *our* contribution to the problem.

By fostering our own spiritual growth (by first enduring the pain of honest self-analysis) and changing ourselves, we open the door for the other to change. We actually change others by first changing our own actions and reactions toward *them*. This gutsy process nearly always involves change that means putting the needs of the other ahead of our own. A husband, for example, who tries to improve his wife's inattention to detail in household tasks by the use of sarcasm is doomed to failure and frustration. He may succeed, however, upon realizing that his own need for a meticulous house is disrupting his love of and respect for his wife. By asking her what he can do to help in the matter, he opens himself up to changing his own actions toward her. Improvement on her part now becomes a possibility. Of course, she may inform him that the most helpful thing he can do is to shut up. Whatever works, works. We come back to the same principle – our best chance for changing others resides in first changing something about ourselves that's contributing to the problem, and this "something" nearly always involves putting our own needs aside temporarily while we put the needs of the other first. This is what Jung meant when he said that to overcome neurosis we must first deal with the pain of relationship problems by recognizing our own contributions to the difficulty. When we avoid this pain by denials, drugs, alcohol, excuse-making, and blaming others, we set ourselves up for more pain later on as we deny ourselves the opportunity to learn from our mistakes.

Stephen Covey makes similar points when discussing his research on effective versus non-effective persons. Effective individuals are "inside-out" people. They assume that by first changing themselves they can change the world around them for the better. By contrast, non-effective persons feel that the locus of control is outside of them – that the other person, or the system, must change first before they can be happy and productive. Since this rarely happens, non-effective persons end up feeling victimized by others. Or, they feel well only if others treat them well. Their emotional state is determined for them by "the other(s)."

> This is the true joy in life – being used for a purpose recognized by yourself as a mighty one... instead of [being] a feverish, selfish little clod of ailments and grievances complaining that the world will not devote itself to making you happy.
>
> George Bernard Shaw

In far too many marriages, the wife and husband think of their best times, their happiest times, as being their courtship era, the time before they had children. These folk are missing out on one of the greatest eras in marriage, the time of *growing up together* by growing out of the narcissism of "romantic love." The romantic love of the courtship era is always fleeting, for it contains the seeds of its own destruction in its inherent narcissism. Romantic love appears to be selfless love in its obsession with the other, but this is both part illusion and part self-delusion. It never lasts, nor should it. True love, true intimacy with the other, is based on growing up together, which requires "testing by fire," learning how to deal with adversity together. The couple that suffers together but then finds the way to transcend the suffering are on their way to true love. Those who do not learn to deal with adversity together become fixated in self-defeating patterns of relationships. It is a marvel to see elderly couples who have weathered the storms together and still like each other. I have yet to see such couples who were afraid of the end of this life. Their only fear is of the temporary loss of each other.

The early romantic love of courtship is an illusion, because the couple does not yet know if they can handle hardship as a team. But it is a lovely time and should be enjoyed to the fullest. And there is a great nucleus of truth in the idea of "falling in love." It is during this time that the couple often enjoys their first taste of selfless love, each for the other, though for too many couples this is their last taste of selfless love.

When we "fall in love," we see ourselves being adored in the eyes of the other. Our suspicions are now confirmed. We really are the brilliant, gorgeous, lovable persons we always hoped or thought we were. Falling in love is a willowy form of self-love, for we see the glorified image of ourselves reflected back to us in the eyes of the other. We find ourselves deeply in love with this other person, for he is the means and the expression for the unconditional support of our own self-love. The other is greatly admired for she has had the great good sense to recognize how wonderful we are. The unconditional love of each for the other produces feelings of euphoria, for we all long to be loved for being our own, admirable selves, with no conditions attached. Each member of the couple suspends judgment and unconditionally supports and applauds the other. Unrestricted self-love and selfless love for the other temporarily march hand in glove.

Now, if only it could last! But of course it cannot, for it is built on the illusion that unconditional love for the other can last forever, and on the self-delusion that we are perfect in our lover's eyes and thus require no changes, no improvements. When the false ideal falls, the couple can go through a terrible ordeal (from which many never recover), unless each of their maturity levels is adequate to meet the crisis with humor and persistent commitment to the selfless ideal – service to the other comes first.

When the hard times come, as they must, the telling point is the degree to which each can rise above his own self-centeredness in dealing with the shocking discovery (and it's always a shock) of the many defects suddenly found in oneself and one's mate: paradise lost. The self-obsessed find it almost impossible to deal with this shock. They were just getting used to unconditional adoration when suddenly it is taken away. Many celebrities appear to have special difficulty with this normal process. The famous movie star who confides to her interviewer that she's on her fifth marriage because she's hooked on the feelings of falling in love (she's so romantic) is telling us how self-obsessed she is. She's not willing to do the hard, selfless work required to make relationships last.

For some couples, however, the experience of romantic love can serve as an inspiration, an ideal to work back to, but the second time around the unconditional love will not be so unwise. It can also serve as a reminder of all the positive features of the other which initially attracted. These reminders become even more poignant over time as we foster the spiritual growth of the other, for we see those same positive features grow better and wiser with time. We see the warts as well, but they no longer disgust us, for now we see them in the larger, deeper context of the many strengths and loveliness of the other. Eventually, the couple may even return to a stage of romantic love, but this time it is better than the first time. Now it is seasoned with a realistic respect for each other, with shared experiences of coming through difficult times together, and with a fondness for each other based on a conscious decision to ignore (or laugh about) the imperfections, for her overall loveliness overwhelms such matters. These are the rewards that await couples who find the way to deal with adversity together. These rewards are not freely given; they are earned over time through both persons' persistence in the pursuit of the higher ideal of selflessness.

In the pursuit of happiness it is easy to be sidetracked from the ideal of selfless love. Some people believe that "having" a specific other person will make them happy. They earnestly, even desperately, seek the ideal mate in the mistaken belief that if they can just find the perfect other for them, then and only then, can they be happy. If I could just have a woman who looks like *that one*, then I could be a contented man, or so we tell ourselves.

Other folk put their energies into the pursuit of things. If I could just have a house like that one, then I would be happy. If I could just earn that degree or promotion, then I would be complete. If I could just earn such and such income, then my troubles would be over. If I could just buy a 1953 MG roadster, then ... The list is endless of people, places and things which we yearn for because "it" will make us happy, finally. But of course this is absurd, a child's dream. It leads to the "is that all there is?" phenomenon. Lasting happiness is derived from good relationships with others, not things.

Happiness is a simple proposition. It comes from serving others wisely and thereby developing lasting, healthy relationships with other people. Happy families are those where the service ethic is the *modus operandi*. Healthy families may vary in a thousand other ways, but they share this in common: they are motivated by service to the other family members because wise service is routinely observed in the two founders of the family, the mother and the father.

Third Principle: The Importance of Being Different

The main source of tension in marriages is simply that people are different, which is the reason why couples from similar backgrounds with similar beliefs and tastes have a slightly easier time of it than couples from widely varying orientations. These latter couples, however, can have great marriages if they develop the ability to compose their differences amicably.

People differ on a million dimensions, but most differences play off one of two platforms – gender and personality temperament. Sex differences, for example, are a major cause of irritations in many marriages. They are also the stimulus for much of the good humor found in healthy families. A male and female trying to be a team, especially when they are sexually attracted to each other, create both comedy and tragedy together. The so-called "battle of the sexes" has been forever a ripe source of topics for humorists because virtually everyone recognizes the inherent absurdities in male-female relationships. She wants to talk. He doesn't. She wants to feel his sympathy for her position on the matter that went wrong today. He offers no sympathy, but is intrigued with his analysis of the matter and presents her with a detailed plan to solve the problem. She remembers every detail of the first time they made love. He can't remember anything except that it was "great." She is hurt and angry because their relationship is not what it "should be." He tells her that she's making a mountain out of a molehill. She wants to talk about it at 1:00 AM because she can't sleep. He rolls over and pretends not to listen, hoping she'll shut up. She wants to talk about the people she works with. He's bored, but becomes excited when they talk about the day's changes on the bond market. Ample proof of God's great sense of humor is found in the fact that these two alien species, men and women, must work together to create families.

Sex differences come in many forms and often flip flop from one family to the next. Is the woman always the emotionally sensitive one? Is the man always more fact-oriented and seemingly insensitive to the nuances of relationships? Definitely not. Across a thousand families, one sees a thousand permutations of the more commonly observed gender differences. This myriad of combinations, however, cannot obviate the fact that some sex differences are fairly predictable. Women, as a general rule, are more focused on relationships. Men are more likely to go for the facts, the data in the situation, rather than the emotions generated in the people involved. Women are more likely to personalize the incident, whatever it is, whereas men are more likely to objectify it. Most women enjoy exploring and expressing their emotions. Most men find this awkward or boring. Women are much more verbal than men, who on average produce less than half as many words in a day as women. But of course, there are exceptions to these rules, which only makes the whole affair more fascinating.

Some people believe these differing tendencies to be genetic in origin whereas others say they are the products of social conditioning. As we saw in the last chapter, there is ample research evidence supporting the notion that gender differences are the result of a continuous interplay between both genetic and environmental factors. The one undeniable fact is that sex differences not only exist, but are multitudinous.

Failure to deal with this fact in a marriage is a recipe for problems. To the degree a couple recognizes these differences, the greater their chances are of successfully solving these difficulties. *When inherent differences are not acknowledged, there is a dangerous tendency to assume the worst about the motives of the other person.* As noted in the last chapter, this has been one of the great mistakes of modern feminism. By insisting that gender differences were in no way inherent, but strictly due to social conditioning, feminists unwittingly established the grounds in which grudges toward the other person fester and grow, then rigidify. We then automatically assume the worst about our mate's motives. The wife whose husband refuses to talk with her when she needs emotional support may conclude that he no longer truly cares for her. The husband who is embarrassed by his wife's flirtations at parties may quickly conclude that her purpose is to emasculate him in front of their friends. The wife whose husband only touches her when he wants sex may conclude that her husband's only real interest in her is for the sexual relief she provides. The husband whose wife corrects him mainly when they are with his peers may conclude that his wife no longer respects him. All of these inferences may be correct, but they can just as readily be totally wrong.

When a couple studies and understands gender differences, especially as they apply to them, they are far less likely to assume the worst about their mate's motives. A wife may then correctly infer that her husband is reluctant to talk with her not because he's uncaring, but because he simply has no energy for high verbal interactions most of the time. A husband may then see that his wife's flirtations are not designed to emasculate him, but to elicit from *him* attention and recognition of *her* attractiveness. When gender differences are recognized and treated with the good humor they deserve, it becomes much easier to give our mate that most precious of gifts in human relationships – *the benefit of the doubt.*

It is when we develop the ability to resist the holding of grudges and instead develop the willingness to forgive that we are developing true maturity of character. When both the husband and the wife are growing along these lines, then the foundation is being built for a healthy marriage. But this is difficult to do unless both recognize the very real differences between them, and both acknowledge the importance of giving the other the benefit of the doubt when conflict arises. It is very difficult to develop this willingness to forgive, however, unless both partners believe in a just and merciful universe so that it is believed that everyone, eventually, experiences the consequences of their behavior. When both partners truly believe in this ideal, then the need to be judge, jury and executioner disappears. Each partner can breathe more freely, for he or she now knows that the benefit of the doubt will be automatically granted. Failure to do this – holding on to our grudges instead (always accompanied by assigning blame to others) – is the sure sign of an immature person and problems to come in the marriage.

In addition to sex differences, there are also great, inherent temperament differences among people. There is a large, growing body of evidence for the idea that personality temperament is strongly influenced by genetic factors. Bill Cosby once told this story about two of his children. One daughter, he related, was politely born late in the morning. She didn't fuss if her wet diaper was left on for hours. She lay in her crib and cooed while Mom and Dad "slept in." She hardly ever cried, and smiled sweetly and often at an early age. Her parents figured this parenthood thing was a cinch. Lots of fun, too. Then came the next child. She was born at 4:00 AM. She demanded to be fed on the hour or else a bloodcurdling scream screeched through the house. Wet diapers had to be removed instantly. Mom or Dad had to jump out of bed at 6:00 AM to meet her needs or else all hell broke loose.

Parents who have two or more children instantly respond to not only the humor but the truth in Cosby's tale. We come into the world with widely varying temperaments, cognitive styles, and characteristic responses to frustration.

- Some people are extroverts who thrive on contact with people. They quickly become lonely without people around. Their batteries are charged by being in active association with others. Some people, however, are introverts who become exhausted if they must interact with others for very long. They often dread prolonged social contact and will seek out isolation so they may recharge their batteries. When an introvert marries an extrovert, fascinating complications inevitably result.
- Some people are at their best in the mornings, while others reach the peak of their biological clock in the late afternoon and evening. (Woe to the couple where one is a morning person and the other is a night person.)
- Some people naturally yearn for closure in all situations, especially where there is a problem to solve or a job to perform. Others, however, enjoy the process itself of solving the problem and are not strongly motivated to secure closure.
- Some people immediately go to sequential, step-by-step thinking when confronted with a difficulty. They automatically seek to solve problems by deriving a logical plan. Other people, however, instantaneously see the difficulty as a *gestalt*, as a whole thing with many seemingly non-related parts. They deal with the difficulty not so much with a plan, but with a reaction wherein they "wing it" as the process of resolution unfolds. Some people are "feelers" whereas others are "thinkers."
- Some people are primarily concerned with showing others they are all-accepting and offer no threat to others. Their desire is to please and make

everyone happy. These are the "golden retrievers" in Gary Smalley's terminology. Other people are primarily concerned with showing others how competent and accomplished they are. They, too, want people to like them, but they wish first to be admired for their high levels of competence.

- Some people couldn't care less about exercising authority over others, whereas some individuals are driven their whole lives by the desire for more power over others.

The list goes on and on. We are only beginning to understand the many, inherent differences in personality temperament and cognitive style among people. One of the best beginner resources for gaining knowledge of different personality styles and temperaments can be found in the book, *Please Understand Me*.[93] Its authors base their work on the pioneering efforts of Carl Jung, who first developed our understanding of such personality dimensions as extrovert vs. introvert, thinking vs. feeling and intuitive vs. practical, sequential inferencing. These temperament and thinking differences cause much mischief as well as much delight among people. Our mate's personality tendencies may be so different from our own that we may feel at times we are living with an alien from another world.

Most people enter into marriage with some rosy ideal about what the relationship will be or "ought to be like" a few years down the road. This projected ideal almost never takes into account the actual personality tendencies of the selected mate. A new wife, for example, may foresee a relationship five years hence where she and her mate have long, soulful talks by the fireside wherein they discuss *everything*. She neglects to take into account, however, that her husband is an introvert and a thinker. He is, let us say, outstanding in his work, but not very good with intimacy. He catered to her needs during courtship, but now he is obsessed with his career. Only rarely does he desire intimate, long conversations. He wants to be alone when at home so he can think and study. Obviously, some adjustments, painful ones at first, must be made by both partners if each is to have his needs met in this marriage. This adjustment will be made easier if the two partners realize that the one is not out to irritate the other. They each care for the other. But they are two very different people with differing tendencies, needs and reactions. Wise marriage partners are students of each other's tendencies and learn not to put unrealistic expectations onto each other. Again, benefit of the doubt.

When we place too many of our own expectations onto the other, we set ourselves up for heartbreak. This is especially true if we are depending on the other to make us happy. As already noted, happiness comes from serving others, not from expecting others to make us happy. In fact, an excellent definition of selfishness is this – I expect *you* to make *me* happy by meeting *my* needs. In contrast, when we do not expect others to make us happy, their capacity to hurt us is diminished. One of the easiest ways to fall into the "me-first trap" is to place expectations on the other which do not take into account his or her personality and gender tendencies. Do this, and you are bound to be disappointed. When disappointed by our intimate other, it is normal to experience hurt and anger. It is then easy to infer the worst about our partner's motives. A steamroller effect is kicked into gear, for the more we feel anger toward our mate, the more we feel victimized by our mate. Anger, if allowed to go unchecked, always results in self-righteousness combined with a sense of betrayal by the other. *We are victims.* We have been hurt by the other.

"He must have meant to hurt me. If he didn't mean to, that's even worse, that means I'm not important enough for him to think about."

But is this true? Or are we assuming the worst while forgetting about the great personality and gender differences between ourselves and our mates?

When we learn to appreciate the differences between ourselves and others, we are building on the strengths of all the other people in our lives. We then become more open and trusting, less defensive and judgmental. If you cannot bring yourself to value the differences among people, then there is no good reason to hope for good and lasting relationships with others.

Fourth Principle:
Dealing with the Power Struggle Fairly
While Preventing Negative Scanning

The breaking of expectations is especially painful as the couple moves out of the courtship phase and on through the "power struggle" phase of the marriage. The courtship era of romantic love may last a few years or a few hours. The power struggle era typically lasts at least the balance of the first decade of the marriage. And this is when marriages are most likely to fall apart.

The power struggle develops when the couple gets down to the business of adjusting to the demands and sometimes harsh realities of the outside world. This adjustment requires the couple to make *decisions* on how they will use their mutual resources of time, energy and money. Now the fireworks begin, for these decisions have real consequences for each partner. Now the potential for violation of self-ness by the other partner becomes an everyday reality. The power struggle begins.

A waggish acquaintance whom I once interviewed about the success of his long-term marriage told me this when I asked him how he and his wife had resolved their earlier power struggles. He said, "When my wife and I were first married, we decided that she would make all the routine, daily decisions and I would make all the major decisions. Funny thing, after 50 years of marriage there's never been an occasion to make a major decision." Now, to be sure, most husbands when making such comments are patronizing their wives, but this was not the case with this man. He had a profound respect for his wife's contributions to their shared happiness. His little joke helps to point us to the basic problem couples encounter in the power struggle era.

Namely, the impossibility of having a true democracy in a marriage, a fact which the power struggle brings to light. Now, I can hear the screams of protest already from those couples who pride themselves on their modernity. Marriage, they say, should be a democracy based on equal rights of man and woman. True, and it's a great and noble ideal, but it doesn't work that way. The reason it doesn't work, at least not in the absolute sense, is simple. One man, one vote. One woman, one vote. Clean and equal, yes? No. They can easily cancel each other out, hence the power struggle is not resolved by the democratic ideal. He wants it this way; she wants it that way. Neither budges. They're stuck. Imagine a couple at a busy intersection on their way to an important meeting and they're late. She says turn right; he says no, they must turn left. Neither gives; each is convinced he is right and the other is wrong. But theirs is a democratic marriage and they have agreed all decisions must be unanimous. They're stuck. They don't move. Not only do they become mad at each other, but all the people in the cars around them are soon angry with them. The situation is impossible, an impasse.

Successful couples resolve this inherent impasse by determining, over time, the areas of *relative competency* of each partner. A wife, for example, may determine that when it comes to directions and other spatial relations, her husband is usually more competent than she. She may decide to "give in" to her husband on such matters. (Or, she may feel as competent as her mate in this area, but infer that it's more important to his self-concept for him to have priority in this arena, and thus she chooses to "give him" this area of competence, much as a gift to his self.) Or, a husband may see that his wife is better than he at "doping out" other people's motives in business relations and comes to rely on her perceptions in such matters. Each partner develops an awareness of the relative competencies of the other so that the talents of each are well utilized for the common good of the marriage. This is not an easy task, and it takes years of effort to attain a good grasp of relative competencies.

And the task is never finished, for as conditions change with time, the relative competencies of the couple change. Perhaps Dad used to pay all the bills, but now Mom does. Perhaps Mom used to have the final say on all matters pertaining to the house, but now Dad does since he retired. Part of the adventure of marriage lies in the discovery, and then the rediscovery, of the sometimes changing relative competencies of each partner. The couple may wisely decide to discuss all matters of import before final decisions are made so that each has his input into the matter, but if a consensus is not evident then one partner must choose to defer to the other. This temporary deference hopefully is based not on fear of the other, but on recognition of the other's higher level of competence in the area in question.

The power struggle years are by necessity long and often difficult. This is where the issue of selfishness comes into full play. If one or both of the partners must always have matters their way, and only their way; if one or both partners can only see their own position, then the power struggle will eventuate in the dissolution of the marriage. The marriage may not legally dissolve only because one partner decides to give in totally to the dominant one as the only means of saving the marriage. In truth, however, the marriage is dissolved because if one partner is totally dominant the partnership can continue only at the expense of the weaker partner. This is not a healthy marriage, but a one-way street to growing unhappiness for the one who has "given in."

In healthy marriages there develops a profound respect of each for the other. There is a growing recognition of the strengths and particular talents and contributions of each partner. The differences in temperament between the two partners are no longer seen as threats to one's power, one's selfness, but as sources of strength which increase exponentially the couple's capabilities to deal with the world. Differences are then seen not as reasons to fight, but as great resources to be tapped into. In this way couples eventually resolve most aspects of the power struggle in a healthy manner. There will still be irritations of course. ("She almost never gets anywhere on time; he nearly always gets angry if someone contradicts his political views.") But these irritations are seen in their true light – as personality tendencies of the beloved, *not* as deliberate attempts to disappoint us and make us unhappy.

In resolving the power struggle with respect for each other, the couple lays the groundwork for the later stage of true intimacy, which as noted before doesn't normally develop until 15, 20 or 25 years into the marriage. The first stage of marriage is the courtship era when romantic loves holds sway. Romantic love is a form of selfless love that has at its core a peculiar form of narcissistic self-love. This stage never lasts long, for it has within it the seeds of its own destruction. The second stage is the era of the power struggle where the two egos are in ongoing deliberations with each other. The third stage, provided the couple makes it this far, is a time of resolution of the power struggle wherein each partner stops (or lessens) his tendency to project his own fears and needs (his "shadow," as Jung would say) onto the other. Each partner increasingly takes responsibility for changing himself so that the other person's competencies may flourish. Relative competencies are acknowledged. More and more is expected of oneself; less and less of the other. Tolerance expands, love grows. This process eventually leads to the fourth stage (rarely achieved) of true and lasting intimacy – an intimacy based on the mutual respect that comes only from weathering adversity together.

Being able to resolve the power struggle successfully requires that the couple develop the ability to "fight fairly." Some fights are inevitable. The differences of perspective are too serious, or seem so at the time, to resolve through negotiations over the dinner table. If one of the partners has come home for the fifth night in a row drunk and picking a fight, then serious discussions are in order. Will this discussion have a constructive outcome, or will it deteriorate into a shouting match, a grand slammer of an even bigger fight? The outcome mainly will depend on whether or not the couple has developed the ability to fight fairly (and presuming, in this instance, they are both sober at the time of the "fight"). Fighting fairly means:

- Continually bringing up past grievances does not routinely occur. This attitude makes it impossible to focus on the current issues in a fair-minded way.
- The *never* and *always* words are precluded. "You *never* do this" and "you *always* do that" are inherently unfair and cause in the listener feelings of being the object of unjust perceptions ("Some nights I do come home sober!").
- Listening to each other without constant interruptions. The interrupter who lets fly his counter slam before the other person even finishes his point cannot fight fairly. Few habits are more likely to cause anger during a discussion than this one. Effective problem solving requires that each person hear out the other person. To interrupt shows an obsession with our own views while showing contempt for the other. It also denies us the opportunity to infer the motives of the other by hearing him out in full.
- Most of all, granting the other person the benefit of the doubt; especially, with regard to the true motives behind his actions. These motives must be accurately ascertained before blame is assigned (or withdrawn). This is rarely an easy task, and one that is made impossible if we immediately assume the worst about our mate's motives. He will then "shut down" on us and become so embroiled in his defenses that we never learn his true intent, which may or may not be blameworthy. He may be crying out for help while we are busy assigning blame for the overt infraction.

In one interesting study conducted at the University of Denver, married couples who were taught how to "argue constructively" (i.e., how to fight fairly) had a divorce rate half as high over a 10-year period as a comparable group of married couples who did not receive this same training. The investigators, headed by Howard Markman, report that teaching couples how to argue well and fairly is more important in holding the couple together, and in producing well-adjusted children, than physical attraction, common interests, or any other factor studied.

When first married, most couples are eager to grant each other the benefit of the doubt. But as expectations are broken and power struggles develop, it is easy to fall into the trap of *negative scanning*. Negative scanning nearly always results in unfair fighting and lousy problem solving techniques. Negative scanning generates the worst poison that can creep into and destroy human relationships – *the holding of grudges*, which is the polar opposite of giving the other person the benefit of the doubt.

Negative scanning is a cancerous process we all fall into from time to time. Negative scanning usually occurs subconsciously. We almost never know when we're falling into it. It is rarely intentional, though it happens in all kinds of relationships: parent-child, boss-employee, friend-friend, wife-husband. *It happens when we intensify our efforts to correct and change the other person.* We may be right or we may be wrong; regardless, we decide to change the other. We then begin to focus our efforts on his objectionable behaviors. We remind the other of his need to change. This reminding readily becomes nagging. In doing this, we forget the cardinal principle of personal change: that we change the other, if at all, only by changing something about ourselves first. We change ourselves, we let go of something about ourselves, so that we help free the other so that he may change. But when we indulge in negative scanning, we give up nothing of ourselves. Instead, we pressure the other to change through exhortations, reminders or threats. *He or she must do all the changing.* But this of course doesn't work; it can only work as long as we have total control over the other person, and we never have total control over our spouse. Our approach backfires. The other doesn't change enough or change fast enough to suit us. It becomes clear we must intensify our efforts. Now we focus even more on the negative aspects of the other so we may "help" him to change. Increasingly, our time and energy are devoted to making the necessary changes in the other. Now the poison of negative scanning sets in. Without fully realizing what we've done, we've slipped into the habit of responding only to the perceived negative aspects of the other. Increasingly, we forget to respond to and acknowledge his many positive aspects. Our energies are focused on his negatives. We must help him to change. He must change.

The loved one knows that something has gone terribly wrong in the relationship. He or she rarely understands it intellectually, but he feels it down to his bones. He knows he's being treated judgmentally and evaluated unfairly. He no longer hears how great he is. Now he only hears from us when he messes up. He is being scanned for his negatives. Most people fight back by negatively scanning the negative scanner. To buttress his positions he must remember every wrong, every infraction of the other. When the fights come, as they must, each partner now throws up to the other the accumulated list of past grievances. There is no forgetting or forgiving. Each now holds a grudge against the other. The positive features of the other slowly sink out of sight as the darker tones of mistrust come to dominate the relationship. They no longer know each other. They only know the negatives of the other and these they know only too well, for they are obsessed with them. It is in this way that two (often well-meaning) people proceed from romantic love to despising each other. Each ends up fulfilling the negative prophecies of the other. Each helps to create a monster of the other. After the divorce the monster becomes a super monster, for now they only interact when there is a conflict over children or money. It becomes almost impossible to see each other in a positive setting; all is negative reinforcing negative.

Negative scanning is the poisonous, subconscious process born of selfishness that generates grudges. Grudges destroy relationships if allowed to go unchecked. They preclude forgiveness and negate effective problem solving. Negative scanning comes about when we try to coerce another into changing to suit ourselves by focusing on his negatives while forgetting about his positives. We then forget about the personality and gender differences of the other. We thereby forget to respect the unique individuality of the other person in his wholeness – his positive features as well as his negative features. We come to practice the worst kind of prejudice toward another person – we respond only to his negatives while ignoring his positives.

In healthy marriages the couple develops the ability to nip in the bud the natural tendency toward negative scanning. They develop, instead, effective problem solving techniques based on the principles of fair fighting. All the principles of fighting fairly are based on the idea of putting the other person first in our hearts. We thereby demonstrate respect for the differences between us, or as Smalley aptly puts it, we *honor* the other person first. The growth of love from romantic love to true intimacy is at every stage dependent on our wisdom in implementing this principle – we foster the spiritual growth of the other person first, then our own healthy self-love follows.

Fifth Principle: The Importance of Touching

The negative scanning trap is best avoided by a conscious effort to look for the positives in our mate and affirm them in some way *every day*. Conscious effort is called for to combat the insidious, subconscious process of negative scanning. Covey does an excellent job of describing how effective persons inoculate themselves against negative scanning in their relationships. They build up what he calls Emotional Bank Accounts (EBAs) with their partners. EBAs are the basis of trust in relationships. If my EBA is strong with you, then I can make mistakes, but be forgiven readily. I will not be judged unfairly. My errors do not kick off the judgmental process of negative scanning. Instead, I am automatically extended the benefit of the doubt as to my motives (my actions may have been stupid but my intent was OK). Knowing this, I can relax and feel free to be myself with you. EBAs are built up by practicing the everyday courtesies and kindnesses, by truly listening to the other (non-judgmentally) so we may better understand our partner, by keeping our commitments to each other, by periodic re-clarification of our expectations for each other, and by sincerely apologizing when we make mistakes.

All this is easier for some personality types to do than others. For some, the conscious effort "to stroke" others everyday is relatively easy, whereas for others this "task" is the most difficult thing we can ask them to do, for it goes against the whole grain of their personalities. It is crucial to recognize these personality differences in helping others to become more consciously supportive of their loved ones. Otherwise, we again fall into the trap of being judgmental and assuming the worst about the motives of others.

The simplest way to stroke others during the day is to physically touch them. A squeeze of the shoulder here, a pat on the back there, maybe a hug, go a long, long way toward building good relationships with others of all ages and both sexes. This is the most basic, the most primitive expression of love. Small children will literally wither away and die if they are not touched and held by others. All primate species huddle and cuddle together. We all need to be *stroked*, not merely to survive, but to flourish.

Physical touching also gives us an instant read of how we're doing with the other person. If we're doing well the other person will reciprocate by touching us back, or by instantaneously smiling at us. He will, in some way, move toward us, if only for a moment. If the other moves away from us upon being touched that is a sure sign something's not right in the relationship. Time to go to work.

The subject of touching quite naturally leads us to sexual intercourse, a rather extreme form of touching one another. It seems almost fashionable these days to downgrade the importance of sex in marriage. The redundant polls in women's magazines on "what makes a marriage work" barely mention it at all, although these same magazines are filled with articles telling women how to make themselves more desirable to men. Perhaps this is the predictable aftermath of the "sexual revolution" of the 70s, which was another product of the wacky 60s. Perhaps it's not mentioned often because few married couples have a good sex life and no one wants to make anyone else feel bad about this. A.I.D.S. of course, has put a damper on the whole subject. Somehow, however, we suspect that the subject has not altogether disappeared in importance.

Healthy marriages are characterized by good sex. I've never seen a healthy marriage that was an exception to this rule, provided that both partners were physically capable of sex. Important disclaimer: every couple has their own definition of good sex. For one couple, once a year is bliss. For another, once a night is not enough. One couple does it this way, another couple does it that way. Such matters are trivial and rarely matter. Good sex is how the couple defines it (as long as they both agree!). All this is hardly surprising. When a couple is enjoying a good relationship, *they want to touch each other*. Sex is a form of touching. Of course, healthy marriages are characterized by good sex. We should be shocked if they weren't.

This brings us to one of the most painful topics in marriage break-up: the loss of sexual attractiveness of one partner for the other. This one hurts, really hurts, and it is the cause of far more marital break-ups than anyone seems willing to acknowledge publicly. It is often camouflaged as the real reason for the divorce. Often both partners conspire (without knowing it) to cover up the real instigator of negative scanning and the consequent divorce: the fact that one partner no longer sexually excites the other. This, though, is simply too painful to talk about directly. They start arguing over the children instead, or money, or whatever – anything except the real cause of the hurt and disappointment. The truth is they're arguing because they are both disappointed by the one's lack of desire to touch, really touch deeply, the other.

This topic richly points up the importance of understanding sex differences in marriage. Otherwise, blaming and assuming the worst about one's partner inevitably results. These differences drive both men and women up the wall, for somewhat different reasons. Men hate this subject because it forces them to admit how hung up most of them are on the physical features of woman. Women assert that men are too shallow to have true, loving relationships based on ideals and values. Men have no defense on this matter except to say that men are men. Sometimes, however, males counterattack by asserting that women should act and feel as men do.[1] This old male strategy actually worked for a few years in the 70s during the heyday of the "sexual revolution." Thanks to the feminist movement's insistence that men and women should be in all ways the same, it became *de rigeur* for young women to be sexually active in an aggressive, almost masculine manner. This fad in social norms faded quickly, however, much faster than the other social fads generated out of the 60s, for it went too much against the nature of most females.

Virtually all women instead focus on sex as a relationship. For women, the physical act itself is a means either to develop a relationship or maintain (confirm) a relationship with the other. Women rarely leave their partner because they sexually desire to "have" another man's body. A woman may leave her mate, however, if the relationship has gone sour and another man offers her the prospect of a more rewarding relationship. The big business of romance novels, whose readership is more than 90% female, thrives in response to women's focus on sex as relationship. These novels provide repeated, vicarious experiences with idealized male-female relationships.

For both women and men sex is a powerful force, but each gender approaches it from widely different perspectives. In successful marriages the partners learn to recognize these gender differences and accommodate to them. This area provides classic examples of how each partner gives up something of himself for the sake of the other, that is, for the sake of the relationship. A woman may agree to sexual intercourse more often than she would otherwise prefer, and throw herself into the act with gusto, simply to please her man. She may even choose to do this when she is not that pleased with the relationship, for this is something she can give of herself to her partner. The man may choose to throw himself into the act with gusto even though his wife's body no longer excites him. He may do this because he wants his wife to feel that she is still a desirable woman, and this gift he can give her. The need for sexual gratification can elicit great selflessness or it can elicit great selfishness. It is a profound test of the maturity levels of the two partners.

Review

In healthy marriages the two partners seek out ways to reaffirm each other, praise each other, stroke each other. In the best of these marriages there is a daily commitment to show respect and support and affection for the other. These partners actually scan each other daily for positive features so they can find ways to stroke each other. Positive scanning has become habitual and they rarely fall into the trap of negative scanning. Each person has become secure in the knowledge of how precious he is in the eyes of the other. Differences are not seen as threats to self, but as sources of strength for the good of the relationship, and are often treated humorously. Life is good. Because the relationship is good. This is the happy end of marriages where couples have been able to put aside negative scanning because both partners have developed the habit of putting the needs of the other partner first.

Imagine a marriage where both partners are at least 25 years of age when they marry and where both are strongly committed to the concept of a Higher Power for good in the universe. They both have faith in the ideal that the universe is just and merciful. They both are committed to make the relationship "last forever." Both are eager to study the other, and themselves, for the sake of the other. They like the idea that their relationship will change with the years, and that acquiring more knowledge about themselves and human relationships in general will be an ongoing activity in their married life. They enter the marriage knowing the dangers of selfishness so they both have a strong desire to become more selfless as they grow up together. Each is willing to "let go" of something of his own if it will help the other to grow. They have mutually shared ideals and they will not hesitate to appeal to those ideals in each other when one of them gets off track. They may or may not love money and things, but they are committed to the ideal of always putting relationships first, things second, and they agree to remind each other of this ideal when difficult decisions arise. They already know there are personality, temperament and sex differences between them. They see these differences not as threats to their happiness, but as opportunities for personal growth in their relationship. They agree always to give each other the benefit of the doubt and to develop effective problem-solving methods. They know this means learning how to fight fairly and avoiding negative scanning. They are committed to the ideal that each day they will find ways to stroke and reaffirm the precious uniqueness and lovability of the other.

Sound too idealistic, even farfetched? It's not. I have seen many couples like this among the thousands of families I've dealt with over the past quarter of a century. They may not have all the above factors going for them, but they have most of them. And they all have this in common – each partner is nourishing the spiritual and personal growth of the other. These are the happiest of people. Their relationships are based on good values and a commitment to make these values work on a daily, down to earth basis.

Imagine also that premarital education programs existed that taught these principles and methods (a few do). We could greatly increase the number of successful marriages. People are rarely prepared for the demands of intimate relationships, for such relationships require that we let go of something of ourselves every day. Few of us know much about how to go about doing this wisely and well, and learning how to do this is a lifelong affair. Through application of these principles, couples can actually accelerate their progress through the power struggle years and attain true intimacy much earlier in the marriage than normally seen. The path to intimacy, however, is filled with dangerous detours, even for the best prepared couples.

Nearly all couples need refresher courses from time to time. In most divorces both persons are usually well-meaning people. Occasionally one person is a "bad guy," but this is rare. More often, divorce is the product of one person becoming so wrapped up in his own needs and concerns that he sets off the vicious cycle of negative scanning without even knowing what he has done. The other person responds in kind and two nice people end up despising each other. Our ignorance of what makes relationships work combined with poorly thought out values "does us in" every time. These are lessons, though, we can learn. The next century will see an improvement in the quality of human relationships as long as we honestly address the twin issues of *knowledge* and *values*.

The Seven Principles of Good Parenting

Don't let the above subtitle fool you. There is no magic formula – no step #1, step #2 – to being a good parent. People are too different to allow for step-by-step formulas. Each child is inherently different and each parent is different. Some children, as we go back for a moment to the tale told by Bill Cosby, are inherently more difficult to rear than others. In each parent-child relationship the parent must feel and think his way along as the child grows. There are, however, a few basic principles that can provide both guidance and inspiration. When parents run into problems, they can refer to these principles and nearly always find the source of their troubles in the failure to pay attention to one or more of these principles. These same principles apply to all human relationships where the goal is intimacy with the other.

First Principle: The Commitment of Time
Without the commitment of time, there simply cannot be a healthy parent-child relationship. Time with the child is of the essence; it is a requirement. In

healthy families parents seek out time with their children and do whatever it takes to make this happen. No one has put this basic fact more eloquently than Scott Peck:

> When we love something it is of value to us, and when something is of value to us we spend time with it, time enjoying it and time taking care of it. So it is when we love children; we spend time admiring them and caring for them. We give them our time.[94]

When we give children our time and attention, two critically important things happen: the child comes to feel that he is a valuable person, and bonding occurs between child and parent.

When the other gives us his time and wants to be with us, then we know we are valued for what we are. For the young child this is critical, for he cannot force himself on the parent unless the parent allows it (although most children certainly will try to do this). The child is utterly dependent on the parent's decision to give or not give his time and attention. Surrogate parents such as grandparents and daycare workers can provide noble substitute service, but only the parent can make the child feel truly loved. Every child has an intuitive grasp of the degree to which he is truly valued by his parent. The child correctly deduces that it is the parent's *time commitment*, far more than his *words*, that tell him his true value in the eyes of the parent. If the child does not learn he is valuable at his parent's knees, then he faces an uphill climb for the rest of his life in his relationships with others.

Children instinctively move to bond to their parents, but this process can be disrupted in a myriad of ways. Healthy bonding is dependent on the follow-through of the time commitment by the parent to the child. In many families today the parents are too busy with their careers and other pursuits to allow healthy bonding to occur. Kent Hayes, in his book *Why Good Parents Have Bad Kids*, goes to the point when he says "The truth is that kids can't bond with a moving target. They can't become attached to someone who is not there, or is only occasionally there. Parents who are preoccupied with their jobs, themselves, or their problems are not available to their children."[95]

The second critical development is this: when a child bonds to his parent he internalizes the values, standards and expectations of the parent. When the parent gives his time to the child and makes the child feel valuable, the child begins to identify with the source of these good feelings about himself, the parent. Because of this identification, the child takes on, as his own, the standards and values of the parent (for good or for bad). This is the single most important piece of learning the child experiences. It occurs subconsciously and lasts a lifetime.

Through bonding the child internalizes – makes his own – the values of the parent. Children who later engage in acts of outrageous rebellion against everything the parents stand for are usually throwing a delayed temper tantrum.

This tantrum is due to the teen's perception that he is not valuable in the eyes of his parents. He therefore rejects their values, their standards, their expectations for him. The parents may protest – "but we gave him everything." Everything, except the most important gift of all – time and attention wisely focused on the positive aspects of the child.

Parents, however, should not panic if their teenager exhibits some rebellion. The lad who spikes and dyes his hair outrageous colors, but still works for good grades at school, is probably not showing a lack of bonding with his parents. In all likelihood he is still identified with his parents' values, despite his outward appearance. For some teens their personalities are such that some rebellion is to be expected. If handled wisely by parents, this rebellion can turn out well for all concerned. Even the most docile of children may require some rebellion so they may question and test their parents' values. Never be afraid of this process. If your values are good, your children will always come back to them eventually, though modified for their own purposes. And remember that some rebellion is not only healthy but inevitable.

> Youth to its own self rebels, though none else be near.
> William Shakespeare

The most important time we give our children is *ordinary, everyday* time. We never know when our child may need us. The younger the child, the more he needs our time and attention, though even teens need far more of our time than they care to admit. Through being with our child we become a student of our child's personality. We can come to know his strengths and weaknesses and where he needs correction versus where he needs our unconditional support. We can learn when to tighten down the consequences for misbehavior versus when to give him our all-out acceptance. We learn how to love him. And we have the energy to do this job thoughtfully, which is very difficult to do when parenting is tacked on at the end of a busy workday. When we spend little time with our child, we inevitably feel guilty about this, as we should. This guilt, if used unwisely, can lead us to indulge our child, most often by pandering to his temper outbursts, or by not correcting him as firmly as we should, or by giving him too many material goods. The main cause of the great tide of insubordination coming from today's youths is absentee parents combined with over-protected children (not allowing them to experience the natural consequences of their foolish behaviors). And these two factors often go hand in glove, since absentee parents are likely to indulge their children out of fear of rocking the boat during the little time they spend with them.

Then there are the *special times*, those memorable experiences which families look back on with laughter. Gary Smalley recommends, with tongue firmly in cheek, that all families go camping together. Every family develops its own history, its own traditions. An important feature of this history involves those times the family suffers together. The family that suffers together bonds together. Camping, with all its potentials for disaster, can occasion much bonding. It is therefore a great experience, or at least it seems so three months later. But, of course, there are many other ways for families to suffer together. The critical point is that families cannot develop a family history unless they spend time together.

Erik Erikson, one of the wiser of the early psychologists, said that everything a child does, especially his play, has meaning and wonder for him. When children perform, whether in a play or sports or whatever, it is important for parents to be there to witness and applaud their child. The parent cannot always be there, of course, but must be there most of the time. This is critical for the child's healthy self-concept, for it tells him he is valuable in our sight. We give his activities, his early attempts to develop competencies in dealing with the world, our precious gift – our time and focus.

When my second son and third child went out for little league football, I dutifully attended the orientation session for parents, fully expecting to be bored. Many times before I had been to such sessions. I was in for a surprise. The coach, who donated hundreds of hours each year to this community service, stood up and proceeded to blister us parents. He said, "I am disgusted with you parents who never come to the games, who are too busy to come. I hope I see all you parents at the games. These boys are performing for you. They may never say it, but they are playing to please you as much as for themselves. Don't disappoint them by not being there to see them perform, win or lose."

Unlike most of the other boys where I grew up, I never learned how to fish and hunt. My father never taught me these things because he himself never learned them from his father. However, my father was a movie buff and football fanatic. He took the whole family to the movies two or three times a week when I was small. To this day I can wax poetic about the movies, and the great football players, of the 40s and 50s. And to this day the first thing my dad and I do when we get together is go see a movie, while on the way to the theater we catch up on all the latest sports news on our favorite teams. It doesn't matter whether the shared activity is camping, fishing, sports or tiddlywinks, as long as parents and children develop some common interests and activities so they build their history and family traditions together.

Often our children will lead the way in developing the family history, as long as we are willing to support their interests. One of my sons at age three became obsessed with trains, or as he called them, choo-choos. He lived to see trains. All he talked about was trains. I figured out the time that a fancy, fast passenger train regularly passed a particular intersection about ten miles from our home out in the country. On a certain day I would take off work early, grab my little son and together we would drive to this wonderful intersection. We parked the car, sat on the hood and waited patiently for the train. At first I asked myself, "What is a grown man, with a Ph.D. after his name, doing sitting in the middle of nowhere in mid-afternoon, waiting to wave at the choo-choo man?" The answer was obvious: I was doing it so my son and I could develop family history together. Well, not entirely. I like choo-choos too.

Second Principle: Good Parenting Is Based on the Healthiness of the Mother-Father Relationship

When the mother and father are in the process of developing a good relationship, the odds are greatly increased that their children's development will benefit as well. There are exceptions to this general rule. I have seen healthy children come out of dysfunctional families and I have seen neurotic children come from healthy families. But these exceptions have been very few in number. Healthy kids, generally speaking, grow out of healthy marriages, which is not surprising considering that the principles for healthy marriages and healthy parenting are similar and complementary. It's often been said that "parents who are happy together have happy children." True, but this needs clarification. It's not always possible to be happy together. No one escapes life's problems and tragedies, large and small. A more accurate statement would be that happy children come from families where the parent(s) are growing up together, problem-solving together, actively nourishing each other's spiritual, personal growth through hard times and good times.

In developing good relationships with others there is a fascinating paradox; namely, *that our greatest personal strength can also be our greatest personal weakness.* This is generally true of most people. For example, I am very effective at researching my position and then verbally presenting my conclusions in a logical and forceful way. I am a strong-willed person who can often persuade others to do it "my way." I am a "doer" who makes things happen. But this also means that at times I can be an opinionated so-and-so who runs over the views of others. I can often persuade and motivate people to do as I wish them to do. I can also suffocate them and turn them away from me without even knowing what happened. My strength, alas, is also my weakness.

This paradox is readily observable in parent-child relationships. The mother, for example, who adores nurturing and giving comfort to her child is running certain risks. She may nurture unwisely and not know it. Does she comfort her child immediately when he runs home crying after a conflict with the neighbor child, even if the conflict was the fault of her own child? Is she unwittingly teaching her child that he can deal with relationship problems by making excuses and always blaming the other? Is her strength also her weakness? Or, the father, whose strength is that he sees clearly when his son needs firm discipline for violation of family rules. He acts swiftly and decisively in such matters. He may, however, become so effective in such matters that he forgets to pay attention to his boy for the many positive things he does. The father unwittingly falls into negatively scanning his son and ends up alienating the boy he loves. The father's strength is also his weakness.

Learning when *not* to use our strengths is as important as learning when to apply them. This is especially true for parents who have developed great interpersonal skills in their work and then apply them at home on the belief (often mistaken) that what works at the office will work as well at home. The parent, for example, who gives great pep talks to his staff of salesmen at work and is credited as an inspirational leader may find his motivational seminars falling on deaf ears at home. Children, especially teens, have a great capacity for shutting off parental preaching: "Well, Dad's on lecture #31-A again today; time to shut down ears."

It is generally true that most people have one personality tendency that is the major block to their own personal, spiritual growth. Often, this "thing" is something we like about ourselves. We don't want to give up this thing to even the slightest degree. This may be our beloved self-righteousness (our conviction we're always right when it counts), or our resentments toward authority which perhaps lead us to drink too much, or our procrastination in meeting our obligations to others, or any number of other traits that engender stubborn *self-pride*. This trait, which we often see as a strength, is the block to our developing good, intimate relationships with others. People who sincerely wish to grow up must honestly search out their major obstacle to growth. By then dealing with this major obstacle head-on, major improvement in our character becomes a real possibility.

Effective parenting requires that each mate be on the alert for those tendencies which are interfering with healthy relationships with the children. In healthy marriages the two partners are each other's best critics. Each has been granted implicit permission by the other to offer corrective feedback to the other, and to do this without fear of retaliative fighting, or sulking, by the other. Simply providing unconditional support for one's mate is a disservice to the other's spiritual growth. This is rationalized as "true love," but it is more often done out of fear than love. We all need corrective feedback. Wise couples seek correction from each other just as successful companies seek corrective feedback from their customers. As the two partners help each other to grow up spiritually they create the supportive, growth-oriented home environment requisite for their children's healthiness.

Third Principle: The Importance of Consistency

Consistency is relative, or rather it should be. A rigid application of family rules is better than no rules at all, but not by much. Here we are speaking not of rigidity, but of a reasonable predictability in how parents respond to their child. All children need structure and a degree of predictability in their lives. It is the parents' job to provide these things. Clearly, this is harder for some parents to do than others, and some children need more structure than others. Parents who lack self-discipline themselves will be hard put to discipline their own children effectively. And parents who are set in their ways will find it hard to be flexible when flexibility is needed.

One of the most common problems of families seeking counseling is a wholesale breakdown in consistency between the two parents. Mom says and does one thing; Dad says and does another. Usually one parent sees the other as too "soft" and permissive while the other sees the first parent as being too "hard" and rigid. The parents are projecting their own, unresolved "power struggle" onto the kids.The kids are keenly aware of these inconsistencies, and early on learn to manipulate Mom and Dad by playing one against the other. The parents are unwittingly teaching their children to be manipulative in their relationships with others.

Often these same parents are not consistent within themselves. Or, one may be totally rigid in how he treats the children. These days, however, it is far more common to see inconsistency, rather than rigidity, in parents. One of the more destructive features in child-rearing occurs when one parent develops the habit of contradicting his spouse's orders in front of the child. The countermand is just as destructive when it occurs behind the back of the spouse. When partners disagree they should, whenever possible, retire to a private room to discuss the matter, or if they need to yell at each other, do so, but not in front of the child. Children are keen students of their parents' behavior tendencies and are likely to latch on to any chink in the parents' armor. This is even more of a problem in today's mixed re-marriages, where the child is dealing with one or two stepparents, new siblings, new grandparents, etc. Parents should strive to present a unified front to their children so the kids can see the parents working together as a team. This gives security and predictability to the child's world, and he respects and needs this even when the parents' decision goes against his own desires.

This point is especially critical when dealing with a difficult child. Nearly every family with two or more children has at least one child who is especially hard to handle. This child may be unusually strong-willed, or an inveterate procrastinator ("lazy"), or he may have a remarkable problem such as a learning disability, medical disability, or whatever. Children with unusual problems or tendencies put stress on parents and sometimes create a breakdown in consistency between otherwise capable parents. When confronted with a child with unusual problems, it is easy for one parent to become overly permissive with that child out of a desire to compensate him for his many hurts. The other parent may react by insisting on more firmness in dealing with the problem child so as not to spoil him. The "inconsistency trap" has now been set and both parents must work hard not to fall into it, thereby worsening the problems of the child. This is where the principles of fair fighting and giving the spouse the benefit of the doubt come into full play. Otherwise, assuming the worst about the other's motives and falling into negative scanning are likely to occur and poison the parent partnership.

This is also where the concept of "relative competencies" can be dangerous if not used wisely. Some families handle these conflicts by one partner abdicating all influence to the other partner where the hard-to-handle child is concerned. This, of course, is one way to stop the fighting between parents. Usually, the abdicator is the father and the "winner" is the mother. Sometimes the abdication is to ease the marital conflict, but sometimes it's a handy excuse for the father to neglect the time-draining child so he can focus on his other interests. I have seen men who were commanding and successful in their careers totally abdicate all child-rearing decisions to their wives. These men were later aghast at the results, but it was hard to feel sympathy for them. It is not by accident that each child has both a mother and a father. A single parent can do a good job if all the circumstances are right, but there is nothing to compare with the effectiveness of a mother and a father working together as a team.

There is one important qualifier to the notion that parents should do their fighting (pardon me, "discussing") in private where conflicts over children are concerned. If the parents have reached the point where they can reliably "fight fairly," then this can and probably should occur before the children. This can be great modeling for the kids. They actually get to see two adults acting responsibly! Just think of the novelty of it – a child witnessing his beloved parents fighting fairly and solving difficult problems together with fairness and graciousness for all. Perhaps, even with a sense of humor thrown in for good measure. Imagine the long-range effects for the child in his own relationships when he grows up in a home where the two parents are mature enough to model for him the principles of effective problem-solving. However, if the parents have not reached this point, everyone is better off if they resolve their conflicts in private as much as possible.

Fourth Principle: The Importance of Touching, Again

There is no greater way to foster a child's spiritual and personal growth than to daily search for ways to stroke his efforts to attain competency, and there is no better way to reward a child than to touch him, hold him, hug him, stroke his hair, squeeze him. A smile, a wink, a victory sign, these are strokes too. Physical contact and associated non-verbal gestures are powerful supports for our children. In many ways these things have a far more lasting effect on our child's development than the words we say as parents. How many of us can remember actual words or statements said to us by our parents when we were young? Some of us are lucky enough to remember a few words of wisdom spoken to us by our parents. All of us, however, remember the demeanor and attitude of our parents toward us. We all remember if and when we *felt* loved and accepted, or rejected. As parents we rarely appreciate the power of our non-verbal signals to our children.

When our daughter was in the sixth grade, she had to give her first speech in public at a school assembly for parents. Several students went before her and they all did well with their short speeches. As each one passed the test, I saw my daughter becoming worried. She was growing afraid she wouldn't do well. The lines of her mouth began to droop down in a classic mimicking of the mask of tragedy. I tried to catch her eye, but she wouldn't look up. Suddenly I saw her whole countenance brighten. She stood up straight and smiled, and it was clear that her spirits had suddenly soared. I knew what had happened. She had caught my wife's eye. Instantly, I looked into my wife's face. She was beaming her beautiful smile to our daughter, who then proceeded to give her speech successfully. No nagging words. No pep talks. No lectures. A smile did it all.

One of the greatest catchphrases to come out of popular psychology in the last two decades is "try to catch kids in the act of doing something good so you can stroke them." This is simple, great wisdom. This is what great parents have always done, though often without thinking about it. Make this into a habit and you have at your disposal an incredibly powerful force for good in human relationships.

Two qualifiers are required for this principle. First, parents who have fallen into negative scanning will often protest they can find little or nothing in their child's behavior that's good and deserving of stroking. In a sense they speak the truth, for the poison of negative scanning is that it blinds us to the positive aspects of the other. We are so focused on the negatives of the other we no longer see his positive actions. We expect that it's only a matter of time before he messes up. The child senses our negative expectancy of him and this elicits from him his worst response. He unwittingly fulfills our negative prophecy for him. Parents who have fallen into negative scanning become capable of stroking their child only by a supreme act of true love. They must choose to "let go" of their acquired prejudices toward their own child so they can once again see his positive features. To change the child they must first change something about themselves, and this something involves giving up their own prejudice as they put their child's needs above their own. This is hard to do, but this is true love (this was the point of the parable of the prodigal son).

Second, some parents buy the idea of catching their child doing good, but with the proviso that the child's action must be perfect, or exactly what the parent expects, before it's worthy of being stroked. Such perfectionists always believe they are acting in the child's best interests by setting high standards for her. There's nothing wrong with high standards, but the child often needs a lot of support along the way to meet them. Some children, by virtue of their personality temperaments, need more support than others. Rule of thumb: it's impossible to stroke your child too much, so do it every chance you get.

Fifth Principle: To Discipline Is to Teach

Discipline is derived from a Greek word that means "to teach," and that is precisely what good, balanced discipline does. When implemented wisely, discipline is love in action. For children cannot survive by strokes alone. As important as strokes are, all children need corrective feedback if they are to grow spiritually and personally. The natural self-centeredness of the child, no matter how adorable he is otherwise, leads him into conflict with other people. We can teach him how to deal better with these painful situations (to which he has contributed), or we can choose to avoid discipline and thus lead him to believe that he is always in the right and that the world owes him a sacrosanct place in the eyes of others. Overly permissive parents practice a subtle, unwitting form of child abuse, for they fail to teach their child the most elementary lesson in human relationships – that the child and his needs are *not* the center of the cosmos. These children are the unfortunate victims of parents who themselves are selfish in that they want to enjoy the good side of parenting, the stroking and supportive part, but refuse to do the hard part – learning how to discipline wisely.

I see *far* more children today who are victims of excessive permissiveness – the classic "spoiled brat" syndrome – than children who are victims of physical abuse. These pathetic kids have greatly increased in numbers in recent years. They mainly come from two-career families where both Mom and Dad are heavily involved with their careers. These parents are often too tired from work, or too afraid, to discipline their child. Afraid, because they spend so little time with their child that when they are with him the last thing they want is a negative confrontation. They bend over backwards to make everything positive. The child, being a child, takes advantage of the parents' indulgences and lack of consequences for misbehavior. He pushes the parents, in part to get a response from them that shows they value him enough to discipline him. The parent grows resentful toward the continued misbehavior and eventually "blows up" at the child out of growing frustration at being pushed around by the "ungrateful" child. Negative scanning then sets in, and parent and child are driven farther apart.

There is no magical formula in applying discipline. There is no magical balance between being too firm versus being all-accepting. Each parent, each child and each set of circumstances are too different to allow one, preestablished procedure to cover all bases. There are, however, a few basic principles that if used as guideposts along the way can be very useful to parents.

- First, discipline is effective to the degree that the parent has become good at positive scanning and stroking his child, and does these things on a highly frequent basis. When the child knows he is valued by the parent he is much more likely to respond favorably to the parent's disciplinary actions. The higher we value the person disciplining us, the more motivated we are to please that person. Almost any discipline method will work as long as the relationship between the parent and child is good. Hardly any method will work if the relationship has gone sour. The *quality of the relationship* is the pivotal issue, and this is dependent on all the principles discussed above.
- Second, all effective discipline involves the application of negative conse-

quences to misconduct. This is true for all ages. Parents who are good at discipline know how, when and where to apply consequences. Nearly all consequences are variations of "Grandma's Rule" (you can have your apple pie *only after* you eat your green beans). Some consequences are intended to be wholly noxious, such as spanking a child's hand when she reaches for a hot iron. Others are designed to teach delay of gratification and the idea of earning one's rewards by good effort. Some consequences occur naturally but can be put to good use by the parents. For example, the child who talks cattily about her friends behind their backs may wake up to discover she's lost her best friend. This was an inevitable, natural consequence to engaging in backstabbing gossip. The parent should allow the child to experience some of the pain of her loss before stepping in to redress the situation. Some parents have a knack for knowing how to handle and apply consequences effectively, whereas other parents are very clumsy or inconsistent or rigid in their application. There are courses available on "behavior modification" in all good-sized towns and cities, and these courses can be very helpful to parents as they learn how to apply consequences wisely.

- Third, the most common mistake in discipline is to apply consequences in an inconsistent manner. The second most common mistake is to overdo the consequence, and this leads to what I call the *punishment trap*. A teen, for example, comes home almost every night past her curfew. The parent warns and admonishes her to get home on time, but the violations continue. With each passing night the parent grows more frustrated and feels more ineffectual. Finally, one night he blows up, yells at his recalcitrant teen and tells her she is now "grounded" for a month. He's going to teach her a lesson once and for all. But will he, or has he overdone the consequence? For now he must be his daughter's jailer for a full month. Resentments between parent and child are likely to grow, and what is he to do the next time she breaks curfew – ground her for three months? This is a classic punishment trap. He would have been more effective if he had intervened much earlier in his daughter's sequence of curfew violations with a one, two or three nights' grounding. When parents don't act early enough in the chain of misconduct (and their attempts to nag kids into being good then fail), they often overreact out of frustration. Application of consequences works best when they are swift and sure and then over with as soon as possible so the parent can more readily return to a positive relationship, with grudges set aside.

- Fourth, there is a considerable body of research indicating that discipline works best when applied consequences are combined with *reasoning* with the child. That is, the parent explains his reasons for the disciplinary act. As children become teens, it is wise to limit the number of rules and let the teenager have some voice in presetting the rules and the consequences for misconduct. It is up to the parents, however, to enforce the agreed-upon consequences. Some well-meaning parents become readily confused on these issues. They allow the child to renegotiate each consequence as each infraction occurs. This is an open invitation to the child to manipulate the parents right and left. Parents then develop feelings of ineffectualness, which is a breeding ground for grudges to develop. Consequences can be renegotiated and reasoning encouraged at a later, safer time, when emotions have calmed down and the risk of teaching manipulation has subsided. Regular family council meetings are often the best forum for such discussions. But renegotiations should never occur in the heat of a confrontation.

In making this point, though, I do not wish to create the impression that telling your child to "do this because I say so" is necessarily bad. Occasionally doing this has some merit. There is value in teaching a child that obedience to higher authority contains its own virtue. However, children will learn even more about the benefits of wise discipline if the reasons for same are explained to them at the most appropriate time.

- Fifth, the most effective disciplinary method over time (also the best method by far for teaching morals and values to your child) is via *modeling*. What the parent models in his everyday actions and attitudes will have the most lasting impact on the developing child. On this point, too, there is a considerable body of supportive research evidence. This is why the parent who comes home every weekend blitzed on alcohol from "happy hour" may have much difficulty trying to convince his son to stop experimenting with marijuana. Similarly, the parent who at home often expresses his mistrust of the motives of his business associates should not be surprised to learn that his own children "instinctively" assume the worst about their friends' and teachers' motives. Parental modeling is powerful, long-lasting stuff, and the process often occurs at a subconscious level. We are often into our thirties before we begin to realize how much we have taken on the attitudes and tendencies of our own parents. And children correctly place more emphasis on the actions and attitudes of their parents than on their parents' words. It is proven that a parent's actions speak much, much louder than his words.

Sixth Principle: The Usefulness of Family Councils

The "family council meeting" is an old notion now being revived by increasing numbers of families. On some regular basis the whole family convenes to discuss individual goals, family goals, current problems and anticipated problems. These meetings may be short or long, once per day, once per week or once per month. The meetings may occur in a car while on a trip, or around the dinner table, or whatever suits the family. Each family has its own version, but the basic idea is to create a forum in which all family members contribute to problem-solving and decision-making in a non-emotionally loaded atmosphere. When the format is fully utilized, it teaches children how to make decisions that take into account others' needs as well as their own. The best benefit for children is not that they participate in decisions, which they do, but that they observe their parents solving problems together as a team.

A family council, however, should not be a true democracy of one man, one vote. Sometimes this democratic principle can be utilized, but at other times it cannot, depending on circumstances. It is nonsense to grant a five-year old equal voting power with a parent on many kinds of important family decisions. The parents are the heads of the family, and it is up to them to maintain the integral structure of the family by using their greater authority responsibly. Parents who gravitate to the true democracy ideal are too often children themselves seeking a way out of parental responsibility.

During the 60s and 70s the democratic ideal as the basis for family life was a hot item in popular psychology. Courses were established all over the country to teach "parental effectiveness"; and some useful communication techniques were taught. Unfortunately, these approaches also harmed many families mainly due to misapplication of the democratic ideal. The notion was espoused that each member of the family, even the smallest of children, should have equal rights and all family decisions should be on the basis of one person, one vote. Where conflicts arose, the use of certain negotiation methods would resolve the problems. These concepts failed entirely to take into account the basic fact of *differing developmental levels* of children. A child at age 4 is clearly not operating at the same cognitive, social and intellectual level of a 12-year-old or the parents. Nevertheless, the 60s notion of "participatory democracy" was often applied to family decision-making. Individual and personality differences among family members were deemed irrelevant, for the same ideology must apply to all equally. All too often the result was families where the child was inadvertently taught to be a master manipulator of others and where the child grew up too fast for his own good.[96] I have seen too many such "modern" families where the parents have abdicated their parental responsibilities in the name of "allowing the child to make his own decisions." It is one thing to encourage the child to participate in decision-making. It is quite another to allow an immature child to hold sway on decisions that have great potential for harm to himself and others. This is another area where ideas from the 60s were poorly thought out and then misapplied, resulting in more harm than good.

The family council idea, when applied with common sense and concern for the differing personalities and maturity levels of family members, can be a boon to the quality of family life. Most importantly, it provides a forum in which parents can model for their children the principles of fair fighting and effective problem-solving.

Seventh Principle: Teaching Spiritual Ideals

The saddest feature of the majority of today's youth is that they have little or no idealism to inspire them. Most are concerned only with making it in the everyday workplace. They have few romantic ideals as did students of the past; these have been decimated by the wreckage of human relationships all around them. Only a minority have religious ideals. Few can become serious about the old humanistic ideals, which were the bread and butter of past generations of students. Today's students are a chilling reflection of their society, especially the yawning values vacuum which has come about in the U.S. over the past 25 years. We have reared a generation of students who have little or nothing that can call them beyond the normal adolescent preoccupation with self. They are well prepared for entry into a world where self-obsession and materialism reign as the everyday normative values.

Our children are being cheated of the adventure of exploring new ideals, questioning old ideals, taking ideals, values and morals seriously. Worst of all, they are poorly prepared to deal with the complexities and obligations of human relationships. Most are nice, rather sweet kids, but without a clue as to what makes a whole person and a good life. Their one outstanding value, as Allan Bloom aptly pointed out, is that they are tolerant.[97] They are the end products of modern humanism – they are tolerant of everything and stand for little. They are the pure products of their parents. They stand waiting to join in the pursuit of material goods with little else to occupy their thoughts and feelings in the meantime. They are a generation of incipient Willy Lomans (*Death of a Salesman*), each able to define himself only through his job.

The more thoughtful of the young know that something is very wrong. They sense the great vacuum, the big hole in their lives, but have no additional sense about where to turn to try to complete their incomplete selves, which would allow them to connect, truly connect, with other human beings. Their need for a spiritual ideal is palpable.

The healthiest families I've seen manage to give their children an ideal to aspire to and live by. This is perhaps the greatest gift we give our children. This ideal is not necessarily couched in formal or systematic terms. It may or may not find expression in a dogma or doctrine. It may or may not find expression in a church. The parents may or may not talk about it a lot. Somehow, but mainly through modeling, they communicate to their children an idealism about life and people that pulls and stretches the growing child to a point outside himself. Their children are tender-hearted and compassionate and yet strong in the true sense of strength. They are the most fortunate of children.

Review

Imagine a child growing up in a home where the parents like each other and nourish each other's spiritual growth through hard times as well as good times. In this home the parents often choose to put time with their child as their first priority. This child rediscovers every day, through his parents' actions, how valued he is in their eyes. These parents provide a reasonably consistent structure for the child to function in, and they often apply this structure with a sense of humor. Every day they show the child affection. They touch and stroke him. But, marvelously, they do not indulge their child; they practice the five principles of effective discipline. They model how to solve problems for their child via family councils. And, they teach their child there is more to life than pursuing self and material goals. They point him to higher ideals and values, and they do this mainly through the modeling they themselves provide in their daily interactions with each other and with other people.

Imagine, if you will, how healthy this child will be as an adult. He will enjoy good relationships with others and deal well with life's many adversities. He will be well equipped to start his own family and pass these blessings on to the next generation.

Our current time of spiritual and idealistic lethargy will not last much longer. The pressures are building to create a *Zeitgeist* out of which will emerge a new ethic. It has always been true that man cannot live by bread alone. If this new ethic combines the best of the old fashioned values with the best of the new knowledge about human relationships, our children can look forward to far better conditions in which to rear their own children.

Summary

Marriages and families bring out the best and worst in individuals. The key is to maximize the best aspects and to use the worst as growing blocks – not stumbling blocks.

It's easy to deal with the positive elements of ourselves. It's important to deal with the negative – that is, face the pain for what it is and work through the problems, instead of ignoring or denying their existence.

With this as a framework, a variety of principles emerge targeting both the issues of a fulfilling marriage and positive parenting.

A solid marriage relationship provides the backbone of a healthy family environment. Five principles which serve as guidelines for couples are:

1) Learn how to love your partner as a means of establishing self-love versus the "love myself first" orientation produced by the 20th Century Myth.
2) Prepare to deal with adversity as a normal aspect of the relationship, and use problem-solving of painful challenges as a way to grow together.

3) Discover the differences between partners, so that particular behaviors and actions can be understood, accepted and enjoyed instead of being judged as "good" or "bad."
4) Become aware of each other's strengths and how one person's abilities may handle a specific situation better than the other's - in lieu of challenging one another in a relationship power struggle.
5) Touch each other consistently, providing the tactile component so important to our sense of well-being and acceptance.

A healthy relationship following these guidelines will lead naturally into positive parenting, which focuses on such fundamentals as:

- Making a quantity and quality time commitment to your children.
- Providing consistency to children so they understand the boundaries without being rigid.
- Nurturing through touching.
- Establishing a healthy disciplinary teaching system, which will cope with the child's natural self-centered tendencies.
- Holding regular family meetings to discuss wants and needs of all members.
- Teaching a spiritual idealism, giving children the incentive to strive for lofty accomplishments.

---

1   One of the most persistent male fantasies, one that helps make pornographers rich, is that of the Amazon woman who ravishes men because she desires a man's body just as men crave a woman's body.

Chapter Seven

The Schools
From Family to Organizational Change

Our public schools can be lastingly reformed only by parents. Reforms generated from within the current system inevitably melt away – back into the system itself. We will see real change only when parents demand that ultimate authority be removed from central administration and returned to parents themselves. Parents working with empowered principals can radically change our schools from within. In this chapter we'll describe one way this can be done.

As noted in chapter four, *as the family goes, so goes the society*. Societal progress is based on progress in the quality of family life, which in turn is based on the personal growth of individuals.

The quality of our schools, however, is a direct reflection of the state of society so that the above dictum is modified to read, *as the society goes, so go its schools*. Our schools are a mirror of both the positives and the negatives of our society. Ultimately, the quality of our schools depends on the strength of the families providing students to the schools. But there is much that schools can do to reinforce and support families that simply isn't being done well now due to deficiencies in our school systems. Many of these deficits are due to applications of the 20th Century Myth into our public schools as can be seen in the centralized control and enforced uniformity inherent in socially-engineered education.

If ever there were an example of benign social engineering, public education should be it. Through our publicly-funded schools a large sector of the population, children ages 6-16, are coerced by government mandate to attend school whether they like it or not! Surely this must be one example of social engineering where the positives outweigh the negatives. Well, perhaps, but there are many, many problems with our public schools.

This particular form of social engineering does not have a long history. Even in Western industrialized nations mandatory, publicly-funded education for all young people did not come into effect until the 19th Century, and in some cases not until the 20th Century. Looking back over this short history, it seems that public education, at least in the U.S., reached an apex of quality and effectiveness in the mid-1900s and has since been deteriorating. In the 1940s, 50s and 60s, a great many communities took great pride in their local schools. Since then we have witnessed the well-publicized decline in SAT and ACT scores among high school students that occurred primarily in the 70s and early 80s. The sudden, dramatic upsurge in incidences of physical violence, tardyism, absenteeism and drop in teacher morale that occurred in the late 60s and 70s has also been well-documented. Rarely, today, does one hear people in a community pointing to their public schools as a source of great pride (with the exception of real estate agents trying to close a house sale). There are still, however, a great many private schools which enjoy great support from the community of families they serve.

Overall, private schools have not experienced the same decline in status as public schools. Most private schools are still seen as providing quality education. Most tend to embody many traditional values, such as demanding that students work hard and be held accountable for all their actions in school. Private schools, though, are perceived as being "for rich folk only," and thus not available to middle-class and poor families. Although this latter perception of private schools is often erroneous, it has helped fuel the popular notion that only the rich can afford good schools for their children, while people of average income must suffer along as best they can with the local public schools. But is it possible to take the features that make private schools successful and apply them to our public schools? We will probe this question many times in this chapter.

For example, both James Coleman and Abigail Thernstrom have documented how much better inner city youths do in Catholic than in public schools. Single-parent black and Hispanic students in inner city Catholic schools perform much better on standardized measures of math and language, and graduate on time at rates far higher than comparable populations in the public schools. Why? Because of school unity and values, say Coleman and Thernstrom. The principal hires the staff who must endorse the school's ideals. Teachers speak with one voice and get to know their students (and vice versa). Students find themselves in a safe, orderly world run by adults, not kids. Teachers push students to excel. And, as Thernstrom notes:

> The demands upon the Catholic school students extend to their relations with others and their spiritual growth. The moral seriousness of these schools stemming from their religious commitment makes them willing to dwell on such values as respect, self-respect and responsibility – topics they touch upon in every class. "We aim to create competent, decent, loving human beings," one teacher explained.
>
> These Catholic schools provide no bilingual education – despite their significant Hispanic population. They don't fret about black teachers for black students; role models come in all colors. And they don't hesitate to separate fast from slow learners. But kids in different tracks learn basically the same material – at a different pace.[98]

The U.S. has been wracked by one negative report after another on the condition of the nation's public schools. There is a growing consensus that today's young people are less well-educated than the previous generation. Educational standards in the public schools have slipped, and for the first time in national history we've produced a generation of people more ignorant and less skilled than previous generations. There are three main reasons why public schools are not doing the job expected of them: centralized authority, expanded functions, and the failure to teach values and morals effectively.

Public schools, first of all, suffer from exactly the same problems that afflict all government bureaucracies. Public schools are government bureaucracies. They are funded by the taxpayers and operate as a virtual monopoly (only 10% of U.S. children attend private schools). Especially in urban areas, public schools are run through central offices with centralized patterns of authority that usually contain many layers of bureaucracy. Central administrators readily confuse standardization of service with quality of service. They use centralized purchasing techniques to purchase uniform educational materials. These central offices require that the same curriculum, same materials and same standards be implemented on a uniform basis throughout their school systems. These same standards, often mandated by the federal government, are implemented as much as possible on a national basis. And as the role and power of the federal government has increased dramatically since the 60s, the public schools have become even more entangled in bureaucratic rules and regulations. The goal of much of this increased standardization was worthy, namely, to eliminate all forms of discrimination. A chief effect, however, has been to nullify innovation and create a mediocre level of service for all. Controversy is spiked and everything must hew to a "party line." Teaching methods are inevitably affected once texts are increasingly standardized by state mandate. Public schools used to be thought of as outreaches of local government. Now, many public school administrators think of themselves as controlled more by the federal government than by local government.

These same points are well made by John Chubb and Terry Moe in their long-term study of over 500 American high schools (published by the Brookings Institution). Their report at first seems unremarkable, for they find the same factors reported by numerous other investigators. Namely, that effective schools are characterized by principals who are strong leaders, who in turn foster attitudes of professionalism among teachers, who in turn place high academic standards on students. They report that these factors are found mainly in schools relatively free from centralized authority. Principals, parents and teachers are free to run their own schools. Ineffective schools are run from above by centralized bureaucracies. At this point, however, Chubb and Moe depart from the usual reports that only offer ways to improve the current methods used by schools. They instead go to the heart of the matter. They assert that the only way to reform our public schools is to free them from central administration and instead put accountability back where it belongs – with the parents, principals and teachers of each school. In this chapter we will describe one way this can be done.

The second major factor working against our public schools is that since the 60s they have been required to expand their functions well beyond their original mandate. Now they perform more and more functions previously performed by parents or other agencies. Public schools thus find themselves increasingly required to provide everything from babysitting services to the health, moral and sex education formerly said to be the province of the home. As families have deteriorated, the schools have been asked to perform more and more parental functions. As one black educator notes:

> Education reform involves, not programs and systems, but restoring ourselves, our values. For 20 years and more, we Americans have lazily turned over to government institutions the social and moral decisions we should have the courage to make for ourselves. Education is one glaring — and negative — example of the trend. Our assumption: With all their expertise, federal, state and local governments can educate our children better than we can.
>
> Wanna bet?[99]

> Craig Bowman

It's a wonder that public schools do as well as they do considering the constraints under which they work. It is characteristic of the 20th Century Myth that whenever social problems arise or when our attempts at social engineering cause unexpected problems, we turn to even more social engineering for solutions.

Public schools *were* our best examples of social engineering that worked and *were* sources of community pride. But then they became everyone's favorite resource for solving social problems. Not surprisingly, they don't work nearly as well as they did in the past. We want our schools to be mom, dad, priest, psychologist, and policeman, as well as teacher. And then we blame them for failing at an impossible mission. In a recent study of some of Denver's housing projects, it was found that nearly 85% of young people who should have been on track to receive diplomas had instead dropped out or flunked out of high school. In one sample only 21 of 131 potential graduates of the class of 1990 graduated. Two-thirds of these homes were headed by single mothers and virtually all were poor. High rates of dysfunctional families, however, are not confined to low-income project areas. Dysfunctional families are found in all strata of society and increasingly the children they send to school lack the self-discipline, work ethic, and regard for education required for the schools to do their job of education. A teacher who works with the above project kids puts it this way: "When you work with a kid for nine months, it's like giving birth. Then something happens and the kid decides to drop out. It really is depressing when you see all that potential go to waste. It's really painful."[100] And, Craig Bowman again goes to the heart of the matter:

> Bring education back into your home and stop this '60s myth that 100% of learning takes place at school. Yes, it's inconvenient to turn the TV channel from Roseanne to The Civil War, or to turn it off altogether on a school night. It's as painful, too, to enforce a study time every school night as it is to wean that 16-year-old off cheap, poorly written love novelettes and onto some difficult to read classics.
>
> That brave, single black mother – I'll call her Sojourner Truth for her softspoken courage – comes to mind who wouldn't let her sophomore son wear earrings, didn't have a great deal to spend on fancy clothes. But rather than save and buy a car when he turned 16, she bought him a computer and insisted he enroll in advanced classes in computer, English, history and science.[101]

This brings us to the third major reason why our schools are failing our children – the failure to teach sound values. All schools and all teachers teach morals and values all day long. Schools used to be explicit on these matters. Prior to the 1960s, they stated plainly what they believed in, what they stood for, and how they were going to implement their values, morals and standards on an everyday basis. Schools, of course, still model values and standards, but they live a lie, for they try to insist that they do not impose values on students, that all value notions are treated the same, with equal respect, and that it is up to each student to choose the morals that best suit him. Schools cannot avoid the fact, however, that students soak up the implied values and morals represented by the school in its attitudes and acts, no matter how muddily expressed they may be.

And what are these values and morals? In the main, they are the ragtag end products of modern humanism, popular psychology and popular sociology, i.e., the spinoffs of the 20th Century Myth that inevitably reinforce a self-centered view of the world. As one professor of adolescent psychiatry puts it, young people today "face a garbage culture with no values to latch on to, and so they're preoccupied with themselves."[102]

Not all modern schools, though, are so ambivalent about the teaching of morals. Earlier we noted Thernstrom's study of inner city parochial schools' success with disadvantaged youth. She attributes much of their success to the "...moral seriousness of these schools stemming from their religious commitment [which] makes them willing to dwell on such values as respect, self-respect and responsibility – topics they touch upon in every class." And these are the schools, though inexpensively run, that the data overwhelmingly indicate do a better job of educating young people from disadvantaged homes.

Prior to the 1960s, public schools also took strong stands on issues of morality and personal values and the teaching of same. But moral relativism, the fountainhead of the 20th Century Myth, ripped this moral base apart in the 60s. Almost overnight, public schools were prohibited from teaching right versus wrong. All values were suddenly relative to the individual. Public schools were exhorted to teach *values clarification* instead of values. Values clarification was, and is, moral relativism run amok. It taught that each person, even small children, should choose freely the values by which to live their lives. Schools were not to take a stand on right versus wrong, since there was no absolute right or absolute wrong. Schools simply were to assist each child to clarify the particular values of his choosing. This approach produces children (and adults) who are obsessed with their personal *rights* (what's the value in it for me?), but who have a diminished sense of their *responsibilities* to others.

Values clarification was so obviously morally bankrupt that it passed from the scene, but it lives on in many guises in today's schools. Teachers are still afraid to take stands. They still say, "it is not for me to tell you what values to live by; you must choose for yourself." All values are considered to be relative to the individual or to his subculture. Indeed, many teachers themselves are so much the products of the 20th Century Myth that they have only a vague understanding of what their own values are and where their values came from. Values teaching in today's schools is often a matter of the blind leading the blind. Kids need mentors desperately. But where are their mentors? Their parents are too busy working and their teachers don't know what to believe or what to teach anymore. Such are the products of the 20th Century Myth.

One of the more pernicious aspects of all this is that we have lost the sense of a commonly shared morality. Now it is every person for himself. My values come first, then yours. When communities lose their sense of shared values – the sense of a common public trust – then a deterioration in both manners and morals inevitably follows. Self-centeredness, masked as personal expression or personal preference, both rules the day and ruins the day.

Schools do not have to stand for the mishmash that currently passes for values education. It is true that public schools will always be at a disadvantage in comparison to religious schools on these matters. Religious schools can state boldly that values and morals come from God and that the Divine Source always stands ready to help us to lead a good life, one that serves others as well as ourselves. But public schools, as Thomas Lickona argues in *Educating for Character*, can teach the concept of Natural Law – that there is a universally agreed upon morality that transcends all cultures, all times and all people.[1] They can also teach that this universal morality must be agreed to and acted upon if we are to gain respect for ourselves and show others the respect and love we wish for ourselves. Schools can also teach that this universal morality is required if we are to have a true sense of community wherein each person gives up something of his self-ness every day for the sake of bettering the common good for all. The schools can also teach, if they are intellectually honest, that the values of the universal morality have nearly all been derived, historically, from the traditions of the world's religions. We do our children a great disservice when we fail to teach them these concepts. We leave them with little more than a cynical, self-absorbed materialism to build their lives around.

Lickona's book details dozens of methods used by innovative, courageous teachers around the country to teach morals and values to today's students. He discusses Natural Law, the universal morality, and how it can be taught so that students may see the logic and force of it. He also points out how it can be taught so as *not* to violate our constitutional requirement of separation of state from religion. He then provides teachers and parents with a variety of ways to teach our most basic values and standards effectively.

Parents must demand to know from principals and teachers these things: What values are you going to teach our children? How are you going to teach these values? How can we help? Most parents want their children to be taught good values. Given a voice, they will demand that schools return to an explicit teaching of values, morals, standards, and a sense of the common good. These discussions will be hot and fast, but well worth the trouble, for they will provide the forum to bring teachers and parents back onto common ground where both are explicitly standing for the same basic values. This could be the single best benefit of turning ultimate school control over to neighborhood boards, a proposition discussed later in this chapter. At any rate, it is incumbent that our public schools be put to the test on these issues. They owe it to us and to our children to be explicit on the values and morals they teach. On what basis do they teach these values? How are they going to teach these values? How can we help?

Despite all the handicaps we've placed on them, our schools are one form of social engineering that's salvageable. The degree to which they are salvageable is conditioned on three factors: (a) the condition of our homes and families, (b) the extent to which the federal government is *not* allowed to dictate policies, standards and procedures to schools, and (c) the degree to which higher values in our society eventually replace baser, materialistic values. Schools do not operate in a cultural vacuum. They are a direct expression of the current mores and general state of society. Put bluntly, if our homes and families continue to deteriorate, if the federal government becomes more and more dictatorial toward local schools, and if there is no replacement of materialistic values with higher values, then all we do to improve our public schools will have little or no effect. But if these three factors improve to any degree, then we stand a good chance of reforming and rejuvenating our public schools. The good news is that the knowledge to do this is already in hand.

There are nine basic steps of reform that could be taken by any school district anywhere, anytime. Here's more good news. None of these steps costs more money. This is, as always, a major consideration since it's unlikely that any major source of new funding will be forthcoming for the public schools in the foreseeable future. Also, there is no data to indicate that putting more money into public education produces increases in the quality of educational services. During the 70s and early 80s, a time in which teachers' salaries increased the greatest, student achievement scores declined the greatest. No one can say for sure if this correlation was the product of a cause and effect relationship, but the fact of this correlation is certainly not encouraging. It must also be noted that at private schools, where the quality of education is typically better, teachers are paid considerably less on average than public school teachers. Even teachers at the more successful private schools are usually not paid as well as their counterparts in the public schools. If only it were true that the morass of problems in our public schools could be solved by throwing more money at them! But the reality is that monetary considerations are not the primary determinants of the *quality* of education.

We'll now turn to a discussion of the nine steps which provide a new beginning for public education. These options mainly have to do with reorganizing the lines of authority and accountability in our public schools. *This reorganization extends to public schools many of the benefits enjoyed by the more successful private schools.* Many of these ideas were implemented years ago at Denver Academy, the school I founded in 1972. They have worked remarkably well for many other schools, both public and private, that have tested these ideas. We start with the key figure in any reorganization plan: the school principal.

First, the Principal Is Given the Freedom and Authority To Be in Charge of the School

The most consistent finding in the research comparing effective versus noneffective schools has been termed the "principal factor." The single best predictor of an effective school (versus an ineffective school) can be found in answering this question: how dynamic and influential is the principal? This factor recurs time and again regardless of the socioeconomic class or racial composition of the schools studied. It cuts across all lines.

The distinguishing characteristic of successful principals is that they have a philosophy of education which they communicate effectively to the teachers and support staff of the school. They are able to "sell" their teachers on the desirability of implementing the particular vision of education the principal espouses, for they know how to reward teachers and students for accepting their vision of what education should be. They thereby create an atmosphere of high morale and enthusiasm among teachers and staff. To create an effective school, the staff of the school need a cogent, cohesive picture of what the principal wants them to create. A wise principal involves his or her teachers in every step of the implementation and further development of the school's philosophy and methods.

It is interesting that no particular philosophy of education predominates among the successful principals. There may be some common factors among their various philosophies, but as yet these factors have not been delineated by the research. No one has discovered the "magic formula" for the betterment of all education. The field is wide open for exploration, innovation and much, much more research. The key to effective school programs is not so much the particular philosophy of education espoused by principals as it is their ability to persuade and motivate teachers to adopt and implement their philosophy.

Giving principals authority to run their own schools requires other changes in present conditions. First and foremost, principals must have the authority to hire and fire the teachers in their schools. I can hear the gasps now from those readers who are ardent members of teachers' unions. Hopefully, they will hear me out. We cannot expect principals to develop creative, dynamic schools while at the same time demanding that they accept whatever teachers are assigned to them via the district's central office. That "Catch-22" is precisely the kind of double bind that makes centralized bureaucracies so ineffective. Principals should also be granted the authority to award merit raises to outstanding teachers in their own schools. Principals must have greater control over school budgets than they have now. If we wish to give principals the freedom to develop their own schools, then they must have the responsibility and accountability that goes with that freedom. These are precisely the same freedoms and the same responsibilities enjoyed by headmasters of all good private schools.

There is nothing radical here. This has been tried and proven effective ten thousand times over in the private sector. In good private schools, headmasters are given the authority to run the school in accordance with the stated philosophy and goals of the school. They select, hire, and fire teachers. They are provided with considerably more discretionary power over the school's budget than public school principals. The headmaster of a private school is thus provided with both the freedom and the means by which to accomplish his or her goals. He is then held accountable for his actions. If his efforts do not please the community he serves, he is replaced. He is accountable in the best sense of the word: either he does his job or he is sacked. The boards of trustees of effective private schools, and the communities of families they represent, make every effort to provide headmasters with all the resources they need to accomplish their goals. They, in turn, make sure that their teachers and staff are provided with the resources and encouragement they need to accomplish these same goals. Accountability, true accountability, is built into the system from start to finish. The students are accountable to the teachers, who in turn are accountable to the headmaster, who in turn is accountable to the board of trustees, who in turn represent the community of parents and families paying for all these services.

This form of accountability is very different from that found in government bureaucracies such as public schools. Accountability in public schools usually comes down to filling in endless forms on various important matters so that government auditors will be pleased when they discover file cabinet upon file cabinet full of forms properly filled in. The information on these forms has only a distant relationship to everyday reality. These form-filling-in activities require a lot of time on the part of teachers and staff. An inevitable by-product of this inane practice is that teachers lose valuable time that would be better spent with students. This is one of the most common and justified complaints heard from public school teachers. Putting principals truly in charge of their own schools would institute the same kind of meaningful accountability already enjoyed by the better private schools.

A positive by-product of the above change would be to attract a larger number of dynamic people into the field of education. There is no need to increase administrators' salaries in order to draw a higher proportion of effective persons into public education. This same goal can be accomplished by offering people the opportunity to create and lead their own schools. There are many, many young people who would be drawn to the field of education if they saw it providing opportunities for effective leadership and creativity in an important social institution. Education today attracts a disproportionate number of people who are drawn to it for the safety and security it provides. Public education, once the teacher has obtained tenure – which normally takes only three years – provides a decent salary, decent fringe benefits, short work days, short work years (you can get by working eight to nine months of the year), and job security for life. Not a bad deal, even though the salary is low in comparison to that of many other college graduates. But these are not the kinds of working conditions that attract the more creative and dynamic personalities. We need a higher proportion of such people in the field of education if we are to prosper as a society in the years to come. We can attract more such personalities into education without having to increase salaries dramatically. Other lures can be utilized such as offering valid opportunities for creative, aggressive leadership.

Second, Each Principal Is Accountable to a Local School Board Representing Each School in the Community

School boards, especially in large urban communities, are a farce. They are supposed to represent the community's interests and have the final authority in running all its schools. But our urban areas have become so large, and contain within them so many different, antagonistic interests, that it has become impossible to represent accurately "the community." Most school board members I've met have little or no knowledge of the various schools, internal programs, staff personalities and interests in their districts. The issues they deal with are too complex to be dealt with effectively within the context of the typical school board meeting. School board officials are almost totally dependent on information siphoned and prepared for them by central administrators. There is often considerable distrust between the school board and the teachers and local principals. Further, most school boards no longer take a breath without first checking to see if it's okay with their federal monitors, who are often the actual, final authorities in running the school system. Most urban school boards have become little more than politicized snake pits. (If you are in a good mood, don't attend your local school board meeting; the experience will depress you.) Attendance at school board meetings should be required of all civics classes so students can have a real-life exposure on how not to exercise power over others. The notion that a publicly-elected school board represents the interests of the taxpayers and serves as the final authority in matters of school policy still has validity, but only in small towns and in private schools where it takes the form of a board of trustees. In middle-sized communities and certainly in large urban communities the publicly-elected school board has lost its value, its meaning, and, in many cases, even its authority. Nevertheless, we persist in using this form of "governance."

Our communities would be better served if each public school had its own school board. The members of the board would be publicly elected on a rotating basis and only adult members of the community served by that particular school could be elected to the board. The board members would serve with no pay. This local, community board would have the authority to hire and fire its own principal for its own neighborhood school. A new principal would first have to "sell" this local board on his/her view of what "their" school should be. Once the board and the new principal were in agreement regarding how their school should be run, it would be up to the principal to implement this philosophy on a daily basis. He would be accountable to his local board. If the local board did not like the job being done by the principal they would have the authority to replace him. Those local boards that provided the best possible working conditions for principals would, of course, be the ones to attract the best candidates for the job. One of the main benefits of this approach would be to place the final authority for running the school back into the hands of those people who are most directly impacted – the people who live in the immediate community. This concept is now being experimented with in Chicago as a means to break the stranglehold of central administrators over local schools.

This change would not, and should not, eliminate today's centralized school boards. The central or "supra" school board can still serve useful functions. Certain issues, such as health standards and discrimination issues, cut across all schools in a district and may be better implemented by a central board. The current central boards could also serve as a "court of appeals" to resolve differences that would arise among the local boards. And, the central board should serve as the final authority in approving the total budget plan for the whole district, especially in considering different allocations to the different schools in the district. Its main job would be to see that resources are allocated fairly to the local boards. The central school board would still be a political hot seat, but under this plan the central board would perform functions it should be able to perform effectively, which is certainly not the case today.

By transferring much of the power now held by central school boards over to small, local boards we would go far toward making each public school comparable in governance to the more effective private schools. In a sense, each public school would become its own private school, except it would be open to all the students who lived in that neighborhood. The community served by the school would elect its own delegates who in turn would have the final say on the philosophy and goals for that school. Some people in the neighborhood would not like the particular philosophy adopted, or the principal, or the shape of the building, or whatever. They would have the option of freely moving their children to another school whose philosophy was more congruent with their own. At this point it is important to address a serious question that has probably occurred to every reader. Namely, if we return to and develop true neighborhood schools under local governance, what then happens to the goals and ideals of integrating our public schools across racial boundaries?

Third, all Public Schools Have Open Enrollment with Voluntary Busing Replacing Forced Busing

In our desire to bring about racial integration in urban school districts, we turned to a form of social engineering, forced busing, that resulted, again, in our throwing the baby out with the bathwater. Forced busing broke the bond of the local neighborhood with its own neighborhood school. The sense of community involvement and community support in the local school was torn asunder. Families in urban neighborhoods often do not know, from year to year, where their child will be attending school in the city. The presiding federal judge determines which schools require changes in their racial quotas in a given year. Children are yanked up and moved about the city in order to meet shifting goals of racial quotas designed to achieve racial balance.

The present nine-point proposal emphasizes that *each and every public school should strive to be a magnet school.* Each school would have open enrollment so that any child, within the total school district, could enroll at any school, anywhere in the district. Neighborhood children would always receive first priority for enrollment in their own neighborhood school, but each school would be required to set aside additional spaces open to other children from all over the city. Clearly, no racial discrimination would be tolerated with respect to filling the additional spaces. The present, expensive busing system that was developed for forced busing would be utilized to transport children to schools voluntarily selected by individual families. Forced busing would be put to a well-earned termination. It would live on, however, in the social science classes of the 21st Century as an example of how social engineering, even when done with the very best intentions, often produces more negative than positive results.

We can hope that before the end of the 1990s the emotionalism generated by forced busing will have dissipated enough so that the issue can be dealt with rationally. After twenty years of implementation and billions of dollars spent on it, the idea of forced busing is hard to justify on any data basis.

In the late 60s and early 70s, the concept of forced busing was the hot topic in education. Town meetings were then being held in Denver, my new hometown, so that people could voice their views on forced busing. Not that our views really mattered, since the issue was to be decided by a federal judge anyway. Since we had small children, my wife and I attended a few of those meetings. Only a couple of years before, I had been involved in civil rights protests in some of the Southern states. While participating in marches and sit-ins, I had been spat upon by white on-lookers, hauled off to jail, and called a "white nigger" by some of the white observers to these events. Upon attending town meetings to discuss forced busing in Denver, I had an eerily similar experience, but in a totally different context. It turned out that I was one of the few in the audience to question the advisability of using forced busing as the principal means to achieve integrated schools. My position was that magnet schools would prove, over the long run, to be a more effective way of achieving the goal of integration. Magnet schools, I argued, would provide a setting in which black and white students of similar interests would be drawn together to work toward similar goals. Their interactions with each other would thus be voluntary and essentially on an equal basis. Admittedly, magnet schools would take longer to bring about the desired results of integration, but, I contended, they would be more effective in the long run than the "quick fix" offered by forced busing. Much to my surprise I was shouted down in these meetings, mainly by white parents, with cries of "white racist." It was a shock to be called a white racist, especially in light of my previous experiences in the South. "White nigger" had not been so hard to take; I could even take some pride in being called that. But in one year's time, I went from being called a "white nigger" to being called a "white racist" though my views hadn't changed at all. But then the demand for forced busing led to many strange situations.

Forced busing is social engineering gone awry. It is a case where the best intentions were the motivating force, but all the classic mistakes were made again. Typical of social engineering, the subjects (children in this case) were defined not as individuals, but as members of a racial group (class). The subjects are then forced to associate with each other on the basis of dictated quotas for their racial group. As the composition of the neighborhood schools changes, often due to "white flight" to the suburbs, the composition of the racial quotas is changed from school to school and year to year. In many of our larger cities white flight has become such a dominant factor that the number of white students has changed from a majority to a minority, causing innumerable headaches for federal judges as it becomes more and more difficult to reorganize the racial quotas on a year-by-year basis.

Forced busing now has 20 years of history and billions of dollars poured into it. Nevertheless, it is almost impossible to find reliable data to support the idea that the academic achievement of black students has risen due to the circumstances of forced busing. It is also almost impossible to find any reliable data to support the notion that black and white students benefit socially from being placed together under conditions of coercion. In my experience of dealing with thousands of young people of all races over the past 25 years, I have not been able to detect any noticeable decline in racist attitudes. Forced busing has resulted in improved attitudes for some students. But for each of these there is at least one other student who exhibits an increase in racist attitudes. Forced busing has caused a great deal of mistrust and resentment between black and whites, both parents and children. And self-selection has worked in its predictable way. Those whites who stayed in the city and allowed their children to be bused are in many cases whites who were non-racist to begin with. They and their children did not "need" the experience of forced busing to make them into non-racists. Forced busing is a failure. The sooner we face up to this obvious fact and move on to other means to encourage integration the better off we will be as a society. It is to be hoped that the next method we use to work toward integration will have positive effects on our urban educational systems, rather than contributing to their deterioration.

A principle criticism of the magnet school approach is that some neighborhood schools would be more successful than others. More students would want to enroll in these better schools and fewer would enroll in the weaker schools. Now, that's some criticism! Of course some schools would be better than others. That's the whole idea: to find out what kinds of schools work best in which situations. Over the long run, neighborhoods with less successful schools would implement their own versions of the more successful schools. If they didn't, they would run the risk of seeing their neighborhood school shut down for lack of students. The underlying implication of this criticism actually has to do with the notion that poor and/or minority neighborhoods would not be able to develop their own successful school programs. It is precisely this form of patronizing attitude on the part of "enlightened whites" that holds minorities back as much as anything else.

Actually, the idea suggested here has already been in part accomplished. In New York City, the East Harlem School District, the city's poorest and lowest scoring area, has been turned into a model "schools of choice" so successful that it is increasingly attracting upper- and middle-class students from outside the district to enroll there. This district's 20 buildings contain 49 separate schools with different emphases on music, science, integration of all subjects for students who stay together for several years, and many other options. Parents are free to send their children to any school in the district. One of the chief architects of this innovative program was Seymour Fleigle, a former New York City School Superintendent. Here are some of his comments:

> We made our public schools like private schools. Small, with a philosophic base with something to emphasize as a vision or a dream. You'd be shocked at how many schools don't know where they're going because all the principal's energy is spent on day-to-day administrative hassles. I want for poor kids what kids in private schools already have. Choice without quality and diversity is meaningless – letting parents choose among a dozen mediocre schools is no choice at all. The key to creating diversity is to give schools the autonomy to run themselves and the support for them to create unique programs. I see choice as a natural partner with school-site autonomy. Schools need to be free from many bureaucratic restrictions rather than being made responsible for administrating them. Let's give schools a greater autonomy and I expect the professionals to be responsible for creating schools that work. Parents take part in the accountability. Their choice becomes a very strong accountability piece.[103]

The concept of each public school becoming a magnet school in its own right, accompanied by freedom of parents to send their children to the school of their choice, is working in East Harlem. Note however, this critical point made by Fleigle: "Choice without quality and diversity is meaningless." Many urban school districts now allow some degree of open enrollment. This is offered as a sop to parents demanding freedom of choice for their children. But this freedom of choice is often meaningless because all the schools in the district *are alike*. The "schools of choice" concept will not work unless each school is freed from centralized, standardized administration and allowed to develop its own identity.

By allowing parents free choice of schools, we establish the same form of accountability that exists in the private sector. If a given school cannot generate enough good programs with good teachers, then it withers and dies. Of course, in most cases it wouldn't die at all. If the school were losing enrollment and thus losing its budget allocation, the local board would demand that the principal be replaced and the philosophy modified by the new principal so as to attract more new students. In actuality, fewer neighborhood schools would die as a result of this approach than died because of the combined effects of forced busing and white flight.

Fourth, the Principal and Board, Working Together, Have the Primary Responsibility for Developing the Philosophy of Each School

As previously noted there is no "magic formula" that always leads to quality education. No one knows for sure what constitutes the best possible educational format, especially when we attempt to deal with large numbers of students. When students are known as individuals with their own particular pattern of strengths and weaknesses, it is a little easier to design and apply the educational format best for each. Even at this individual level it is easy to make mistakes. There is a great need to find out the best educational format for different children in differing circumstances. Virtually all public schools now follow the same, uniform curriculum. One result of this increased standardization has been that it is now hard to discern any differences between one public school and another. They all have the same dreary, lock-step curriculum, course offerings and uniform texts. Here again we encounter that icon of the 20th Century Myth – that equality must mean sameness, standardization, identicality. A visitor from another planet looking over this scenario would surmise that we have indeed discovered the magic formula for quality education for all. How else could he explain the fact that we have used government authority to pressure all schools everywhere to adopt the same, standardized approaches, curriculum, and texts? It is amazing when you stop to think of it. Our schools cram everyone through the same program on the assumption that this uniform approach is in everyone's best interests although everyone knows this simply isn't true. Many critics have pointed out that our schools resemble factories with their assembly lines run by a time clock.[104] There is much validity to this criticism. Perhaps this particular approach is best for some students, but we can safely assume it is not the best approach for all students.

The approach recommended here would not only welcome innovation in education, but would demand it. This is important since most educators are by nature a conservative lot who are more comfortable sticking with what they already know. They can be shaken out of their inertia only by building incentives into the system that reward successful innovations.

It could be exciting. It could result in an extensive rejuvenation of our public school system. Imagine for a moment, local community boards working with principals to develop the concept of what *their* school is going to be. Imagine the creative tension in that room! It would be valuable to see some schools adopt the *Padeia* proposal of Mortimer Adler. Let's see under what conditions that fascinating concept works well, and where it does not work so well. Some schools might want to stress an experiential approach, or more of a "back to basics" approach, or more of a vocational orientation, or some might decide to emphasize a particular subject matter (music, the arts, science, computers, etc.).

The high school level especially lends itself to this form of experimentation with alternative educational formats. This is not a new concept. In the beginning decades of this century, nearly every large urban school district established specialized magnet schools open to students from all over the city. The experiment, all in all, was going well until it was sacked by the rush to standardize (equalize) all schools.

Elementary schools may not lend themselves to quite as much variation in format, but then we don't really know, do we? Among private schools one sees many variations on the traditional elementary school format. All of these variations seem to have their strong as well as weak points and are certainly worthy of greater study. And, as noted earlier, it is incumbent on the board and the principal to make their values curriculum explicit so that parents, teachers and students all know the morals and standards to be implemented by the school.

In the 80s the two most penetrating critics of American education were Mortimer Adler and Allen Bloom. Both pointed out something with which most people now agree. Namely, that our schools are no longer doing an effective job of teaching students the common values and historical roots of our culture, and for that matter, of world culture in general. Many students show an appalling ignorance of the basic facts of their own existence. It is not merely that they cannot read or write well, or do basic math well; that is bad enough. But many of them demonstrate great ignorance of the history of their own country and of the values and principles on which their country was founded. Most show no understanding of the historical roots of Western civilization, much less world civilization.

It is a strange irony that over the past 25 years, a time in which our schools have become increasingly standardized by government mandate, our children have demonstrated an appalling decline in basic, common knowledge of their own culture. *Standardizing the curriculum via central authority fails even where it should be strongest – in producing a common set of facts and skills known to all students.* This is a critical problem to be addressed by each local school board and its principal. How are they going to deal with this issue? Perhaps the central or "supra" board would have to mandate that certain courses be taught in all schools, at least in all elementary schools. But it is hoped that central boards would not be allowed to go too far in that direction. The collective wisdom of local boards, working with effective principals, is a far more potent force to move our children from their current levels of cultural illiteracy to the higher levels of literacy we desire for them. Clearly, the use of highly centralized administration and standardization of curriculum have failed to bring this about. It appears that they have, in fact, made the situation worse. It is unlikely we will make this problem worse yet by putting authority back into the hands of the people. Some people worry about such an idea since they are concerned that a loss of standardization would lead to chaos. With each school going its own way, they worry that some students would be shortchanged on some subjects, depending on the particular approach of that school. Their underlying fear is that by minimizing standardization schools would become even more unequal in product than they are now.

These are legitimate concerns, though I do not believe they are nearly as serious as they may appear to be.

- First, many students are already being short-changed on many subjects by the present system.
- Second, we already know that the present system is doing a poor job of teaching our young people not only the educational tools they need but the basic facts of their own culture.
- Third, it is unlikely that the proposed approach would generate as much diversity as some of us might wish for. The fact is that most educators have a "herd mentality" and are reluctant to stray too far from what they already know.
- Fourth, it is the people themselves who are the most concerned about the lack of training in the basics. They are far more concerned about this issue than most educators. By turning more control back to the people in the local community, it is likely that one of the first changes made would be to place more emphasis on the basic foundations of education. In Denver, as in many other cities, the central school board allowed an elementary school to be redesigned as a "fundamentals" school. This "back to basics" school has proven very successful and very popular. It always has a long line of parents trying to get their children enrolled. Despite its success, the central school board has failed to recognize the validity of parental demand by failing to allow more such schools to be formed. If the people have their way, it is a sure bet that schools emphasizing the "basics" will become more prevalent than they are today.
- Fifth, this proposed approach offers parents who cannot afford private schools something which they do not have today: *choice*. If the parents disagreed with their own school's philosophy or if they were unhappy with the choice of subjects for their child in the coming year, they would have the option of placing their child in another school with a program more congruent with their own beliefs and values. The ultimate authority for *directing* each child's education would be returned to those who should always have this authority: the parents of the child. At the present time, families who cannot afford private schools have no choice. They are stuck with the uniformity and mediocrity of public schools.

Fifth, Teacher Tenure Is Abolished

These proposed changes in our public educational system would work best if we were to abolish teacher tenure. Presently, after a new teacher has worked for two or three years, he or she is granted tenure. For all practical purposes tenure guarantees lifetime job security for the overwhelming majority of teachers. While there may be some legitimate arguments for continuance of tenure at the university level, it is difficult to find one convincing argument for continuing tenure at the public school level. To people outside of education, it has always seemed strange that teachers should be the beneficiaries of lifetime job security when the same is not true for most other persons. Only other government employees in civil service enjoy the sort of lifetime job guarantees extended to public school teachers. Perhaps it is only a coincidence that those branches of government service that utilize job tenure also have the lowest employee morale and productivity. The abolition of teacher tenure could lead to higher morale and, for sure, higher productivity. It might even lead to a badly needed increase in the status of the teaching profession, since it is difficult for most other people to respect those whose work performance is unrelated to their continued employment.

Teacher tenure stands in the way of educational reform. Continuance of tenure means that mediocre and poor teachers, once they have attained tenure, have to be hired by someone, somewhere in the district. This is not fair to other schools and, most important, it is not fair to those students who must suffer through the year with a poor-to-mediocre teacher. And this fact leads us to a not-so-subtle point – continuance of tenure provides teachers' unions with far more power in our public schools than they need or should have. Teachers' unions have repeatedly gone to battle to protect job tenure for poor and mediocre teachers. They justify this practice by asserting that they must protect the weak as well as the strong; otherwise the whole structure of tenure for all could too easily topple and fall. While some teachers are dedicated people who do far more than the minimum required, too many public school teachers are not of this ilk, and these have no inherent right to be paid from the public trough. Teachers' unions, in this and other respects, often pose major barriers to serious educational reforms. They have done a fairly decent job of helping to upgrade teachers' salaries and fringe benefits, but their contribution to the quality of education is questionable. It may be that teachers' unions have outlived their usefulness. At any rate, on the issue of teacher tenure the unions must give way. Their position is indefensible.

In abolishing teacher tenure we would free the marketplace for teachers. Teachers could apply to those schools where they want to teach, while principals could hire those teachers they want in their schools. Again, there is nothing radical here. This is the manner in which virtually all private schools operate. Teachers in the private sector are subject to the same marketplace conditions of supply and demand that affect most working people. Either they perform up to expectations or they have to move on and try to develop their abilities elsewhere.

It would be interesting to see some school districts maintain their relationships with teachers' unions while other school districts terminate their relationships and go to the open market. Over time, valid comparisons could be made and it could be determined if the benefits of teachers' unions outweigh their drawbacks.

Sixth, Teacher Certification by Universities Is Abolished

There is no demonstrable relationship between teacher certification and quality of the teacher. To become a certified teacher one must first endure the education courses of a department of education in a university or college. Education majors are often looked upon as low status individuals by other undergraduate majors. They are often characterized as not so bright students who are taking the easy way out. Schools of education have come under severe criticism for their lackluster, often irrelevant curriculum. Teacher certification was supposed to guarantee that all teachers in our public schools would attain the same high standards in their profession. Instead, it has served to generate professional standards which are minimal at worst, mediocre at best.

Another reason for abolishing, or at least minimizing, the requirement of certification for teachers is the projected teacher shortage. In the 1990s a shortage of certified teachers will arise in most parts of the country. New Jersey has already modified its former certification requirements. Subsequently, a significant proportion of new teachers in New Jersey are now coming from the non-certified pool of talent, and this has been especially helpful in attracting persons of minority backgrounds into teaching. By modifying certification requirements the field of education would be opened to an influx of new talent from other fields. There are many people in other fields who would love to teach. The field of education needs this new talent with its greater diversity of background in the "real" world than that currently offered by education graduates.

Seventh, the Best Teacher Training Is On-the-Job Training that Occurs Within the Local School

In the early 1970s when Denver Academy was started, we quickly discovered that most new teachers, fresh out of the university education departments, did not know how to teach effectively. This situation is just as bad today as it was then. Rare is the new teacher who knows how to step into a classroom and manage it and teach students effectively, much less inspiringly. The few who can do this seem to be "born teachers." But most new teachers struggle, and struggle hard, in their first classrooms. The more dedicated among them eventually learn enough of the "tricks of the trade" to get by, but few ever develop their full potential as teachers. A few others, working harder than the rest, eventually make themselves into good teachers. But most remain at a level far below their actual abilities.

In recognition of this problem, we instituted our own teacher training program in the mid-70s. When new teachers are hired, they must agree to undergo a two- to three-year on-the-job training program. During that time new teachers work as assistants to master (senior-level) teachers. Master teachers are those who have already completed training and have demonstrated an exceptional level of quality teaching across several measurable dimensions. Teachers work hard to be promoted to master teacher, since it means more status, more responsibility and more pay. Master teachers then take under their wings new teachers and teach them the Denver Academy techniques in student management, classroom management, student counseling and content teaching.

One of the most important methods new teachers must learn is how to discipline students. Amazingly, novice teachers have never been taught at the university the basics of effective discipline and associated classroom management. Few people are "naturals" when it comes to discipline. Most of us have to be taught these critically important skills. Without them, any classroom readily deteriorates into a near-riot, regardless of how well-motivated the teacher is. It is hardly surprising that *teacher burnout* is a major problem in the public schools. Anyone "burns out" if he has to teach kids all day long without even knowing the rudiments of effective discipline, much less knowing how to individualize discipline to different students in different circumstances. New teachers at the Denver Academy are not allowed to take over a classroom until they have demonstrated that they understand how to apply the principles of effective discipline, how to manage a classroom, and how to monitor homework effectively. Even then the new teacher is only allowed to take over the classroom for a period while the master teacher observes. Afterwards, the master teacher and teacher intern meet in private so the master teacher can go over his written critique, which focuses on both the positives and the negatives exhibited by the new teacher. In this way the teacher intern receives an almost continuous stream of feedback on what he is doing right versus what he needs to work on so he may attain a level of acceptable mastery in the particular technique. This on-the-job education goes on for one, two, or three years until the teacher intern attains an acceptable level of quality in all teaching skills.

This effort is reinforced by extensive involvement from the administration of the school. Administrators and master teachers conduct weekly didactic sessions in which teachers are presented with the research, rationale and philosophy underlying the specific techniques utilized at Denver Academy. Teacher interns must demonstrate full understanding of this underlying rationale before they can be promoted and then accorded responsibility for their own homerooms. Administrators conduct teacher observations and are required to present model lessons for teacher interns to observe. Both administrators and master teachers are highly involved in the day-to-day running of the school. Another of their chief functions is to attend conventions and workshops, and bring back to the school current information on changes in the field.

And, as noted in the earlier comments by Thernstrom on successful parochial schools, it is critical that teachers create a safe, orderly world for students that teaches respect for others and accountability for one's own performance. At the Denver Academy teachers are very explicit in teaching values and personal standards to students. All courses and interactions with students are infused with the teaching of values.

This whole process produces an exciting, dynamic work environment for teachers. They become highly trained professionals who are accorded the respect and dignity they deserve. Teachers are always either being trained or training others. Quality of teaching is not merely a slogan at Denver Academy. It is the goal and the by-word of every staff member. It is the value that permeates all efforts to provide the best possible services for the school's students.

Eighth, Larger Schools Are Replaced, Over Time, with Smaller Schools

Throughout this century American schools became larger and yet larger. With each passing decade American public schools began to look more and more like factories. Part of this was due to the urbanization of the general population, but it largely came about because of the prevailing ethic: "Bigger is better." Today, high schools of 2,000 to 5,000 students are not uncommon in large urban areas. This gigantism was justified on the grounds that it was more cost effective to build a few huge schools than to build a larger number of smaller, more localized schools. It has never been demonstrated, however, that large urban districts are more cost effective than small school districts. New York City, with its huge public schools, is a case in point. The parochial schools in New York City maintain much smaller schools than the public schools and a minuscule central administration. Not only is the quality of education in these parochial schools (which often have large proportions of minority students) far superior to that of the public schools, but their average cost-per-pupil is less than half that of the public schools. This same point could be made in every large city. Large urban districts with their huge schools generate incredibly high overhead costs, primarily in the expansion of central administration costs. Whatever gains are made through centralized purchasing and fewer buildings are more than offset by the additional overhead costs generated by central administration facilities and salaries.

This proposal is to replace most of our current mammoth school buildings with smaller facilities over the next 30 to 50 years. The replacement costs would be prorated over a period of several decades, as school districts face the need to replace their old facilities with new facilities. In the meantime the concept used in East Harlem, mentioned earlier, could be implemented in any district at no extra cost. Remember that in East Harlem there were several different, smaller programs going on in each of the large school buildings. Smallness can be readily attained even within huge schools by creating several small schools within one large facility.

The design of the new smaller schools is probably best left to experimentation. Clearly, the school buildings built since the 1960s, which mainly look like prison/factories, are not the answer. Neither was the "open school" concept pushed in the late 60s and 70s. Open schools were a classic example of how the field of education is governed by fads and fashions rather than by facts. In open schools, classroom walls were torn down so that several rooms could be combined into one large open room. Teachers minimized their directive instruction and instead assisted students working together in small groups at various learning stations. Students directed their own learning. It was all very trendy and fit perfectly into the ambience of the late 60s. As the 60s faded so did the open school concept. It failed to meet expectations. One of the main problems was that open classrooms turned out to be (now hold on to your hats!) very noisy. Many students found it hard to concentrate in these settings. Many students missed out on directed instruction from the teacher. Nevertheless, because "its time had come" school districts spent billions of tax dollars building open schools and converting old schools to open schools, despite the fact that there was no replicated evidence to support the notion that open schools obtained superior results to traditional classrooms. It was a fad, and a costly one.

Now, there's nothing wrong with experimentation with new approaches to education. Indeed, that is precisely what has been recommended throughout this chapter. But experimentation should be done first voluntarily, on a small scale with built-in objective evaluation to determine its pros and cons. These experiences and the data they generate can then be disseminated within educational circles. In this way a professional field slowly builds up a knowledge base on which it can operate. The field of education has a minimal knowledge base. In the absence of this knowledge, our public schools are highly vulnerable to whatever fad or fashion is making the rounds. Experimentation with innovative ideas is valid only if it has built into it on-going evaluation conducted by qualified, disinterested observers. This principle applies whether we are speaking of school size, building design, classroom size, method of teaching or whatever. If schools are made smaller so they can be more personalized, then let's be sure to evaluate these changes in an objective manner so that the positives and negatives can be determined.

Ninth, Student – Teacher Ratios Are Decreased Over Time

As a corollary to the above point, it follows that quality of education can be improved by improving the current student-teacher ratio. This is one of the secrets of the greater success of private schools. Private schools often have a lower student-teacher ratio than public schools. Teacher and student satisfaction is greater in schools where there is one teacher for every fifteen students versus most public schools where there may be only one teacher for every 20 to 30 students. This is all part of the personalization of education. The more we personalize and individualize education, the better it becomes.

Fortunately, a partial solution to this problem in the public schools looms just ahead. School population is likely to decline over the next two to three decades. There will be a moderate "baby-boomlet" in the 1990s, but after that there is good reason to believe that school population will again decline. When this happens, rather than laying off teachers, it would be wise to maintain the same number of teachers in our public schools. (The tendency now is to lay off teachers while maintaining the same number of central administrators.) In this way, we improve the student-teacher ratio without noticeably affecting the overall school budget.

Better student-teacher ratios are predicated on this idea: the best education is personalized. It was said a long time ago that the best education occurs when a teacher and a student sit on the same log and talk with each other, person to person. The best education occurs when the teacher knows the student well enough to individualize the instruction to the particular strengths and weaknesses of the student. It is best when the student knows that the teacher cares for him as an individual person. Discussions of ideas and ideals are most effective when the teacher knows all the students so he can encourage each of them to become part of the discussion. When learning to write, one must write a lot. Teachers who are seeing 100–250 students per day in huge high schools simply do not have the time to read the amount of writing assignments necessary for students to learn how to write well. *The more highly personalized education is, the more meaningful it is.* Admittedly, some students enjoy snuggling up to their computers for hours on end, but not even the almighty computer can replace the teacher. Our mammoth junior high and high schools are the very ones in which lack of student discipline, truancy and misconduct are most common. The very design and size of our modern schools prohibits personalization. For the vast majority of students, teachers are distant, isolated figures who have little meaning or relevance in their lives. For the vast majority of teachers, who see anywhere from 100 to 250 students per day parading through their classes, most students are just faces in the crowd. Any notion that we can have quality education for our children under these circumstances is patently absurd.

A Special Case-in-Point Is Special Education

In the 1970s the federal government stepped in and with much media hoopla required local schools to meet the special education needs of all students. At first blush this federal requirement, P.L. 94-142, appears noble and just. In practice, however, schools were mandated to accomplish an extremely difficult goal with few additional funds. It was thus required that every child who shows emotional disturbance and every child who exhibits any form of learning disabilities and every child who is retarded and every child who is unmanageable in the regular classroom and every child who is physically handicapped must be cared for and properly educated within the public school facilities.

To make matters worse, a peculiar twist was added to this new law. It was mandated that all special education students must be provided with equal access to the regular classroom. Discrimination toward the handicapped was to be eradicated by requiring all students to be educated in the same setting – the regular classroom. This was and is called *mainstreaming*. It was said to be a concept whose time had come. It was based on the prevailing conviction that equality must mean sameness. There was not one iota of replicated data to support this law, this new form of social engineering, but this did not prevent the federal social engineers from demanding that all handicapped students be placed in regular classrooms to the greatest possible extent.

This concept's "time had come" in large part because it provided a face-saving device for those educators and federal legislators who had already placed the public schools in an impossible situation by demanding they meet the needs of all special education children, but then failing to provide the funding necessary to meet this mandate. Mainstreaming is cheap. It saves money in comparison to the very expensive cost of special education classrooms. By mainstreaming, schools could be said to be meeting the needs of all special education students, while helping the schools out of the impossible dilemma in which they had been placed by earlier mandates. All of this maneuvering was readily enshrouded in the slogans of the new ethic: "equal access," "the same educational opportunities for all," etc.

This idea had some merit to it. It certainly deserved to be experimented with on a small, voluntary scale and objectively evaluated over a number of years. Instead, it was mandated on a uniform, nationwide basis. Unfortunately, it has not worked well. For every study that finds positive results there are studies reporting negative results. There is no consistent evidence to support the putative benefits of mainstreaming, but there are considerable negative and contradictory data.

Personally, I have seen thousands of children hurt deeply by mainstreaming. In my professional life I have worked with many children with learning disabilities. Many years ago I lost count of the children and teenagers I saw who had been humiliated by other students and even their teachers when forced, via mainstreaming, to go into the regular classroom. A child with significant learning disabilities cannot function well, if at all, in the regular classroom. The same can be said for most other handicapping conditions as well. Learning disabled students require highly-specialized teaching techniques that often have to be taught on a one-to-one up through a four-to-one student-teacher ratio. With few exceptions handicapped students are at a cruel disadvantage in the regular classroom. This mandate is unfair to both teachers and students. Nevertheless, the gods of social engineering had to be served, in the name of good intentions of course, and mainstreaming became the law of the land. Millions of school children were thus forced together under conditions that benefited very few.

Instead of each public school trying to be all things to all people, both the schools and handicapped children would be better served if a few schools in each district specialized in education for specific handicapping conditions. These schools would thus be magnet schools for children with specific handicaps. There are financial incentives already in place to support such efforts since schools receive higher government stipends for educating the handicapped. A public school, for example, might decide to offer a program for the learning-disabled as part of its total program. This school would then specialize in such education and would offer "a school within a school" for the learning-disabled. Students would be mainstreamed into the larger school program only when they were ready. In this plan many handicapped children would be bussed to a specialized school outside their local area. This, for most families, would be a small price to pay to secure the quality education their children deserve.

This, again, is an adaptation of the private school model to public schools. In the private sector a special education school will usually educate children with only one kind of handicapping condition. Their energies are thus focused. There is no foolish attempt to be all things to all people. Actually, public schools with a specialized "school within a school" would have an advantage over their counterparts in the private sector, since the public schools would have the capacity for mainstreaming (when it was truly called for) built into the same facility.

The Voucher System

This concept is not part of this nine-point reform plan, but it deserves mention. The voucher concept is simple. It proposes that each family be awarded credit, each year, for the amount of money required to educate their child in their local school district. The family can then "cash in" their credit in their local school, or in some other school in the same district, or in another school district. Ideally, the voucher system would work best when implemented on a metropolitan-wide basis. In many proposals private schools are included so parents could send their child to a private school if they were willing to pay any extra charges.

There are two major thrusts behind the voucher concept. First, it is designed to give parents the maximum possible number of choices of schools in which to place their child. Second, it is designed to stimulate competition among schools so that the factors of supply and demand would force public schools to upgrade the quality of their programs.

The voucher concept is attractive on several counts, notably in its promotion of true choice of schools for parents and in its breaking of central administration's grip on local schools. Despite these attractions the idea has been strongly opposed, especially by teachers' unions and school administrators. Some of this antipathy is simply the predictable response of any entrenched bureaucracy to protect its own (near) monopoly. But the critics also make some valid points. They argue that poor families would use vouchers to transfer their kids to schools, public or private, in the "better" parts of town, thus causing the further decline and eventual closing of neighborhood schools in poor areas. They also argue that the voucher concept is in reality a scheme to transfer public funds to private and parochial schools (though no evidence has been presented to indicate that private schools are behind the notion; it's mainly been pushed by dissatisfied parents whose children attend public schools).

The nine-point reform plan proposed here contains all the advantages of the voucher concept without the putative disadvantages. It maintains the current distinctions between public and private schools; there is no mixing of funds. It provides local schools in poor areas with a real opportunity to develop quality programs of their own while still providing voluntary busing for those parents who choose, for whatever reason, to send their children elsewhere to school. This nine-point reform plan encourages the re-energization of our public schools without pitting them against private schools.

Review

This program for reform is a frontal assault on what are seen as the principal causes of the deterioration in our public schools since the 1960s. It was during the 60s that the 20th Century Myth became the driving force in our public schools. This Myth inevitably brought with it the increased emphasis (1) on the use of social engineering to solve all problems, (2) on the centralization and standardization of authority, (3) on increased uniformity across all systems, which was premised on the notion that equality can be defined only in terms of sameness, (4) on moral relativism as the basis for teaching values, and (5) on the treatment of children, not as individuals, but as members of groups and classes. We will not reclaim our schools until these elements of the 20th Century Myth have been peeled away and replaced with the assumptions and values which underlie traditional liberalism. Traditional liberalism, born of the Enlightenment, focuses on freedom of choice by the individual. It couples this freedom with the requirement for individual accountability in all cases, while placing as much power as possible in local rather than centralized governance. It emphasizes the individual, the family and the neighborhood, not government, as the resources for alleviating society's ills. This is our heritage, and it is the loss of this heritage which has led our schools into their present quagmire.

Is the proposed nine-point program a panacea for public education? No, any proposed solution to human problems is fraught with negative consequences, unintended or not. This proposal is more a beginning than an end, more a start than a solution. It openly admits that we do not know the best teaching methods, the best school design, the best curricula, the best philosophy of teaching for different students. It encourages us to initiate experimentation on these questions, but on a responsible basis – it requires us to evaluate objectively our attempts at innovation.

Probably the biggest omission in this proposed approach is that it does not offer a resolution to the problem of how to deal with the incredible ignorance so many students display toward their own cultural and historical roots, much less their appalling lack of basic academic skills. This defect is due to the following assumption: that we do not know the best way to teach all students the basic skills and common knowledge they deserve to know. This proposed approach is designed to stimulate, instead, a nationwide, ongoing effort to determine the best teaching methods to achieve these goals. And it is set up to involve as many people as possible in this ongoing debate and research effort. This is too important an issue to be left to "experts" only.

It is good to remember that quality education for all people is still a new idea. Quality education for the masses is no doubt easier to pull off in highly homogeneous societies such as Japan. In the United States we are dealing with a far more complex task. We are aiming to provide quality education for the most diverse student body on earth, and we have a meager knowledge base from which to launch this great effort. This last point cannot be stressed strongly enough. Our knowledge base is weak. As long as this vacuum exists, other forces will fill it – namely the fads, fashions, prejudices and political pressure groups that now dictate change and curriculum in our public schools. This situation will remain until we generate a reliable information base on which informed decisions can be made, and this will not happen until we free our schools from their present constraints. We have a full century's work ahead of us. But that's okay, because by now we know that *there are no quick fixes* when we are dealing with human beings and human problems. The next century offers great opportunities to upgrade our public schools, but only if we free them to do their job, and our families do their job.

Summary

Public schools have become bureaucratized, controlled from afar by federal government dictates, and overloaded with functions once handled by parents. For these reasons, schools have become too burdened to deal with localized needs and issues effectively.

In addition, schools have been directed by governmental authorities to teach generalized ideas of values, suggesting that each person make choices from there. This has become so watered down that the concept of "values" is ineffectual and the "mentors" who teach them are ineffective. In fact, many teachers are unaware of their own values – making it even more difficult to impart any clear ideas to their students.

To save the public school system, our families need to get healthy again, impart higher values – instead of materialistic ones – to children, who can then bring this firm foundation into the classroom. And, control must be returned to the local community working with empowered principals in settings where accountability is set up along lines similar to those found in effective private schools.

A nine-point proposal for educational reform will set the public school system on the right course. This program:

- Provides parents with something they don't have at the moment – freedom of choice as to which school their child will attend on a yearly basis.
- Stimulates diversity among schools so that the choices available would require parents to make meaningful, hopefully tough decisions.
- Encourages racial integration, but on a voluntary, individual choice basis rather than on a mandated, racial quota basis. It takes advantage of the busing systems already in effect to ensure that children of poor families would have access to all schools.
- Transfers significant authority from central administration to local, neighborhood community boards.
- Provides principals, teachers and the people in local neighborhoods with the opportunity to develop a school of their own philosophy and values. It provides principals with the means by which to implement the stated philosophy and values of each school.
- Reduces the role of the centralized school board and restricts it to those functions it should be able to handle. It also reduces the role and authority of central administration with its complex web of multi-layered, ineffectual bureaucracies.
- Places pressure on teachers' unions to either put up or shut up as to their role in upgrading the quality of education for students, especially on the "hot topic" of teacher tenure.
- Encourages innovations and experimentation in education, but only as long as innovations are objectively evaluated.

- Suggests the development of smaller schools and better student-teacher ratios over a reasonable period of time.
- Encourages the minimization of current teacher certification processes, replacing them with on-the-job teacher training. It opens teacher and administrative ranks to new sources of outside talent by changing the current certification process.
- Fosters the development of special education programs as "schools within schools" and reduces the role of federal mandates for handicapped children.
- Does all these things without substantially changing the current size of school budgets and sources of school funding.

The underlying premise to these proposals is that the best hope for our public schools is to start running them along the same general lines as the more successful private schools. This concept thus extends to the public schools the advantages (both the freedom and the accountability) now enjoyed by successful private schools. And this means, first and foremost, that ultimate authority in each public school is placed into the hands of parents and other concerned citizens drawn from the local community.

---

[1] For example, the Universal Declaration of Human Rights, adopted by the United Nations in 1948, states that all human beings have the right to life, liberty, freedom from personal attack, freedom from slavery, presumption of innocence until proven guilty, freedom of religion, freedom of speech, etc. Another example: The Ten Commandments, in some format or another, are recognized by virtually all world societies as containing universal validity.

Chapter Eight

Lessons of the 20th Century
Toward the 21st Century

There is good reason to be optimistic about the 21st Century, for the lessons of the 20th Century are obvious. For the most part, these lessons are replays of ancient scenarios from past centuries done up in modern form. If this is true, then we obviously haven't yet learned (and applied) the lessons of history. True, but we now have two advantages that should help. Speed of communication has increased at a phenomenal rate worldwide. Ideas, as well as products, can and do use these circuits for fast communication among peoples. And second, our eyes were blinded in the 20th Century by the notion of the "inevitability of progress." Most of the time we truly believed that what we were doing was all new, that it had never been done or thought before, and that if something was "modern" it had to be better than its predecessors. Belief in this assumption was made easier by the great progress in technology made throughout the century. Our technological advancements often blinded us to the fact that our social realities, and even our social experiments, were often throwbacks to earlier eras. The person flying from New York to Stockholm in only eight hours may marvel at such technology while not realizing that the socialist Utopia he's flying to has been tried – and discarded – many times before in history. This naiveté is dissipating. It reached its apex in the middle of the century and has been on the decline since. Now there is a growing awareness that our technology has far outstripped our social and interpersonal realities and innovations. We can no longer equate technological progress with social progress. And we now know that technological progress can even bring with it social regression. Are people doing business with each other through computers better off or worse off than people doing business face to face? It all depends.

The ease and speed of our communications, along with the realization that technological progress does not inevitably correlate with social progress, should combine to make it a little easier to apply the lessons of the 20th Century. To some degree, however, each new generation will insist on repeating, in new form, the mistakes made by past generations. However, unless we apply the lessons learned during this century of unprecedented bloodletting and mayhem, we allow the suffering to pass on to our descendants.

First Lesson: Freedom and Equality Are in Perpetual Conflict

Will and Ariel Durant, after two lifetimes of study of the history of man, contended that the greatest lesson to be learned from history was that freedom is always sacrificed in the pursuit of equal outcomes.[105] In the 20th Century, man has most earnestly pursued the goal of equality for all. In their great experiments with socialism, 20th Century men and women have tried to create utopias with equal outcome, the same outcome, for all. The goal of equality, though, is always in conflict with the goal of personal freedom. The more socialistic the society, the more likely that personal freedom will be inhibited. This lesson is not unique to the 20th Century:

> Inequality is not only natural and inborn, it grows with the complexity of civilization. Hereditary inequalities breed social and artificial inequalities; every invention or discovery is made or seized by the exceptional individual, and makes the strong stronger, the weak relatively weaker, than before. Economic development specializes functions, differentiates abilities, and makes men unequally valuable to their group. If we knew our fellow men thoroughly we could select thirty per cent of them whose combined ability would equal that of all the rest. Life and history do precisely that, with a sublime injustice reminiscent of Calvin's God.
>
> Nature smiles at the union of freedom and equality in our utopias. For freedom and equality are sworn and everlasting enemies, and when one prevails, the other dies. Leave men free, and their natural inequalities will multiply almost geometrically, as in England and America in the nineteenth century under laissez-faire. To check the growth of inequality, liberty must be sacrificed, as in Russia after 1917.[106]

The 20th Century has provided more direct comparisons of socialism versus capitalism than any other time period. We can therefore compare South Korea versus North Korea, West Germany versus East Germany (or for that matter, Western Europe versus Eastern Europe), Taiwan, Hong Kong or Singapore versus mainland China. There are many such examples where one side chose capitalism, the other socialism; and yet, both sides had similar histories, similar initial levels of technological advancement, similar levels of initial capital and comparable family, cultural, and educational levels. One such comparison can be seen in the production and distribution of food, a most elementary social function. Throughout this century, wherever nations turned to state-managed agriculture, productivity declined so much that states which had previously been exporters of food became importers of food (e.g., USSR, Poland, Rumania, Bulgaria, Iran, Iraq, Syria, Burma, India, Ghana, Tanzania, Argentina, Brazil). By contrast, societies that retained capitalistic agriculture, such as the United States, Canada, Western Europe and Australia, continued to produce food surpluses. Indeed, food production in the capitalist countries often kept the people in socialist countries alive.

It is clear that capitalism has far outperformed socialism. And not only on materialistic grounds. In terms of the quality of life, as well as the overall standard of living, capitalist societies have outperformed comparable socialist societies. Whether in South Korea or West Germany, people have been freer – their personal freedoms and civil liberties better protected – than in North Korea or East Germany. *There is a positive correlation between capitalism and personal freedom.* Capitalism, after all, is dependent on the freedom and accountability of the individual for advancement of society's aims. Socialism, in contrast, assumes that the individual must be subservient to the aims of the State. Even in those few exceptions where socialism has been happily infused with democracy, in Sweden for example, this same principle applies. The people of Sweden are far more controlled and inhibited by their government than are the people of Switzerland, another small country, but one that has achieved an even higher standard of living without Sweden's socialistic controls and regulations.

The problems encountered by the socialist approach are not new. Socialist systems have been tried many times in history going back at least to the state-run economy of Sumeria over 4,000 years ago. Rome tried socialism under Diocletian in the decades following A.D. 300, but the task "...of controlling men in economic detail proved too much for Diocletian's expanding, expensive, corrupt bureaucracy, ...taxation rose to such heights that men lost incentive to work or earn, and an erosive contest began between lawyers finding devices to evade taxes and lawyers formulating laws to prevent evasion."[107]

About every 1,000 years China has experimented with socialism. Every experiment failed and resulted in a return to some form of capitalism. China's last great attempt at socialism (prior to today's Communist China initiated in the 1940s by Mao) was begun in A.D. 1068 by the emperor Wang An-shih. He wanted to protect the lower classes from the rich and lessen the concentration of wealth in the hands of the few. He ordered the state to "...take the entire management of commerce, industry, and agriculture into its own hands..." with the aim of preventing the "working classes...from being ground into the dust by the rich."[108] Wang's noble experiment was in turn ground into dust by the usual villains: high taxes, disincentives to work, and an ever-growing, corrupt state bureaucracy. It seems, as the Durants put it, that mankind must forever choose between private plunder or public graft. Private plunder has proven less offensive to more people in more societies over time.

All this, however, is not to say that capitalism, even when softened by democracy, is all that superior to socialism. In every known case socialism sprang up in reaction to the abuses of capitalism. Capitalism seems to be the more natural mode for man. It is more congruent with the nature of man and thus more likely to evolve under natural, unfettered conditions. But under capitalism the natural inequalities of men often create societies where a few people control most of the resources. These few persons all too often show a greed for more power that precludes others from access to these same resources. In enlightened capitalism, these destructive tendencies of the elite are countermanded by universal education and equal opportunity for all. Otherwise, unnatural growths such as socialism are bound to arise in reaction to the abuses of capitalists. The new socialist state then demands equal outcomes for all, which restricts unduly the freedoms of the people, thereby re-instigating the vicious cycle again.

While there can be no doubt that the profit motive is essential to the long-term productivity and financial feasibility of a society, there can also be no doubt that the profit motive, unrestrained by higher principles, leads quickly to abuse. And here we are speaking of the higher values that respect the divine spark in each and every person, for even the highest principles of democracy are not adequate, in and of themselves, to control the runaway materialism often sparked by capitalism. Plutarch states that in the Athens of 594 B.C. the people, under democracy and capitalism, had become "mad after money" – *pleonexia* (the Greek term for this particular madness) reigned supreme. The rich concentrated more and more wealth in their hands and built luxurious homes, bought expensive jewelry and clothes, and competed with each other in throwing lavish parties while providing nothing for the working-class poor. The gap between rich and poor grew greater every year, while corrupt courts ruled against the poor at every turn, until violent revolution by the poor was imminent. The country was saved only by political reforms led by Solon, an aristocratic businessman who devalued the currency, established a graduated income tax and liberalized the courts.

When enlightened democracy is wedded to capitalism, the results are far more beneficent than those engendered by socialism, as can be seen today in many countries of Western Europe, North America, and the Pacific Rim. Hopefully, the 20th Century has seen the last of man's experiments with socialism/communism. Especially pathetic are the attempts by so many Third World countries, the poorest of countries, to use socialistic models as their way out of poverty. These poor nations were swept up by the prevailing 20th Century Myth and then convinced that some form of collectivism was the answer to their problems. In the 21st Century more progress will be made if Third World countries abandon socialism and instead move to a democratic/capitalistic model with strong emphases on education for all, reduced birth rates, strong family life that respects the roles, functions and rights of women, and civil liberties for all. These four factors comprise the greatest drain on the psychological and spiritual resources of Third World nations. Equal opportunity must be their focus, not guaranteed equal outcomes (that inevitably lead to disincentives to work and corrupt, overblown state bureaucracies).

Though socialism was imbued with a mythical status in this century, the fact is that its origins are ancient. It is based on a primitive ethic often tried and then discarded in the past – the rule by state over all, enforced equality of outcome, imposed homogenization on the many by an elite few, group rather than individual accountability. It is the abuse of capitalism, however, that brings on these pathetic experiments in state-controlled living. Capitalism can flourish with the greatest benefits for the largest number of people only when the profit motive is wisely conditioned by the service motive. Someday there will be sufficient numbers of capitalist leaders motivated by spiritual ideals as well as profit. Then we shall see what capitalistic democracy is really capable of achieving for the largest possible number of people. In the meantime, we learn this lesson: that socialism results in too great a loss in personal and civil liberties, more so than most people are willing to tolerate; and it makes democracy, with its dependence on the personal freedom of individuals, difficult to attain.

> All deductions having been made, democracy has done less harm, and more good, than any other form of government... Under its stimulus Athens and Rome became the most creative cities in history... Democracy has now dedicated itself resolutely to the spread and lengthening of education... If equality of educational opportunity can be established, democracy will be real and justified. For this is the vital truth beneath its catchwords: that though men cannot be equal, their access to education and opportunity can be made more nearly equal. A right is not a gift of God or nature but a privilege which it is good for the group that the individual should have.[109]

It has been shown repeatedly in history that societies flourish best under conditions of peace, non-protectionist free trade, and respect for the rights and dignity of the individual. How many times must we relearn these same lessons? The most successful societies in the 21st Century will meet these criteria in the context of capitalism conditioned by democracy. They will focus on the family as the primary social unit. And they will regard voluntary service to the common good as the highest duty, while regarding each person's quest of spiritual meaning as the greatest value in life.

Second Lesson: The Harm Done by Ideologues Is Incalculable

The harm done to families and individuals by too much government is in direct correlation to the degree government is controlled by ideologues.

Whether right-wing or left-wing, whether humanistic or religious, ideologues have done incalculable harm throughout this century. The same could be said for any other century except that never before have ideologues held such total, state power in so many different parts of the world as in the 20th Century. Ideologues are those people whose beliefs are both fixated and self-righteous; who define the world in accordance with a rigid set of views and then brook no dissent from those views. People as well as places are redefined by the ideologue's world view. As an individual, you matter only to the degree you are "for" or "against" the ideologue's viewpoint. You are redefined either as a "good person" (for) or a "bad person" (against). If it turns out that you are a bad person, then in the eyes of the ideologue something must be done about you. At the very least you must be re-educated so that you become "enlightened" (you come to see the world as the ideologue does). If this doesn't work, or if you have already been classified as a member of an unacceptable group or category, then you may have to be eliminated in some manner. No one stereotypes others more readily than the ideologue. No one dehumanizes others as rapidly or as effectively.

Paul Johnson is the historian of the 20th Century who most trenchantly documents the destructiveness of the ideologue addicted to the power of the state:

> The state was the great gainer of the twentieth century; and the central failure... The state had proved itself an insatiable spender, an unrivaled waster. Indeed, in the twentieth century it had also proved itself the great killer of all time... What was not clear was whether the fall from grace of the state would likewise discredit its agents, the activist politicians, whose phenomenal rise in numbers and authority was the most important human development of modern times... They marched across the decades and the hemispheres: ...Sun Yat-sen and Ataturk, Stalin and Mussolini, Kruschev, Ho Chi Minh, Pol Pot, Castro, Nehru, U Nu and Sukarno, Peron and Allende, Nkrumah and Nyerare, Nasser, Shah Pahlevi and Ghadafy, usually bringing death and poverty in their train.[110]

Johnson asserts that the 20th Century has taught us that the best answer to state-created evil and waste resides in respect for the dignity of the individual and "a society in which the family, as opposed to the political party and the ideological program, was the starting point for reconstruction."[111]

Third Lesson: Rapid Change Usually Causes More Harm than Good

Ideologues nearly always make the mistake of requiring that change be all-encompassing and be made immediately. They are blind to the obvious lesson that social change that occurs rapidly too often causes more harm than good. At the risk of sounding curmudgeonly, this point must be made: social change that occurs quickly often brings about more negative than positive results no matter how noble the intent may be. Our basic social institutions – our families, schools and courts – are by nature conservative, wrapped up in a thousand traditions. These traditions are in constant need of challenge, lest they become hidebound and suffocate us. But these traditions arose because they serve useful purposes. It is good to be open to the changing of roles and functions, but if we rip our traditions apart and throw them out overnight we run a severe risk of regressing in the name of social progress. We then find ourselves devising a set of apologetics to explain the embarrassing results. This observation of the harm often brought by too rapid change falls hardest on the young and on those in social need, who understandably don't wish to hear this.

Probably the most embarrassing fact for those who demand radical change overnight is the repeated tendency of those who advocate the overthrow of the current condition to abuse power later in much the same manner as the prior rulers. As the Durants put it, "Nothing is clearer in history than the adoption by successful rebels of the methods they were accustomed to condemn in the forces they deposed." Thus a Fidel Castro foments a violent revolution in Cuba against the "capitalist oppressors of the people," but once he gains power he uses it to oppress the people even more than the previous rulers, and throws in a wrecked economy for good measure. The example of Castro in Cuba has been repeated innumerable times in history. Those who advocate overnight changes, risking violence "if necessary," are the most prone then to repeat the same mistakes (only in new form) of those who were previously despised. The 20th Century abounds with example after example of this process, since in this century society after society has experimented with radical change of basic social institutions. Many societies have been remade almost overnight, and nearly all suffered more than they gained.

> Mao was for radical reform. Many of the independent warlords were for radical reform... All these honourable gentlemen protested that they were working, and killing, for the good of China and her people. The tragedy of inter-war China illustrates the principle that when legitimacy yields to force, and moral absolutes to relativism, a great darkness descends and angels become indistinguishable from devils.[112]

Proposed social changes, especially those supported by *government power*, should be subjected to several conditions. New programs should be experimented with first on a small scale and, wherever possible, with volunteers only. Second, independent evaluators should be engaged to provide a wholly independent study of each new program. Third, a "sunset law" provision of 3, 5, or 10 years should be preestablished. Based on the results provided by the evaluators, the elected legislators would decide at the predetermined "sunset" whether the pros of the new program warrant its continuation. The methodology underlying these three steps is already available. Sunset provisions should also be applied to all ongoing government programs in human services so that a continuous accountability check is built-in. The burden of proof should reside with the programs themselves on the need for their continuance. The data, however, must in all cases be provided by independent evaluators. Such an approach would help to curb some of the more blatant excesses and abuses in state-sponsored social experimentation. The abuses caused by well-meaning social services that become entrenched bureaucracies supported by special interest groups are too numerous to mention. We do not have to tolerate these abuses. This proposed approach would approximate Karl Popper's dictum that social change works best when it occurs a piece at a time and is forced to prove itself as it goes. (His corollary dictum was that social change brings the worst results when it is based on sweeping ideological assumptions imposed too rapidly on a society.)

Reformers who fail are usually those who move too fast and quickly antagonize far too many interest groups in the process. Their reforms, no matter how well-intentioned, then fall apart as quickly as they arose.

Social change works for the better, that is, shows a higher gains-to-costs ratio, when these conditions are met:

1) When equality of opportunity is striven for while state-imposed equality of outcome is eschewed.

2) When state-sponsored social engineering is kept to a bare minimum and carefully monitored and evaluated.

3) When social change is based on testable ideas, not on grandiose ideological formulations that purport to explain all social phenomena; and when the leaders of change are not ideologues, but are open to the concept that their ideas must be tested.

4) When change is slowed to a reasonable pace that takes into account already established procedures and traditions.

5) When change is based on assumptions about human nature that are valid, or at least submitted to test first.

6) Last but not least, social change works best when the dignity of the individual is the center value; when it's recognized that in the last analysis the only real societal change is found in the personal growth of individual human beings.

Fourth Lesson: The 20th Century Myth Foments War-Making

In the last 3,443 years of recorded history, only 268 have not seen war.[113] It is clear, though, that no other century has seen anywhere near the carnage observed routinely in the 20th Century. Over 100 million human beings have been slaughtered in this century, easily the largest blood bath in history. Much of this increase in death and destruction was due to the great scientific and technological advances of this century, which have made war more destructive than ever before.

But there's more to the excessive war-making of the 20th Century than mere improvements in technology. The dominant ideologies of this century foment war. Most have been humanistic ideologies, expressions of the 20th Century

Myth, that focus on the material world of the here and now; that is, they have been *time-dependent*. Aldous Huxley contrasts for us the effect of time-dependent approaches to those he characterizes as eternity-oriented:

> The aim of all revolutions is to make the future radically different from and better than the past. But some time-obsessed philosophies are primarily concerned with the past, not the future, and their politics are entirely a matter of preserving or restoring the status quo and getting back to the good old days. But retrospective time-worshippers have one thing in common with the revolutionary devotees of the bigger and better future; *they are prepared to use unlimited violence to achieve their ends.* (Italics mine.) ...And because the ultimate good lies in time, they feel justified in making use of any temporal means for achieving it....From the records of history it seems to be abundantly clear that most of the religions and philosophies which take time too seriously are correlated with political theories that inculcate and justify the use of large-scale violence.[114]

Huxley goes on to point out that not all religions have been time-dependent. Some are eternity-focused. They teach that any person can choose to identify with the divine spark within, so that this Ultimate Good can be realized "as a fact of immediate experience." When eternal life becomes a present reality, then ideologies that demand instant change lose their appeal. That is, time loses its ability to dominate us.

> Unlike early Judaism, Christianity and Mohammedanism (all of them obsessed with time), Hinduism and Buddhism have never been persecuting faiths, have preached almost no holy wars and have refrained from that proselytizing religious imperialism, which has gone hand in hand with the political and economic oppression of the coloured peoples.[115]

Certain Christian sects (e.g., the Quakers) also teach an "eternity-now" approach to life that is not time-dominated. Eternity-now approaches foster a greater quality of tolerance and forbearance for others. Beginning in the 1700's the Quakers...

> believed that the inner light was in all human beings and that salvation came to those who lived in conformity with that light and was not dependent on the profession of belief in historical or pseudo-historical events, nor on the performance of certain rites, nor on the support of a particular ecclesiastical organization. Moreover, their eternity-philosophy preserved them from the materialistic apocalypticism of the progress-worship which in recent times has justified every kind of iniquity from war and revolution to sweated labor, slavery and the exploitation of savages and children —

(and the current neglect of children – author's note) – has justified them on the ground that the supreme good is in future time and that any temporal means, however intrinsically horrible, may be used to achieve that good. Because Quaker theology was a form of eternity-philosophy, Quaker political theory rejected war and persecution as means to ideal ends, denounced slavery and proclaimed racial equality.[116]

Many modern states rose to power on the back of humanistic ideologies that strove to create utopias on earth, *now*. These ideologies have all been products of the 20th Century Myth. They share this characteristic with certain religions – that they have "the answer" for all mankind and they are thus duty bound to impose their world view on everyone else *now*. Such an attitude readily foments war on others. The ideologies spawned by the 20th Century Myth are as judgmental and damning of others as the religions they were intended to replace. Since it is clear that time-dominated ideologies have caused war and violence and terrorism on an unprecedented scale, it seems appropriate to re-evaluate the finer points of the eternity-now philosophies (see chapter three), which offer a better hope for peace and freedom for all.

There are several other steps that would help make the 21st Century more peaceful, less violent than the 20th Century. One of the most useful of these steps is to encourage free and open trade across all nations, freed from local and national tariffs. A free marketplace which encourages international businesses and cross-country commerce will do more to encourage world peace than all the current peace movements put together. When nations are tied together financially and commercially, they are loathe to go to war against each other; and the negative aspects of nationalism are more easily controlled. Today's peace movements are well-intentioned, but base their appeals on a vague humanitarianism ("we're all in this together") that counts for little when financial and commercial interests are brought into play. And all too many peace movements make the mistake of those who too urgently seek change – they antagonize the very interests whose support they need to accomplish their goals. The last few decades have seen a growing trend toward internationalism in business, more openness of markets and freer trade. It is good to encourage these trends in the cause of world peace.

A second major step would be to encourage the continued development of a world language. At this time English is the most likely candidate to become the world's language. It is already spoken worldwide in circles of international commerce and transportation (e.g., air traffic controllers and pilots worldwide use English as their common language). Language differences constitute one of the most frustrating barriers to understanding among peoples, and there is only one way to resolve this problem – one common language spoken by all. This concept in no way negates the teaching and use of other languages. The beauty and diversity of the world's languages can not only survive but flourish within this concept. Each local culture can teach its children its own language, while insisting that all learn the world language fluently. The little country of Greece is one of many examples of this new model. Greeks still learn Greek, but all school children must learn English as well. A common world language will go far in creating an atmosphere conducive to ongoing world peace.

A third step is to build on the first two steps by encouraging the trends toward international exchange programs in all fields – the arts, sciences, business, education, religion, competitive play, student exchange, living abroad, etc. Travel should be considered an indispensable part of education. Travel, however, is enlightening only to the degree the traveler integrates himself into the local culture and people. "Travel" by tour group (with one's own nationality only) is a misnomer.

The fourth step is a long way off, but can be encouraged in the form of certain current trends. Namely, world peace will not become a permanent reality until all nations give up their claims to "sovereignty" (the right to bear arms in the form of their own, national militaries) to the one sovereignty of a single world government. Clearly, this momentous change is not likely to occur for several centuries. The initial steps are already in motion, however, and deserve encouragement. The economic unification of Western Europe in 1992 is the first of several such alignments that will occur in the 21st Century. The Eastern European countries will likely join this new pact in due time (after they have gone through some difficult transitions moving from communism to capitalism), so that at some point in the next century, a United Europe could surpass the United States as the world's primary economic power. Of course, the United States may join with other countries in this hemisphere, while Japan is likely to become more aligned with other Pacific Rim nations. Alignments among Third World countries will become a must if they are to have any hope of competing in this new world of trade and commerce.

In future centuries these economic alignments are likely to evolve into "superstates" that will be the next step toward eventual world government. The replacement of national sovereignty with one world sovereignty will be spurred on more by economic than by ideological considerations.

The potential for war-making among the new mega-nations will be enormous, especially if they are caught up in time-dominated ideologies, religious or humanistic.

This development is a major reason why the lessons of the 20th Century on the abuses of state power are so critically important. Unless these lessons are applied, the potential for abuse of individual citizens and families of these new mega-nations will be unlimited. The Orwellian year of "1984" may have passed, but we have not yet escaped the threat of "big brother," especially since democratic capitalist societies have shown some of the same tendencies toward abuse of state power as collectivist societies.

As these new superstates emerge, it will be even more critical for their citizens to remember the importance of this principle – that the only proven way to control government power is through a system of carefully monitored checks and balances. Each branch of government must function within its own boundaries and submit to the power checks of the other branches. The separation of powers between local government and those of the superstate will be an ongoing battleground in the 21st Century. As the superstates emerge, they will be sorely tempted to run roughshod over the legitimate power of local and regional governments. The restrictions on the powers of the superstate must be explicit and adhered to or else there will be continuous warfare between local government and federal government. The great abuses of state power observed routinely in the 20th Century make us shudder when we think of the greater potential for abuse by the coming superstates. But the superstates are coming; and they are probably a necessary step toward eventual, unified world government, so it's best that we prepare ourselves to relearn old lessons in new contexts.

The fifth step is the most far-reaching of all, for it is strictly a matter of individual free will. Peace on earth will not come until some significant proportion of the world's people truly practice faith in a Supreme Being who is the loving Father-Mother to all people. A person can believe many, many different things in his spiritual life, but this he must believe to be at true peace with others – that all people are brothers because all are the sons and daughters of God. This is the value that will eventually create a world in which "good will to all men" reigns as well as "peace on earth." As noted in Chapter One, the cutting off of the Brotherhood of Man from the root concept of the Fatherhood of God was the main cause of modern humanism's descent into power politics. If this statement – that the Fatherhood of God is the basis for the Brotherhood of Man – is *truly* believed in one's heart of hearts, then it becomes impossible to *initiate* violence toward any other brother. All other steps toward world peace are dependent for their success on the degree to which this spiritual principle is operative in the hearts and minds of the people involved. The following principle (where the "super-sovereign" is denoted as God) is as true for nations as it is for individuals, and perhaps even more so for superstates competing with each other on a free and equal basis:

> Freewill beings who regard themselves as equals, unless they mutually acknowledge themselves as subjects to some supersovereignty, some authority over and above themselves, sooner or later are tempted to try out their ability to gain power and authority over other persons and groups. The concept of equality never brings peace except in the mutual recognition of some overcontrolling influence of supersovereignty.[117]

By encouraging the trends toward freer trade, international commerce, one common world language, exchange programs in all fields, and foreign travel, we can all work toward world peace. The intermediate steps toward eventual world government, wherein all nations would give up any and all claims to maintain their own militaries, should be encouraged only as long as such potential superstates can be prohibited from the great abuses of state power so evident in the 20th Century. And, most important, world peace and goodwill toward men are ultimately dependent on individual free will. That is, peace among men is utterly dependent on the proportion and position of people who faithfully commit themselves to this ideal: that it is God's will that we freely choose to treat all our brothers and sisters as His beloved children. Without this foundation, we posture and flounder while taking one step backward for every one step forward.

Fifth Lesson: The 20th Century Myth Ends in Worship of Self

In the first half of this century, as noted by Erich Fromm in his signal work on modern times, we "escaped from freedom" into the worship of the State. When that approach failed, we regressed farther to the worship of Self. If patriotism is indeed the "last refuge of the scoundrel," then Self worship is the last refuge of the desperate – the person desperate to believe in *something*.

This vacillation between State worship and Self worship is the inevitable consequence of belief in the 20th Century Myth. The true believer is caught like a yo-yo between these two points. When his State disabuses him, as it must, all he has to fall back on is the only reality that his relativism allows him to believe in – his Self. This sole point of reference is the fountainhead of the 20th Century Myth.

This worship of self, this confusion of moral relativism for tolerance, created a receptivity to the pseudo-scientific pretensions of the 20th Century Myth. And this in turn damaged our basic social institutions producing the "cynicism and shallow sophistication" so characteristic of the 20th Century. But in all this we have been somewhat naive, for there is really nothing new here. Many past societies have gone through similar periods of transition from religion to paganism back to religion again. During these transitions it is common for the generations involved to be somewhat unhinged, as noted by the Durants in their description of the ebb and flow of past human societies:

> Caught in the... interval between one moral code and the next, an unmoored generation surrenders itself to luxury, corruption, and a restless disorder of family and morals...

They further note that throughout history, religion prevails

> ...in periods when the laws are feeble and morals must bear the burden

of maintaining social order; skepticism and paganism... progress as the rising power of law and government permits the decline of the church, the family, and morality...[118]

So it seems that each generation rides its own notch on this pinwheel of cyclical movement from religion to paganism back to religion again. But does this mean that progress in the social realm is always an illusion? Can't progress ever be real? Does our so-called social progress always have to be in the form of one step backward for every one step forward? Will it ever be possible for human beings to act wisely in some consistent manner? Is it required that we now return to some form of "theological terror" as recompense for the savagely learned lessons of the 20th Century? Or can we do better? Can we, for example, learn something from the great teachers of mankind so that we piece together a spiritual underpinning that liberates the best in the human spirit, rather than encasing that spirit in fear and rigidity?

Sixth Lesson: The Need for Spiritual Meaning Does Not Disappear

True religion is slow in growth and, when once planted, is difficult of dislodgement; but its intellectual counterfeit has no root in itself; it springs up suddenly, it suddenly withers.[119]

It is probably true, as historian Paul Johnson suggests, that there are fewer atheists today than a century ago. For, the second half of the 19th Century saw the acme of atheism in intellectual circles – a product of the then growing optimism that man-made reason, through the applications of science, would solve man's problems and even create utopias on earth. It was during this same period that the thought of Marx, Freud and Nietzsche came of age – the three atheists who collectively contributed more than anyone else to the formulation of the 20th Century Myth. That ethic now stands discredited in the eyes of all except the few remaining zealots, though it lives on in various forms in most of our social reform movements. The great hope of the 20th Century – that man through the agencies of his beloved state could create heaven on earth – is either dead or moribund in the minds of most people.

People are thus less confident now than they were a hundred years ago of the beneficent results of science. And this development naturally leads to a reconsideration of things spiritual. Yet, many people find that they cannot go back to the religions of their traditions. With each new generation in the 20th Century, the proportion increases of those people whose minds are open to spiritual concepts but who find that they cannot return to the orthodoxy of the churches.

The followers of Moses are said to have wandered in the desert for decades looking for guidance, sustenance and ultimate truth. A similar situation exists in the 20th Century, where millions wander in search of guidance and spiritual sustenance. Our 20th Century philosophies have been lame in response, ranging from logical positivism (the last great attempt to apply Reason to all arenas of human thought) to existentialism (an extension of Nietzsche's nihilism). They sprang up suddenly, then just as suddenly withered.

The greatest lesson of the 20th Century is that God will not go away. Man has spent this century trying to replace God with one manmade system after another. We declared Him dead. Or we simply considered that He was no longer relevant to our everyday concerns and problems. But He wouldn't go away. None of our substitutes provide enduring sustenance to the human spirit – that never-ending quest to understand truth, beauty, and goodness.

If it is true that we are to return to some sort of spiritual basis for human society, then the least we can do is put our best foot forward. What can we learn from the great spiritual teachers? What do we already know? What would human society look like if it were guided on a daily basis by these same, great teachings? Is this the ennobling ideal we now lack? Can this be the vision that our children can pass on to their children? Isn't it evident that this is what's missing? Clearly, the self-obsession fostered by modern humanism that passes for self-growth is not the answer to what ails us.

> Even the skeptical historian develops a humble respect for religion, since he sees it functioning, and seemingly indispensable, in every land and age.
> There is no significant example in history, before our time, of a society successful in maintaining moral life without the aid of religion.
> Will and Ariel Durant

Summary

What we call social progress is mainly illusion. We take one step forward, then almost immediately cancel our progress by taking one step backward. The overall quality of our lives, our relationships with others, thereby remains static. Though in this or that area of living we emancipate ourselves, we find that the anxieties, fears and nagging doubts in the other areas soon crowd in and continue to rule us as much as ever. This is exacerbated to the extent that we base our personal growth on erroneous definitions of reality, such as the 20th Century Myth. All growth is based on how we apply our personal values in everyday life. These values are derived from our assumptions about the nature of reality. What is real? What is not? What we believe Ultimate Reality to be determines our values and ultimately sets the direction and attitude of our lives. The closer we align ourselves with the true nature of Ultimate Reality, the more real and lasting is our personal growth. All else is illusion, which ultimately feeds disillusionment and cynicism about ourselves and other people.

Real social change, then, is based ultimately on the personal growth of individuals. And there are as many different ways to pursue truth as there are individual human beings. It is for this reason that in this look at the 20th Century we have worked our way through the major changes in the social realm back to the individual. Even those changes and corrections at the social level that exemplify the highest ideals will have little lasting effect when society contains too few individuals trying to function at that same high level of idealism. And this observation brings us back to the theme of this book:

> It is, unfortunately, only too clear that if the individual is not truly regenerated in spirit, society cannot be either, for society is the sum total of individuals in need of redemption.
>
> Carl Jung

There is nothing new here; history is replete with examples of this principle. When the great pharaoh Ikhnaton and his beautiful queen Nefertiti moved the ancient Egyptians from primitive polytheism to the worship of one god and to reforms in family life, it seemed that a miracle of progress had occurred. But within a few years after his death, the vast majority of people returned to primitive worship; they were not ready for Ikhnaton's reforms in religious values or social practice. The most brilliant example of a man ahead of his time was Jesus. His teachings on love, personal development and man's relationship with God and his fellow man were far ahead of his time, and ours too. The teachings of the ancient wisdom seem to stand outside of time. They are often found in the past, yet they are always ahead of their time and, unfortunately, of our time as well.

An optimistic assessment of the 19th and 20th Centuries would be that man has been in the throes of a kind of prolonged adolescent rebellion. That is, we have been reacting against and finally throwing off the old, primitive idea of God as a rigid, punitive and "unscientific" Father. Perhaps we are now ready to trust in that idea of God that all the great teachers of the ancient wisdom have always taught – that God is a loving, merciful Father-Mother spirit who is the Ultimate Reality, and that we become real and lasting to the extent we join ourselves to the great God of all.

If this assessment proves valid, then the 21st Century will be characterized by this paradigm shift – a moving away from excessive materialism in our thinking and acting, and a moving toward the personal quest for spiritualized meanings and values. It is personal spiritual experience with God, not theology or ritual, that provides the energy, the motivation for such a dramatic change in focus. A paradigm shift of this nature would produce dramatic changes. (The impact of one Mother Theresa is mind-boggling.) If the number of persons who are simplistically spirit-led increases even modestly, the impact on society will be enormous. This new energy would redirect our social institutions, especially in keeping them focused on the higher, more ideal values. For it is not the purpose of religion to become a political or social party that attempts to force change on society. Rather, the role of religion is to remind us of our supreme values, thereby keeping all parties focused on the degree of congruence between our ideal goals and the means used to reach those same goals. Our social systems fall off track and become self-serving, even abusive of the people they serve when so few individuals in these systems really have faith in the higher values that supposedly underlie them. We then resort to means that contraindicate our ends. And this is true whether we're speaking of our families, our schools, our relationships with others, or our political and legal systems. We can tinker with these systems all we want, making this change or that, but until the persons involved in these systems practice faith in the higher values, real social progress will continue to elude us. It all comes back, just as it should, to the actions of individual persons.

Epilogue

The remaking of America can occur only if enough people seriously reexamine the very finest features of our heritage – that heritage born of the Enlightenment with its ethical and spiritual roots in the ancient wisdom. We were the first modern nation conceived as a grand experiment in the implementation of high ideals. We have a long way to go to complete the experiment. We will fail in this task if we continue to respond to the siren call of the 20th Century Myth. This Myth will always sidetrack us with its call for quick fixes, its excessive use of central authority to force change from the top down, its dreary emphasis on sameness of outcome in all things, its focus on group identity and collective responsibility rather than individual accountability – all leading, ironically, to a descent into me-firstism. The finest of our traditional values reject relativism and instead call us to the pursuit of the Absolute, but with supreme respect for the particular nature of each person's quest. It is only through tolerance and forbearance for each person's quest of the Absolute that we can eventually attain caring communities where service to others is the first value in all activities.

With the new interest in the spiritual orientation to life will come new as well as old problems in all spheres of life. People will always struggle with the natural tendency to be ruled by material demands, or by dogma and creed. It will always be scary (at first) to put one's trust, one's destiny, one's faith in the hands of the Divine Source. But these adversities are no cause for alarm, for they create great opportunities for growth. Our lives and times are not meant to be easy. They are meant to provide the beginnings of our greatest adventure.

> When we look back, we realize that the things which come to us when we put ourselves in God's hands were better than anything we could have planned.
>
> Bill Wilson

> Belief fixates; Faith liberates.
>
> Urantia Book

Notes

1) Hettner, Litteratur des 18, Jahrhunderts, III, 2, p. 170.

2) Statement made in the fifth part of *The Joyous Science*, translated as *The Gay Science* (New York, 1974). Also see Kaufmann, Walter. *Nietzsche: Philosopher, Psychologist, Antichrist*. Princeton University Press, 1950, 1974; and Magnus, Bernd. *Nietzsche's Existential Imperative*. Indiana University Press, 1978.

3) Johnson, Paul. *Modern Times, The World from the Twenties to the Eighties*. Harper & Row, 1983, p. 698.

4) John, C.G. *The Undisclosed Self*. Mentor Books, 1957. Also see *The Collected Works of C.G. Jung*. Bollingen Foundation, 1961-67. The best primer is *On Jung* by Anthony Stevens. Routledge, 1990.

5) See Walter Lipman. "The Permanent New Deal." Yale Review, 24 (1935), pp. 649-67; and Paul Johnson. *Modern Times*. Harper & Row, 1983, ch. 7; and John M. Keynes. *New Republic*. July 29, 1940.

6) See ch. 6 in Paul Johnson's *Modern Times*. Harper & Row, 1983. Arcadia was a district in ancient Greece proverbially known for the innocent, contented simplicity of its people.

7) Adler, Mortimer. *Desires, Right & Wrong, The Ethics of Enough*. Macmillan, New York: 1991, p. 1.

8) Knott, Paul D. *Student Activism*. W.C. Brown, 1971.

9) Raybon, Patricia. *Rocky Mountain News*, May 23, 1990.

10) See Walter Laqueur. "Reflections on Youth Movements." *Commentary*, June, 1969.

11) Feuer, Lewis S. "Students and Revolution: Patterns of Irrationality." *Survey*, 1968.

12) Ibid.

13) Same as #10 above, pp. 19-20.

14) See p. XV in *Out of Revolution* by Eugen Rosenstock-Huessy. Argo Books, Norwich, Vermont, 1969.

15) *The Urantia Book*, Urantia Foundation, Chicago, 1955, p. 2082.

16) See, for example, Emmet Fox. *The Sermon on the Mount*. Harper & Row, 1934.

17) See, for example, Butterworth, Eric, *Discover the Power Within You*. Harper & Row, 1968, 1989.

18) See, for example, MacDonald, George. *Life Essential: The Hope of the Gospel* (ed. by Rolland Hein). Harold Shaw Publishers, Wheaton, Illinois, 1974.

19) See, for example, Girzone, Joseph. *Joshua and the Children, A Parable*. MacMillan, 1989.

20) Huxley, Aldous. *The Perennial Philosophy*. Harper & Row, 1944, 1945.

21) *A Course in Miracles*, Foundation for Inner Peace. Glenn Ellen, California, 1976.

22) See #15 above.

23) As reported in the *International Herald Tribune*, October 16, 1991, p. 8.

24) Ibid., see #20 above, p. VII.

25) Lewis, C.S. *The Great Divorce*. MacMillan, 1946.

26) Covey, Stephen. *The 7 Habits of Highly Effective People*. Simon & Schuster, 1989.

27) Wilson, Bill. *Alcoholics Anonymous*. Alcoholics Anonymous World Services, Inc., pp. 8-9.

28) Ibid., pp. 10-11

29) Ibid., p. 12

30) Wilson, Bill. *As Bill Sees It*. Alcoholics Anonymous World Services, Inc., 1967, p. 95.

31) See #27 above, p. 13, p. 14 and pp. 60-61 and 62-63.

32) Jampolsky, Gerald. *Goodbye to Guilt*. Bantam, 1985, pp. 2-3.

33) As reported in Jacobi, Jolande. *The Way of Individuation*. Meridian, 1983, p. 16.

34) As reported in *Bill W.* by Robert Thomsen. Harper & Row, 1975.

35) See *The Collected Works of C.G. Jung.* Bollinger Foundation, p. 334.

36) See #30 above, p. 171.

37) See #20 above.

38) See #17 above, p. 1.

39) See #30 above, p. 38.

40) See #15 above.

41) James, William. *The Varieties of Religious Experience.* Harvard University Press, 1985.

42) As reported in #20 above, pp. 113-114.

43) See #32 above, pp. 17-18.

44) See #20 above, p. 73.

45) See #17 above, pp. 132-133.

46) See #15 above, p. 1102.

47) Saxe Commins and Robert Linscott, ed., *Man and the Universe, the Philosophers of Science.* Washington Square Press, 1969, p. 428.

48) Ibid., p. 450.

49) Ibid., p. 390.

50) See #15 above, p. 1118.

51) See #15 above, pp. 1453-1454 (please note that the quotes are not in direct sequence).

52) See Rimland, B. (1982) in *Searching for Joy* by David G. Myers in #53 below.

53) See David G. Myers, *Searching for Joy, Who Is Happy and Why* (working title unpublished manuscript). Hope College, Holland, Michigan, July 1991; and Spilka, Bernard, et al. *The Psychology of Religion, an Empirical Approach.* Prentice-Hall, 1985, pp. 105-107.

54) Ibid., pp. 104-107.

55) Ibid., pp. 104-105.

56) Ibid.

57) Ibid.

58) *Save Our Children*, report prepared for the Speaker's Staff and Appropriations Staff, Florida House of Representatives, Tom Gustafson, 1989.

59) Report by the House Select Committee on Children, Youth and Families as reported in the *Rocky Mountain News*, March 19, 1990, p. 20.

60) Hodges, William F. *Intervention for Children of Divorce*. John Wiley, 1986, pp. 8-62.

61) Weitzman, Lenore. "The Divorce Revolution." *Free Press*, 1985.

62) Bloom, B.L., Asher, S.J. & White, S.W. (1978). Marital disruption as a stressor: a review and analysis. *Psychological Bulletin*, 85, 867-899.

63) Ibid., see #60 above, p. 10.

64) Ibid., see #60 above.

65) Geridubaldi, J., Cleminshaw, H.P., Perry, J.D. & McLoughlin, C.S. The impact of parental divorce on children. Report of the nationwide NASP study. *School Psychology Review*, 1983, 12, pp. 300-323.

66) Evans, A. & Neel, J. School behaviors of children from one-parent and two-parent homes. *Principal*, 1980, pp. 38-39.

67) Ibid., see #60 above, pp. 204-208.

68) Ibid., see #60, second edition.

69) Wallerstein, Judith S. & Blakeslee, Sandra. *Second Chances*. Ticknor & Fields, 1989.

70) Ibid, p. 297 and p. 308.

71) See, for example, Hetherington, E.M. Effects of parental absence on personality development in adolescent daughters. *Developmental Pathology*, 1972, 313-326.

72) See, for example, Glenn, N.O. & Shelton, B.A. Pre-adult background variables and divorce: a note of caution about over-reliance on explained variance. *Journal of Marriage and the Family*, 1983, 405-410.

73) Hepworth, J., Ryder, R.G. & Dreyer, A.S. The effects of parental loss on the formation of intimate relationships. *Journal of Marital and Family Therapy*, 1984, 73-82.

74) Raschke, H.J. & Raschke, V.J. Family conflict and children's self-concepts. *Journal of Marriage and the Family*, 1979, pp. 367-374.

75) See #60 above.

76) Private diary

77) See Joan Beck, *Chicago Tribune*, in the *Denver Post*, April 8, 1982, for additional examples of the inherent absurdity of the quality time notion.

78) Blankenhorn, David in the *Rocky Mountain News*, July 22, 1989, p. 57.

79) The scientific research on this topic and all related topics in this chapter is extensive. The best single source for the layman to learn about this research is *Brain Sex: The Real Difference Between Men and Women* by Anne Moir and David Jessel. A Lyle Stuart Book, Carol Publishing Group, 1991.

80) Ibid.

81) Ibid.

82) Ibid.

83) See #15 above, p. 928.

84) See #15 above, pp. 932-936.

85) Stevens, Anthony. *On Jung*. Routledge, Penguin Books Limited, 1990, p. 131.

86) Charen, Mona. Creators Syndicate. *Rocky Mountain News*, May 3, 1990, p. 71.

87) Study by Edith V. Fienst reported in the *Rocky Mountain News*, May 3, 1990, p. 71.

88) All the De Tocqueville quotes that follow are from *Democracy in America*, De Tocqueville, Alexis. ed. by Richard Heffner. Mentor, 1956, 1984.

89) Meadows, Bonnie J. "The Correct Connection: On the Evolution of a New Psychology for Women." *Care Network*, Westminster, CO, September/October 1990, pp. 6-7.

90) Whitmont, E.C. *Return of the Goddess: Femininity, Aggression and the Modern Grail Quest.* Routledge and Kegan Paul, London, 1983.

91) Ibid., see #53 above.

92) Ibid., see #26 above.

93) Keirsey, David, & Bates, Marilyn. *Please Understand Me.* Prometheus Nemesis Book Co., 1984.

94) Peck, Scott. *The Road Less Travelled.* Touchstone, Simon & Schuster, 1978, p. 22.

95) Hayes, E. Kent. *Why Good Parents Have Bad Kids.* Doubleday, 1989, p. 204.

96) Elkind, David. *The Hurried Child.* Addison-Wesley, 1981.

97) Bloom, Allan. *The Closing of the American Mind.* Simon & Schuster, 1987.

98) As reported in the *Rocky Mountain News.* May 12, 1991, p. 85.

99) Bowman, Craig. Column in the *Rocky Mountain News,* August 29, 1991, p. 72.

100) As reported in the *Rocky Mountain News.* June 3, 1990, p. 31.

101) Ibid., see #99 above.

102) Comment by Dr. Harvey Greenberg. *Educating for Character.* Thomas Tickona. Bantam, 1991, p. 83.

103) As reported in the *Honolulu Advertiser.* November 13, 1989, p. A-3.

104) See *Megatrends* by John Naisbitt. Warner, 1982 and *The Third Wave* by Alvin Toffler, Bantam, 1980.

105) Durant, Will and Ariel. *The Lessons of History.* Simon & Schuster, 1968.

106) Ibid., p. 20.

107) Ibid., p. 61.

108) Ibid., pp. 62-63.

109) Ibid., p. 78-79.

110) See #3 above, p. 729.

111) Ibid., p. 581.

112) Ibid., p. 201.

113) See #105 above, p. 81.

114) See #20 above, p. 193.

115) Ibid., p. 194.

116) Ibid., p. 195.

117) See #15 above, p. 1487.

118) See #105 above, p. 93.

119) Newman, John Henry. *The Idea of a University*. London, 1853, as reported in #3 above, p. 699.

Notes